From
SHILOH
to
SAVANNAH

From
SHILOH
—— to ——
SAVANNAH
The Seventh Illinois Infantry in the
Civil War

D. Leib Ambrose

Introduction and notes by
Daniel E. Sutherland

NORTHERN ILLINOIS UNIVERSITY PRESS

© 2003 by Northern Illinois University Press

Published by the Northern Illinois University Press, DeKalb, Illinois 60115

Manufactured in the United States using acid-free paper

Main text was originally published in 1868 as *History of the Seventh Regiment Illinois Volunteer Infantry, From Its First Muster into the U.S. Service, April 25, 1861, to Its Final Muster Out, July 9, 1865.*

Library of Congress Cataloging-in-Publication Data

Ambrose, D. Leib (Daniel Leib), 1843–1922.

[History of the Seventh Regiment Illinois Volunteer Infantry]

From Shiloh to Savannah: the Seventh Illinois Infantry in the

Civil War / D. Leib Ambrose; introduction [and annotations]

by Daniel E. Sutherland.

    p.   cm

"Originally published in 1868 as History of the Seventh Regiment Illinois

Volunteer Infantry from its first muster into the U.S. service, April 25, 1861,

to its final muster out, July 9, 1865"—T.p. verso.

Includes bibliographical references and index.

ISBN 0-87580-309-1 (alk paper)

1. United States—Army—Illinois Infantry Regiment, 7th (1861).

2. United States—History—Civil War, 1861–1865—Regimental histories.

3. Illinois—History—Civil War, 1861–1865—Regimental histories.

I. Sutherland, Daniel E. II. Title.

E505.5 7th .A43 2003

973.7'473–dc21

2002032664

CONTENTS

INTRODUCTION

Daniel E. Sutherland

In the original introduction to his history of the 7th Illinois Infantry, Daniel Leib Ambrose proclaimed that the "history of one [regiment] is the history of all." Ambrose was right enough as concerns the common experiences of most of the Civil War's combat regiments, and that was largely what he meant to convey. He was also being overly modest, however, for the value of any story is created by its author, and it would be a mistake to regard Ambrose's account of the 7th Illinois as just another regimental history. Hundreds of such chronicles were published in the decades following the Civil War, several dozen for Illinois regiments and batteries alone. These accounts would be supplemented over time by hundreds more published memoirs, wartime diaries, and collections of official and private correspondence. Yet for accuracy, historical insight, and comprehensive coverage, Ambrose's work easily rates near the top of the heap.[1]

Like many Illinois soldiers who fought for the Union, Daniel Ambrose had been born farther east, in his case, Highland County, Ohio. His United Brethren clergyman father moved the family to Logan County, Illinois, in 1855, when Daniel was twelve years old, in search of cheap land. The Ambroses eventually purchased eighty acres and settled down on a farm two miles west of Mount Pulaski. One of Daniel's six younger brothers recalled the move as "the great family event" and early life on the farm as "hard and . . . unremunerative." By 1860, however, the family property was worth $2500, and there was money enough to employ a hired woman; with ten family members by that time, Mrs. Ambrose no doubt needed the help. The Ambrose boys—two of whom also became clergymen—worked hard, but they must also have received an above-average education, given their father's profession and Daniel's later success as a journalist and author. There is even evidence that Daniel returned to Ohio to attend Otterbein College—affiliated with the Church of the United Brethren—for a year before the Civil War.[2]

Education and youth were cut short by President Abraham Lincoln's call for army volunteers in April 1861. The 7th Illinois, despite its numerical designation (a gesture of deference to the six Illinois volunteer regiments that had served in the Mexican War), was the first of six infantry regiments rapidly raised by the state. Ambrose, at the age of eighteen, became one of the original privates in Company H when the regiment was sworn into U.S. service on April 25. Two of his brothers also later joined the regiment. Ambrose served in Company H throughout the war without serious injury and with well-deserved promotion through the ranks. He became a sergeant in early 1864, following his reenlistment that winter, and was elevated to first lieutenant in July, the youngest commissioned officer in the regiment. There are postwar references to him as Captain Ambrose, but the captaincy was most likely an honorary title, perhaps a result of his participation in one of the several veterans' organizations to which he belonged.[3]

Ambrose appears to have managed his reintegration to civilian life without incident. Some men, having acquired intemperate habits or violent ways while in service, found themselves in trouble with the law, unable to hold jobs, or incapable of maintaining marriages after the war. Other former soldiers suffered physically, emotionally, or psychologically from the trials of campaigning, captivity, or combat. Many of those men never recovered their health, and of course not a few veterans returned home minus a foot, hand, leg, or arm. Ambrose escaped all such misfortunes. He embraced friends and family (as did his two brothers) in high spirits and as a hero who had helped to save the Union and abolish slavery. In time, as mentioned, he served proudly in several veterans' organizations, including the Grand Army of the Republic.[4]

Too young to participate in politics before the war, Ambrose also returned to civilian life as a confirmed Republican. This probably had been the party of his father. Coming from German stock, the Ambrose family had supported the abolition of slavery, which had also been the position of the United Brethren. The family also happened to be friends with a distant relative of Abraham Lincoln, and one of Daniel's brothers recalled accompanying their father to hear the future presi-

dent deliver a campaign speech at the Logan County court-
house. In any event, a combination of politics and journalism
shaped Daniel's postwar career. Completing his studies at Otterbein College shortly after the war, Ambrose was back in Logan County by 1867, when he purchased the *Intelligencer,* a
Republican newspaper in Lincoln. He moved the paper to Win-
chester, in Scott County, in 1869 and changed its name to the
Star. The enterprise folded a year later, at which time Ambrose
appears to have taught school, although exactly where and for
how long is uncertain.[5]

He made his next known move to Springfield, Sangamon
County, in 1872, to reenter the newspaper business. Ambrose
worked at the *Illinois State Journal,* the capital city's longtime
Republican organ, as a printer until about 1878, when he became city editor of the *Sangamo Morning Monitor*. Unlike
every other newspaper with which he was associated, the *Monitor* was "Independent," but the corruption in public life during
the Gilded Age—highlighted by the scandals of President
Ulysses S. Grant's administration—made it vocally anti-
Republican in the 1870s. Ambrose could only have worked for
such a newspaper had he, too, become momentarily disillu-
sioned with his party. Being particularly interested in state
politics, he reported on the Illinois legislature during the
1870s and 1880s as a special correspondent for newspapers in
Chicago and St. Louis. Ambrose became city editor of the local
paper in Chillicothe, Missouri (the rest of the Ambrose family
had already moved to that state), in the late 1880s, but he returned to Illinois in 1895 to live permanently in Canton, Fulton County. There, he worked, by turns, on several newspapers—most notably the *Daily Register*—and served during the
last decade of his life as the staff correspondent in Canton for
the *Peoria Star*. He also served during that same decade as the
probation officer for Fulton County.[6]

Ambrose took time to marry and start a family in the midst
of this hectic career, although his private life was marred by
tragedy. His beloved bride Fanny Tichenor of Macon County,
Illinois, died of "brain fever" at age twenty-four in 1879. The
couple had been married for only six years. They had produced
two sons and a daughter, and the daughter, Clara, lived with

and cared for her father, who remained a widower, through the last three decades of his life. The youngest child, whose birth in late 1878 probably led to Fanny's fatal illness, died four months after his mother. Ambrose never recovered fully from this double blow. He had been devoted to Fanny, even going so far as to desert the United Brethren and join her Methodist Episcopal denomination after their marriage. An aunt, Clara Leib, moved in with the family to help operate the household and raise the children until daughter Clara came of age. Ambrose died of heart failure at his rented house in Canton, located at 224 West Pine Street, on February 15, 1922. He was buried at Oak Ridge Cemetery, in Springfield.[7]

Ambrose wrote two books after the war. He compiled *Under the Gas-Light; or, Lights and Shadows in the State Capital of Illinois* in 1879 from a series of articles he began writing for the *Sangamo Monitor* the previous summer. A product of his self-described "rambles" as a correspondent through Springfield, the sketches still evoke a feel for the social and political life of the old town. The articles—thirty-one of which appear in the book—range widely in subject and tone, but most of them advocate some type of social reform. They reflect on politics and politicians, the gap between the rich and the poor, the plight of orphans and prostitutes, the evils of drink and lechery, and the virtues of education and hard work. Ambrose lost Fanny and his infant son midway through the original newspaper series. References to their deaths even appear in some of the later articles, which suggests that Ambrose continued with his "rambles," the writing of the series, and the publication of the book as ways of keeping busy and putting his personal tragedies out of mind. In any event, he dedicated the book to Fanny's memory.[8]

Ambrose's other book, published eleven years earlier, was *History of the Seventh Regiment,* which he apparently wrote upon returning to Illinois from Otterbein College. Given his age (mid-twenties) and the research resources available to him, it is an impressive piece of work. Unlike the authors of regimental histories written later in the century, Ambrose could not consult the many wartime memoirs, reminiscences, and official records that would be published after 1870. In-

stead, he relied on his own memory, what documents he could
gather from former officers in the regiment, and the recently
published Illinois adjutant general's report on the state's role
in the war. The adjutant general's report provided him with a
fairly reliable chronology of the regiment's travels and actions
as well as a complete regimental roster, which Ambrose included as an appendix to his book.[9]

One cannot help but wonder what personal sources Ambrose may also have used to write his *History*. It seems rea-
sonable to assume that he corresponded with his family during the war and that at least some of those letters had
survived. Perhaps, too, he had access to a diary written either
by himself or a comrade. Yet Ambrose does not mention using
any such documents, and there is no evidence that they ex-
isted. Even to this day, no diary, journal, or collection of correspondence spanning the entire history of the regiment is
known to exist. Ambrose did employ the format of a diary to
write his narrative, but he likely relied for chronological accuracy on the adjutant general's records and documents kept by
the regiment's officers.[10]

Ambrose probably chose the diary format for his narrative
because he wanted to be precise about events and to "give a
complete and accurate history of every man . . . without favor
or partiality." The use of daily entries also conveys a sense of
intimacy and immediacy, as though one *is* reading a private
journal. Additionally, Ambrose writes primarily in the present
tense, even to the point of feigning ignorance about events
that, according to the date of any particular entry, would not
occur until later in the war. As one reads the *History*, it is easy
to forget that Ambrose wrote with the full knowledge of how
and why his story would end. To his credit, Ambrose also uses
this personal approach without making himself or his own experiences the focus of the narrative. Indeed, we learn next to
nothing from his book about the man who wrote it. Other than
to include his own name on lists of promotions, Ambrose remains invisible in the scenes he describes.[11]

That Ambrose had few models for his work makes his
achievement all the more noteworthy. Just a handful of Civil
War regimental histories had been published by 1868. Only a

dozen Illinois histories—the volumes Ambrose would have been most likely to consult—had appeared, and only two of that lot could be considered genuine histories, as opposed to personal accounts or reflections on the war. Nor did these earlier authors describe the *entire* war, as Ambrose would do. They had either published their books before the war ended or wrote about regiments that did not take the field until after the autumn of 1862. For all that, Ambrose's work is remarkably free of factual errors. His most common failing is occasionally to mention comrades by their military rank at a time before they had, in fact, achieved that rating.[12]

The men of the 7th Illinois enlisted originally for only three months of duty, most of which time they spent at Camp Yates, in Springfield, and at Mound City, Illinois. They did not venture south of the Ohio River until July 1861. Thereafter, like the majority of the Union soldiers from Illinois, they served almost exclusively in the western theater, most notably in Tennessee, Mississippi, Alabama, and Georgia. The regiment operated as part of a "district" command for the first part of the war, but beginning in the spring of 1862 it formed part of what would become the Army of the Tennessee. Ambrose's own narrative will describe the daily movements and actions of the 7th Illinois, but a brief summary of the regiment's service may help to place it in the context of the Union's wartime military strategy.[13]

The North's chief concern in the spring and summer of 1861 was to maintain control of the border slave states—Missouri, Kentucky, Maryland, and Delaware—that had not joined the Confederacy. The 7th Illinois joined operations in the South that summer as part of this holding strategy, first in Missouri, then in Kentucky. Ambrose and his comrades were ordered in July 1861 to travel from Mound City to Fort Holt, Kentucky, but they did not reach their destination until early October. Ambrose's *History* contributes immediately to the historical record by explaining the cause of this delay, which is obscured in most official documents. It seems that the 7th Illinois was diverted to Missouri while en route to Kentucky in order to pursue the Confederate partisan leader Meriwether "Jeff" Thompson. This was a telling assignment as things turned out, for the regiment would spend large parts of the coming years tracking and fighting rebel raiders, partisans, and guerrillas east of the Mississippi River.[14]

By the time the 7th Illinois reached Kentucky, Confederate forces had been occupying the far eastern part of the state for a month, thus endangering Kentucky's hopes to remain neutral in the war. The entrance of rebel troops into Kentucky meant that the United States had to fight to control this politically and militarily vital stretch of the border—and, incidentally, the birthplace of both Abraham Lincoln and Jefferson Davis. Even so, as winter set in, there was no serious combat between the armies there for the remainder of the year, and the 7th Illinois endured several months of boredom.

Ambrose conveys a good sense of the monotony of this period, the tedium of the constant drill, the problems men had in adjusting to military discipline, the construction of winter quarters, the campfire speculation about the regiment's ultimate destination, and the bursts of excitement that accompanied occasional reconnaissance patrols into enemy territory. Indeed, he enriches such times of relative inactivity throughout his narrative by providing details about the private side of soldiering. Bits and pieces of army life, often forgotten in the whirl of momentous military battles and political debates, fill this history. The pride regiments took in their reputations on the drill field, the concern men demonstrated in sending their pay home to family members, the importance soldiers attached to letters received from those same loved ones—all loom large in the lives of Ambrose and his comrades. With his journalist's eye for the colorful detail or anecdote, he shows readers a side of the war left out of official histories, as in this chance remark made under the date of December 22, 1862: "Our camp now puts one in mind of an Illinois farm-yard, roosters crowing and hens cackling all over camp. The roosters the boys are training for game-cocks."

The 7th Illinois did not experience any hard campaigning or combat until early 1862, when it joined the Union advance against Forts Henry and Donelson. This campaign marked the first Federal effort in the western theater to invade a Confederate state, Tennessee. It also, incidentally, announced a new phase of the war. While the Confederacy seemed content to sit on the strategic defensive in the West, the Union hoped to break the stalemate on the border by pushing the rebels out of Kentucky. They would do so by seizing control of three major rivers that offered natural invasion routes into the heart of the Confederacy: the Mississippi, Cumberland, and Tennessee. Forts Henry and Donelson blocked access to the latter two rivers near the Kentucky-Tennessee border.

Neither here nor elsewhere does Ambrose provide detailed tactical explanations of battles or graphic descriptions of combat. He left that part of the war to the generals in their memoirs. He is content to state clearly and accurately his regiment's role in the fighting. Ambrose is scrupulous about listing members of the regiment who were killed or wounded in each action as well as mentioning men who were cited for gallantry or who played conspicuous roles in the war. He often uses these occasions to provide biographical information about many of the regiment's officers, and he leaves no doubt about which higher-ranking leaders of the army he admired. Ulysses S. Grant, who commanded the Henry and Donelson expedition, is the first person Ambrose places in this pantheon of military heroes, to be joined later by Grenville M. Dodge, William S. Rosecrans, and, most especially, William T. Sherman.

It also becomes evident at this point in his narrative that Ambrose is something of a romantic. He scatters stanzas of poetry throughout the *History*, much of it selected from popular works of the day, to which he added several poems written during and after the war expressly for the *History* by a former comrade, Solomon F. Flint. Even more striking is the way in which Ambrose embellishes his own prose with the romantic imagery that defined the era's popular literature. Such passages are most apparent when he relates the regiment's combat experiences. His colorful and emotional descriptions of the battles substitute for more detached analysis. Ambrose does not so much explain the fighting as re-create the atmosphere in which events occurred. For example, under the date of April 6, 1862, he offers the following vision of his regiment's initial contact with Confederate forces at the battle of Shiloh, its next action after capturing Fort Donelson: "How can we describe the sound of a storm of grape and canister, cutting their hellish paths through serried ranks of human beings. . . . Many are the storms flying around the Seventh now. Thicker and faster they come, but these noble men who bore that riddled flag over Fort Donelson's walls, struggle on."

The victories at Forts Henry and Donelson and at Shiloh sparked a string of Union military successes in the West and the trans-Mississippi region. The Confederates abandoned Nashville a week after the surrender at Donelson. New Orleans was captured in late April, and Memphis surrendered in early June. The defeat of the rebels at Pea Ridge, Arkansas, in March 1862, solidified those triumphs by preserving Missouri for the Union. Northern troops had made remarkable territorial gains in just five months, especially when compared to the sluggish performance of Federal armies in the East. They now controlled the prized rivers of eastern Tennessee as well as both ends of the Mississippi River, where Vicksburg stood as the only major obstacle to their domination of the Mississippi Valley.

The men of the 7th Illinois thus formed part of an extremely confident Union army as they pursued the Confederates from Shiloh into northern Mississippi. They participated in the battle of Corinth, in October 1862, but the regiment's role in the war then changed dramatically over the next fourteen months. While most Union troops in the West were redeployed to operate against Vicksburg, or to defend Kentucky, or to push the rebels out of central and eastern Tennessee, the 7th Illinois was assigned to occupy and maintain the Union's tenuous hold on northern Mississippi, western Tennessee, and northern Alabama. They spent the rest of 1862 and all of 1863 tracking, capturing, and fighting Confederate raiders and guerrillas in those states.

The frequency with which Union regiments participated in antiguerrilla operations is surprising. Dozens of regiments and thousands of soldiers spent large parts of the war in this way, generally, as was the case with the 7th Illinois, in protecting Union supply and communication lines along railroads and rivers. As Ambrose demonstrates, most Union soldiers resented these thankless and dangerous assignments, which prohibited them from participating in the *important* fighting of the war. In the case of the 7th Illinois, this meant missing the battles of Perryville, Stones River, Vicksburg, Chickamauga, Chattanooga, and the opening months of the Atlanta campaign.

The regiment not only operated for long periods detached from the rest of the army but also functioned as mounted infantry. Union field commanders believed that the only chance they had of defeating Confederate cavalry and swift-moving rebel irregulars, who were almost always mounted, was to place a portion of their infantry on horses and mules. Confederate general Nathan Bedford Forrest and his subordinate commanders, Philip Dale Roddey, Jacob D. Biffle, and Adam R. Johnson, became the principal nemeses of the 7th Illinois, and the men spent considerable time and energy trying to round up the leaders of local, largely independent, guerrilla commands.

Thus, Ambrose's *History* offers two very different views of Union military operations. On the one hand, he shows the 7th Illinois functioning as a traditional infantry regiment during the first eighteen months of the war, a role most of the regiment would resume in the last year of the conflict. On the other hand, he also introduces readers to the shadowy irregular war of bushwhackers and raiders. The contrast is stark. The guerrilla war appeared to have no rules. It was defined by ambushes, sneak attacks, arson, lynchings, mutilations, and depredations. While Ambrose and the 7th Illinois enjoyed some success waging this style of warfare, it was a wearing experience, and it led the men to take a hard—even bitter—attitude toward Confederate combatants and noncombatants.

Despite these harrowing months in the hills and swamps, most men in the 7th Illinois reenlisted at the end of 1863, which entitled them to a month's leave at home. Upon their return to duty, they resumed their old job in western Tennessee and northern Alabama until June 1864, when the regiment was ordered to rejoin the Army of the Tennessee at Rome, Georgia, and participate in Sherman's advance against Atlanta. In doing so, the regiment contributed to a new—and final—stage of Union strategy. The failure to conquer the Confederacy after three years of fighting had increased Northern dissatisfaction with the Lincoln administration and threatened the president's bid for reelection. Lincoln installed

Ulysses Grant as the commanding general of all Union armies in early 1864 and told him to bring the war to an end. Grant responded by abandoning the Federal strategy of attrition, which sought to wear down the Confederacy by gradually defeating its armies in the field, to a strategy of exhaustion, which made the economic resources and security of the civilian population equal targets with the armies. The object was to destroy so much rebel property and penetrate so deeply into previously untouched parts of the Confederacy that civilian morale would collapse and the material means of supporting the South's armies would disappear. The new strategy also coordinated the movements of eastern and western Union armies as never before, so that the thinning ranks of Confederate soldiers could not adequately respond to the multiple threats. A series of destructive raids and the movement of Union forces against a series of strategically important geographical points, including Atlanta, would be the means of accomplishing all of this.

The Georgia campaign provided the 7th Illinois with its most intense combat—and highest casualties—of the war at Allatoona Pass, in October. Forty-five years after publishing his *History,* in a Memorial Day speech delivered to his local Grand Army of the Republic post, Ambrose still considered this fight—"one of the greatest battles of the century"—to be his regiment's finest hour. He and his comrades then joined the march from Atlanta to Savannah and through the Carolinas. Several companies were again mounted during the Carolinas campaign, so that the regiment operated in divided fashion—part of it mounted, part on foot—until the surrender of Gen. Joseph E. Johnston near Bentonville, North Carolina, in May 1865. After participating in the Grand Review of the Union armies in Washington, D.C., the regiment traveled to Louisville, Kentucky, where it performed guard duty until sent home to be discharged in July 1865.[15]

The details of all this form the heart of Ambrose's comprehensive narrative, but he does more than just compile the facts of his regiment's biography. Along the way, he also provides valuable glimpses of what he and his comrades thought about the causes of the war and the political and social issues it had raised. For example, Ambrose leaves little doubt about why these Midwestern lads volunteered to fight their countrymen to the south. The "wicked enemies of freedom," whose rebellion against the United States was nothing but rank treason, had to be squashed (July 7, 1861), he asserts. "The world seems to be standing still, watching and waiting to see the triumph of freedom and self-government," Ambrose declares in his entry for May 6, 1862. Nor does he mince words in declaring who started the war. "[T]he South's ignorant classes have been deluded by wicked and unprincipled men," he states in his entry for October 8, 1862. "Oh! wicked men! why did you fling these dark curtains around this people? Why did you whelm this fair sunny south in cruel, desolating war, and cause your beautiful innocent ones to cry for bread?" His attitude had softened but little even several decades after the conflict.[16]

Ambrose—and, by implication, his comrades—had no patience with traitors in the North either. He denounces on several occasions the treacherous intentions and actions of the Copperheads, or Northerners opposed to the Union war effort, whom he describes as "contemptible in nature, pusillanimous in soul, with hearts as black as the 'steeds of night'" (December 24, 1864). Soldiers like Ambrose loathed these enemies more than the gray-clad men they fought with rifle and cannon. Indeed, the numerous times Ambrose pauses in his account of military events to harangue the Copperheads suggest that he may have intended to make a political statement in those parts of his *History*. Clement L. Vallandigham, a former Democratic Ohio congressman who was arrested for "expressing treasonable sympathy," convicted, and banished from the Union in 1863, was the best known Copperhead and a particular target of Ambrose. Illinois had its own share of malcontents, however, and Ambrose describes how in January 1863 the entire 7th Illinois signed a petition that protested the "traitorous conduct" of all Illinois politicians—mostly Democrats—who opposed the war.[17]

Some understanding of the political leanings of the 7th Illinois may be gained by considering where the men resided before the war. The vast majority of its volunteers hailed from the central and northern parts of the state, which were strongly pro-Union and mostly Republican in 1861. The ranks were filled with men from such places as Coles County (Company B), Kane, Kendall, and DuPage counties (Company C), and Sangamon County (Company K). Virtually every man in Ambrose's Company H came from Logan County, and the majority of those men, like himself, had enlisted at Lincoln. The people of the southern tip of the state were less predictable in their political leanings. Many of that region's residents were openly secessionist, with some men even joining the Confederate army, although the government moved quickly to occupy the area and had few problems securing loyal recruits from there. The 7th Illinois drew only a very few men from southern Illinois.[18]

Most of the regiment's men also seem to have endorsed President Abraham Lincoln's decision in the autumn of 1862 to make black emancipation a national war aim, although this is one instance when Ambrose betrays the fact that he is writing several years after the war. His entry for January 1, 1863, the date the Emancipation Proclamation was to take effect, predicts that "the time will come when all will view this proclamation as the most powerful blow against the slave-holder's rebellion." He also waxes poetic when mentioning the noble intent of emancipation in that same passage ("To-day we are reminded that Lincoln's great proclamation takes effect. A chained race is declared free"), and he concludes his *History* by calling the war "America's great crusade for freedom, truth, and the rights of men!" But Ambrose is honest—and quite correct—in acknowledging that many men in the regiment opposed fighting a war to free southern blacks, and many a heated debate over the wisdom of the act warmed that winter's nights in camp.[19]

Ambrose also accurately depicts the increasingly harder attitude that he and many other Union soldiers took toward Southerners as the war dragged on, as their own hardships increased, and as more of their comrades fell victim to the war. Men who may have felt some guilt earlier about confiscating or destroying civilian property believed by late 1862 that traitors must be punished and that the physical destruction of the South—like the abolition of slavery—would hasten the end of the bloodshed. His own regiment's experience with the brutality of guerrilla warfare partly explains its darkening mood. When Confederate guerrillas returned captured Union foragers and pickets to camp minus a nose or an ear, the desire for retaliation grew strong. In 1861, the men of the 7th Illinois treated the theft of a few chickens or a hog as a lark, and their officers, while "officially" forbidding such actions, often ignored the pilfering. By 1863, that earlier sense of mischief had vanished. "'Confiscation and extermination' is our motto," Ambrose declares. "Anything to weaken this inhuman rebellion" (January 13, 1863). By the time the army marched through Georgia and the Carolinas, Ambrose and his comrades gloried in the destructive swath they created. They proclaimed William T. Sherman "the boldest, most fearless and most consummate leader of the nineteenth century." Upon entering Savannah, on December 22, 1864, Ambrose rejoices, "We behold rebellion dying. The tramp of armies; the burning of cities; the destruction of railroads, have ruined Georgia."[20]

Even so, Ambrose fails to broach some subjects, although his omissions tell us something about his purpose in writing the *History*. For instance, it is well known that the majority of soldier deaths in both armies came from sickness and infectious diseases, but Ambrose never mentions this aspect of the war. Even when noting the first members of the regiment to die, in May 1861, he fails to state the cause of death, which was very likely measles or dysentery. Ambrose probably believed such inglorious deaths, with no hint of romantic sacrifice, would diminish the memory of those men. Similarly, he skirts the subject of desertion. We know that desertion ran high in some Illinois regiments, more than 13,000 during the course of the war, and even the regimental roster, which Ambrose appends to his *History,* identifies a number of such shirkers in the 7th Illinois. Ambrose wanted people to remember the regiment as a band of heroes, however, with nary a dishonorable man in the lot. Consequently, as in his handling of the earliest deaths in the regiment, when he mentions the first instance of a man being court-martialed and dismissed from the army—in June 1861—Ambrose states neither the man's name nor the charge against him.[21]

Similarly, Ambrose avoids the subject of black troops. This gap might be explained by the fact that the 7th Illinois had no direct contact with black regiments, but the subject was certainly discussed in camps, and opinions about the introduction of African Americans into the army were just as divided as on the subject of emancipation. Even men who endorsed their recruitment did not always do so for noble reasons. For example, some members of the 7th Illinois welcomed black soldiers as cannon fodder that might spare their own lives. "What do you think of the 'Negro Regiment Bill?'" a member of the regiment wrote to a friend in February 1863. "Some of the soldiers make some few trivial objections but as a general rule most all say that if a negro can stop an enemy's ball, why let them go and do it." Interestingly, too, the early months of 1863, following the enactment of the Emancipation Proclamation and the initial recruitment of black troops, witnessed a sudden—and large—increase in Illinois desertions. Yet Ambrose chooses not to introduce the controversial topic.[22]

If Ambrose had written his *History* a few decades, rather than just a few years, after the war, we might conclude that these gaps in his narrative were caused by loss of memory or a desire to promote sectional reconciliation by deemphasizing some of the war's less honorable and more divisive elements. Yet his recounting of events is sharp and clear, and, as shown, he blames the South in no uncertain terms for having caused the conflict, and he loudly celebrates the demise of slavery. Consequently, his reluctance to discuss such topics as desertion and the contribution of Union blacks soldiers comes more likely from a determination to honor, if not glorify, his comrades, most of whom were still alive in 1868.

In summary, Ambrose's *History* offers several rewarding perspectives on the Civil War. Quite apart from being the only complete history of the 7th Illinois Infantry, it enhances our broad understanding of military operations in the western theater, which historians increasingly regard as the theater of the war where the Union ultimately achieved victory. Ambrose is accurate not only in his facts but also in his depiction of the common Union soldier's experience in the conflict. For even though he ended the war as a junior officer, Ambrose rendered most of his service—more than three years of it—as a private soldier and noncommissioned officer. Accounts of the war by such veterans are rare, and this alone makes his interpretation of events valuable. Ambrose also presents the story of men whose principal contributions to victory came not on the war's storied battlefields but in the precarious role of guerrilla hunters, as they performed the essential tasks of protecting the army's lines of communication and holding on to dearly bought territory. Without such Union regiments as the 7th Illinois, the Civil War could have been even longer and deadlier than it became. Without such accounts of the war as this one by Ambrose, our impressions of the conflict would be woefully incomplete.

• • •

The text of Ambrose's *History* is presented here largely as it first appeared in 1868. Obvious misspellings and erratic punctuation caused by typesetting errors in the original book have been silently corrected. Errors of fact are addressed in the endnotes. The endnotes also supplement Ambrose's narrative by providing information about many of the people and events he mentions and by citing reports, correspondence, and other documents not available to him in 1868.

The 1868 edition includes a roster for the 7th Infantry, but because it is an unofficial version it is not reprinted here. The official roster may be found in the 1886 *Report of the Adjutant General of the State of Illinois*, containing reports for the years 1861–1866 in 8 volumes, revised by Brigadier General J. W. Vance (Springfield: H. W. Rokker, State Printer, 1886). Indexes and rosters are also available on the websites of the Illinois Secretary of State and the National Park Service.

Two people deserve recognition for their assistance in preparing Ambrose's *History* for republication. William Furry, assistant director of the Illinois State Historical Society, unearthed and made available to the editor valuable biographical information about Daniel Leib Ambrose. His generosity has greatly enhanced our knowledge and understanding of Ambrose's life before and after the war. Mary Ann Pohl of the Illinois State Historical Library provided copies of the letters of David B. Givler, Company C, 7th Illinois, and information about the wartime members of the Illinois state legislature. This information has been extremely useful in helping to determine the accuracy of parts of Ambrose's narrative.

NOTES

1. For a comprehensive listing of histories for Illinois regiments, see William B. Tubbs, comp., "A Bibliography of Illinois Civil War Regimental Sources in the Illinois State Historical Library: Part I, Published and Printed Sources," *Illinois Historical Journal* 87 (1994): 185–232.

2. *Canton Daily Register,* Feb. 16, 1922; U.S. Bureau of the Census, *Population Schedule of the Eighth U.S. Census: Illinois, 1860,* National Archives microcopy 653, roll 200, p. 252; Matthias Hattaway Ambrose, "Ambrose Family History," 4, 5–6, typescript of Feb. 4, 1910, in possession of Arlene Johnson Herriman.

3. *Canton Daily Register,* Feb. 16, 1922; Ambrose, "Family History," 5; Victor Hicken, *Illinois in the Civil War* (Urbana: University of Illinois Press, 1966), 2.

4. Some of the problems of readjustment faced by returning Union soldiers are mentioned in Larry M. Logue, *To Appomattox and Beyond: The Civil War Soldier in War and Peace* (Chicago: Ivan R. Dee, 1996), 86–89; Paul A. Cimbala and Randall M. Miller, eds., *Union Soldiers and the Northern Home Front: Wartime Experiences, Postwar Adjustments* (New York: Fordham University Press, 2002), chaps. 10–12.

5. *Canton Daily Register,* Feb. 16, 1922; Ambrose, "Family History," 5; Franklin William Scott, *Newspapers and Periodicals of Illinois, 1814–1879,* rev. ed. (Springfield: Illinois State Historical Library, 1910), 224, 358.

6. *Canton Daily Register,* Feb. 16, 1922; Ambrose, "Family History," 6; Scott, *Newspapers and Periodicals of Illinois,* 39, 280, 321–22, 325.

7. *Sangamo Morning Monitor,* Mar. 8, 1879; U.S. Bureau of the Census, *Population Schedule of the Tenth U.S. Census: Illinois, 1880,* National Archives microcopy T9-0249, vol. 50, p. 206A; *Schedule of the Fourteenth Census of Population: Illinois, 1920,* microcopy T625, roll 369, enumeration district 75, p. 1; *Canton Daily Register,* Feb. 16, 1922. Ambrose appears never to have owned a house. All references to his status in city directories and on census rolls show him residing either at a hotel or in a rented house.

8. D. Leib Ambrose, *Under the Gas-Light; or, Lights and Shadows in the State Capital of Illinois* (Springfield: T.W.S. Kidd, 1879), preface. The book's publisher, Kidd, was the editor and publisher of the *Monitor.* William Furry has made a careful analysis of both this book and the Ambrose marriage in "Remembering the Rambler: The Sad Story of Daniel Leib Ambrose," *Illinois Times* (April 25–May 1, 2002): 11, 13, 15–17.

9. D. Leib Ambrose, *History of the Seventh Regiment Illinois Volunteer Infantry* (Springfield: Illinois Journal Company, 1868), introduction; *Report of the Adjutant General of the State of Illinois,* 3 vols. (Springfield:

Baker, Bailhache & Company, 1867). For later additions to the regiment's history, see Tubbs, comp., "Bibliography, Part I."

10. Most surviving manuscript sources for the regiment are listed in William B. Tubbs, comp., "A Bibliography of Illinois Regimental Sources in the Illinois State Historical Library: Part II, Manuscript," *Illinois Historical Journal* 87 (1994): 277–324. Another useful source is David B. Givler, "Intimate Glimpses of Army Life during the Civil War," typescript in Illinois State Historical Library, Springfield. The Givler manuscript, which is a combination of memoir, diary, and letters written by a member of Company C, is not listed by Tubbs, but Hicken uses it effectively in *Illinois in the Civil War*.

11. E. Merton Coulter, *Travels in the Confederate States: A Bibliography* (1948; rpt., Baton Rouge: Louisiana State University Press, 1994), 4–5; Ambrose, *History,* introduction.

12. The two histories Ambrose would have found useful were written by Louis A. Simmons for the 84th Illinois Infantry and Wales W. Wood for the 95th Illinois Infantry. Interestingly, the author of a history of the 40th Illinois Infantry published in 1864 was written in the form of a diary, although the author, Ephraim J. Hart, also devoted much attention to his personal experiences. The Simmons and Hart volumes are described in Coulter, *Travels in the Confederate States,* 124, 229.

13. For the official record of the regiment's initial term of service as three-month recruits see Janet B. Hewett et al., eds., *Supplement to the Official Records of the Union and Confederate Armies,* 100 vols. (Wilmington, N.C.: Broadfoot, 1994–2001), pt. 2, 8:512–22 (cited hereafter as *OR Supplement*). The best account of Illinois military participation in the war is Hicken, *Illinois in the Civil War*.

14. No mention of these weeks in Missouri appears in the regiment's official Record of Events. See *OR Supplement,* pt. 2, 8:480–511. A reliable summary of the regiment's movements is provided in Frederick H. Dyer, *A Compendium of the War of the Rebellion,* 3 vols. (New York: Thomas Yoseloff, 1959), 3:1046.

15. D. L. Ambrose, "Memorial Day Address Delivered by Captain D. L. Ambrose, Princess Theatre, Canton, Ill., May 30, 1913," 4, in Illinois State Historical Library, Springfield.

16. Ambrose, "Memorial Day Address," 5, pays brief homage to the Confederate soldiers who opposed the regiment at Allatoona Pass ("among the best and most heroic soldiers that ever made a battle record"), although such a characterization also enhanced the courageous stand of the 7th Illinois on that day. Ambrose, like many other soldiers on both sides during and after the war, was also more likely to acknowledge the courage of the enemy soldiers he fought than to recognize the legitimacy of the rival nation. In any event, in that same speech (3), Am-

brose continued to regard southern secession as an act of "treason" only slightly less despicable than the activities of American socialists and anarchists in 1913.

17. Hicken, *Illinois in the Civil War,* 141.

18. Hicken, *Illinois in the Civil War,* 2, 4–5, 12–14.

19. Hicken, *Illinois in the Civil War,* 128–31.

20. Ibid., 79–81.

21. Ibid., 17, 139–40; Bob Sterling, "Discouragement, Weariness, and War Politics: Desertions from Illinois Regiments during the Civil War," *Illinois Historical Journal* 82 (1989): 239–62.

22. Hicken, *Illinois in the Civil War,* 133–39 (quotation on 137).

From
SHILOH
to
SAVANNAH
The Seventh Illinois Infantry in the
Civil War

TO THE

Fathers, Mothers, Wives, Sisters and Orphans,

OF THOSE

OF THE

SEVENTH REGIMENT ILLINOIS VOLUNTEER INFANTRY

WHO FELL IN AMERICA'S GREAT STRUGGLE FOR
FREEDOM AND HUMANITY

THIS VOLUME

IS RESPECTFULLY INSCRIBED

BY

THE AUTHOR.

INTRODUCTION.

Histories of wars are seldom written by eye witnesses of the scenes which they attempt to depict, and the events which they pretend to describe; but are generally made up from the statements of those who wish to gain notoriety, and are embellished by the aid of the writer's imagination. To write a perfect history of the late terrible war in the United States, would seem, from the attempts already made, to be an impossibility. With one writer we have a good account of the great achievements of the Army of the Potomac, but all other armies are ignored. Another faithful historian will give a correct narrative of the war, and to follow him will be to follow the fortunes and misfortunes of Butler, Banks, Pope and Fremont. In all of these, none of less rank than a brigade commander receives special notice, unless, perchance, he happens at some time to meet the author under peculiarly favorable circumstances. While it cannot be said that the history of one army is the history of all armies, yet it may well be said that in the hardships, dangers privations and glories of one good soldier, we have the history of every good soldier who belonged to the Union army. They all bore the same burdens, fought the same, or similar battles, and had adventures identically the same. So with companies and regiments, which are the foundation of armies. The history of one is the history of all. In the following pages, the reader will find recorded the trials and hardships, together with the pleasures and duties of every regiment which bore a gallant part in the great struggle for nationality. It is our design in giving a history of the Seventh Illinois Volunteer Infantry to give a complete and accurate history of every man who had the honor of a membership in it, without favor or partiality. And in so doing, we have called to our assistance the different officers who commanded the regiment, who happened to have in their possession material points of history which we were not able to obtain. If anything has been omitted, it has not been intentional; yet, with all the various shiftings of the scene, it would be remarkable if nothing were omitted.

The narrative commences with the formation of the first company, and runs through the three months, three years, and veteran service, and ends with the final muster-out of the survivors at Louisville, Kentucky, July 9th, 1865.

In the list of casualties some names that will be looked for will not be seen. We very much regret this, but owing to the incompleteness of the Adjutant General's report, we are unable to furnish them: scarcely any note is made there of our noble wounded. Where the blame lies we do not pretend to say.

To the officers of the regiment, for encouragement and aid; to Lieut. S. F. Flint, for valuable poems, written expressly for these pages; and to Rev. W. R. Goodwin, Pastor M. E. Church, Lincoln, Illinois, for services rendered in reviewing the manuscript, we make our sincere and grateful acknowledgments.

We now throw ourself upon the generosity of the public, disclaiming any pretensions to literary merit, hoping that we will be dealt with gently.

Respectfully,

D. L. A.

CHAPTER I.

[April 15, 1861–July 25, 1861]

The Storm that for years had been brewing—Lincoln's Election—The Inauguration—The wild frenzy of the South—The Fall of Fort Sumpter—The Commencement of the War—The first call for troops—The first muster in of the
Seventh—The Three Months service—Their Re-enlistment.

For thirty years the leading spirits of the South, with slavery in full feather, wrote every day of the inviolateness of secession, and the divinity of human bondage. The leading spirits of
the North, champions of universal freedom, advocates of a
broad and comprehensive democracy, read every cruel, vaunting
word as fast as it emanated from the oligarchy; hence sprung
the agitation of the slavery question. Thus the great conflict between liberty and its opposing element began. Looking from the
watch-tower, they had seen the South for years rule the nation,
and by this rule, which was a rule for the interest of the slave
power, the argus eyes of liberty's sentinels discovered that the
proud edifice of liberty was threatened. They beheld not afar
the rock that was threatening to split it in twain, and thereby
whelm a struggling people into a wild, dark night of war. The
fair goddess sat weeping as she beheld the danger. Tears fell
like dew drops, when the harsh music from the lowly bonds-
man's chains was wafted to her ears from Pennsylvania Avenue. It was in the last days of Buchanan's administration
when the promulgators of the great principles of universal
brotherhood to man, saw most clearly the yawning gulf over
which the great Union hung. The people having educated themselves out of their mutual indignation to a grand abhorrence,
and out of this grand abhorrence to a grand agency, with a voice
whose echoes rolled around the world, proclaimed ABRAHAM
LINCOLN their leader. A revolution that had been brewing ever
since Calhoun's day, was now threatening. A wild frenzy was
now holding and controlling the general mind of the slave
power. Declarations to the effect that they would not submit to

abolition rule were boldly made throughout the South. LINCOLN beholds the gathering storm. He imagines he hears afar the thunders of war and revolution. He starts for the Capitol; but ere he starts, says: "I hope there will be not trouble; but I will make the South a grave-yard rather than see a slavery gospel triumph, or successful secession lose this government to the cause of the people and representative institutions." Thus spoke the great apostle of freedom before leaving Springfield. Inauguration day is drawing nigh. The waves of revolution seem rolling. The fostered coals in the hot-bed of treason are being fanned into flame. At last the fourth of March, 1861, dawns. LINCOLN is inaugurated. His inaugural address savors of conciliation. He seeks to stay the angry storm that is brewing. His heart goes out "with malice towards none—with charity for all."[1] But his words of christian beauty, coming from a heart whose dimensions would embrace the whole world and have room for more, has no effect upon the Southern heart. They say, "this has been our darling scheme for thirty years. We will not abandon it now. We will sever this Union. We will crush her laws. We will trail her flag." LINCOLN enters upon his duties; curtains of gloom are flung around him. But in Him who bid faith lean upon His arm and hope to dip her pinions in His blood and mount to the skies, he trusts.

The secession movement had been inaugurated. Five months had intervened since the ball commenced rolling. Five months of turmoil—five months of uncertainty to the republic. The fearful clouds grow darker.

On the night of the thirteenth of April, 1861, a glaring light might have been seen flashing along the horizon's bar down by the Atlantic. The fourteenth dawns, and from the ramparts of Fort Sumter war's dread tocsin is sounded. "Fort Sumter has fallen!" The beautiful banner of stars has been struck by a traitorous foe. The gauntlet has been flung. The ship of state rocks wildly. Soon it is swept from the ocean, over the mountains of the north, telling an anxious people that "the flag has been struck down to-day." The North's powerful millions seem to surge like tall, dark pines swayed by a fierce wind, and we imagine we see the march and tramp of a grand army that will make pale the nations of the earth. The news goes home to

Europe, and a voice comes rolling back, like the organic swell of ocean's thunder, "Save, Oh! save, the American Union!" It comes not from kings, queens, and popes, but from the struggling millions, from the chained slave, from Russia's serfs. But ere this news went across the waters, the President made the call for seventy-five thousand troops, and ere this voice rolls back, there are citizen soldiers in America marshaled for the fray, rushing on to the rescue. Like a grand legion they move to save the flag—save the Republic from drifting back apace towards anarchy and universal night. In every city and hamlet in the north, drums are beating for volunteers. Their notes are heard among the pineries of Maine—heard among the Green Mountains—heard where the Hudson flows—heard where Liberty's great cradle first rocked. Simultaneous with the east, the same living spirit burns in the west. The prairies of Illinois seem blazing with the patriots' fire. Tramp! tramp! is the music rolling from the great west, forboding to traitors the doom of disaster.

The first from the great commonwealth of Illinois, who harkened to the call "to arms!"—who harkened to the appeals that came from the tombs of the silent, sleeping warriors of the revolution, were the men who composed the Seventh Illinois Volunteer Infantry. They were the first to offer their services after the President's proclamation; the first to enter Camp Yates.[2]

The Springfield Grays, afterwards company I, commanded by Captain John Cook, was the first company in the regiment to tender its services to the country, and the Lincoln Guards, afterwards company E, commanded by Captain Wilford D. Wyatt, was the first company in the regiment to march into Camp Yates, escorted by one platoon of the Grays, commanded by Lieutenant T. G. Moffitt. The Springfield Grays tendered their services to Governor Yates, April 15th, 1861. The Lincoln Guards tendered their services and marching into Camp Yates April 19th 1861.

April 24th.—Up to this time, companies from Elgin, Carlinville, Aurora, Mattoon, Lincoln, Litchfield, Bunker Hill and Sangamon, have marched into Camp Yates.

April 25th.—To-day the Seventh Illinois Volunteer Infantry is Mustered into the United States service by Captain John Pope, United States Army, with the following officers:[3]

Colonel.—John Cook, of the Springfield Grays.
Lieutenant Colonel.—Wilford D. Wyatt, of Lincoln Guards.
Major.—Nicholas Greusel, of the Aurora Company.
Surgeon.—Richard L. Metcalf.
Chaplain.—Jesse P. Davis.

COMPANY A.
Captain.—Edward S. Joslyn.
First Lieutenant.—Reuben H. Adams.
Second Lieutenant.—James Doudson.

COMPANY B.
Captain.—James Monroe.
First Lieutenant.—Edward W. True.
Second Lieutenant.—Robert H. McFadden.

COMPANY C.
Captain—Samuel E. Lawyer.
First Lieutenant.—Silas Miller.
Second Lieutenant.—Rufus Pattison.

COMPANY D.
Captain.—Benjamin Munn.
First Lieutenant.—Elizur Southworth.
Second Lieutenant.—Mark Miller.

COMPANY E.
Captain.—George H. Estabrook.
First Lieutenant.—Otto Buzzard.
Second Lieutenant.—H. C. Worthington.

COMPANY F.
Captain.—J. F. Cummings.
First Lieutenant—William O. Jenks.
Second Lieutenant.—C. F. Adams.

COMPANY G.
Captain.—William Sands.
First Lieutenant.—David L. Canfield.
Second Lieutenant.—W. G. Kercheval.

COMPANY H.
Captain.—C. W. Holden.

First Lieutenant.—Chris. C. Mason.
Second Lieutenant.—Leo Wash. Meyers.

COMPANY I.

Captain.—A. J. Babcock.
First Lieutenant.—Thos. G. Moffitt.
Second Lieutenant.—Noah E. Mendell.

COMPANY K.

Captain.—Richard Rowett.
First Lieutenant—Manning Mayfield.
Second Lieutenant.—George Hunter.

At this time the firm steps of Illinois' patriot men were heard, keeping step to the music of the Union. In every direction her stalwart sons were seen marching towards the Capitol. The loyal pulse never beat so central and quickening as at this period. After the organization of the regiment, on the twenty-seventh, they are marched from Camp Yates to the armory, where they receive their arms—the Harper's Ferry altered musket—after which the regiment marches to the depot and embarks for Alton, Illinois, where the regiment arrives at 4 P.M., and are quartered in the old State Penitentiary. With men who were eager for war—whose hopes of martial glory ran so high—to be quartered in the old criminal home, grated harshly, and they did not enter those dark recesses with much gusto.

During our stay here, the regiment was every day marched out on the city commons by Colonel Cook, and there exercised in the manual of arms and the battallion evolutions, until they attained a proficiency surpassed by none in the service.

On the nineteenth of May, private Harvey, of Company A, died—the first death in the regiment. The first soldier in the first regiment to offer his life for the flag and freedom. On the second of June, private Dunsmore, of the same company, falls into a soldier's grave. May the loyal people ever remember these first sacrifices so willingly offered in the morning of the rebellion.[4]

On the third of June, the regiment embarked on board the steamer City of Alton, for Cairo, Illinois. Passing down the river, the steamer is hailed and brought to at the St. Louis Arsenal, and after the necessary inspection, proceeds on her way. Pass the steamer Louisiana, with the 12th Illinois, Colonel McArthur, on board, arriving at Cairo on the fourth, and go into camp on the flat ground in the rear of the city and near the levee.[5] This camp is very appropriately named Camp Defiance. From Cairo, on the seventeenth of June, the regiment is marched up the Ohio river as far as Mound City, where it is quartered in a large brick building, on the bank of the river, which the Seventh will remember as Camp Joslyn, named in honor of Captain Joslyn of Company A. These were quiet days with the Seventh. In their ardor they felt in themselves the strength of giants.

June 25th.—Brig. General Prentiss, and Colonels Oglesby and Paine, visit the camp of the Seventh, addressing the men upon the subject of re-enlisting.[6]

June 26th.—A general alarm seemed to prevail to-day, concerning hostile appearances on the Kentucky shore, and in consequence, Colonel Cook sends Captains Monroe and Babcock, with a squad of men, across the river to reconnoiter. They soon return and report all quiet; nothing but the movement of farmers with their stock.

June 29th.—To-day a member of Company F is "drummed out of the regiment" per verdict of Court Martial. Two single lines were formed facing inward, with a space between of about thirty feet. The disgraced soldier was marched along between the two lines, accompanied by two drummers, who kept up a terribly discordant drumming, while the men kept up a hooting and hissing.

Sunday, June 30th.—Divine service at the grove to-day by Chaplain Davis; largely attended by the regiment.[7]

July 3d.—An alarm to-night; "long roll" beaten; the men formed in line; no ammunition; considerable confusion; three rounds issued to the men while in line; false alarm, caused by the firing of the pickets.

July 4th—Dawns gloriously. The national salutes roll from the Illinois shore, sending their joyous music southward, telling a story that runs back to the morning of the Republic. At 10 o'clock the regiment is formed and marched to the grove, where they listen to the reading of the Declaration of Independence by Colonel Cook. Oration by Chaplain Davis. Valedictory by Captain Joslyn.

July 7th.—The regiment's period of enlistment is now drawing to a close, and it has not been out of its native State. The
drums are now beating for volunteers to fill up the call made
on the fourth of May for three years' troops. The Seventh stood
on the banks of the Ohio. They looked southward and they
knew that they had not been down there where the wicked enemies of freedom trailed the old flag. They had performed the
engagements the government had required of them; but san-
guine hearts had been disappointed, and the country was calling again for defenders. The majority of the Seventh say they
will stay; that they will re-enlist; that they will harken to
every demand the country makes for the defense of her honor
and glory. Those re-enlisting are given a short furlough to their
homes, and after returning to Mound City, the regiment is
mustered out of the three months' service the twenty-fifth of
July, and on the same day is mustered into the three years'
service by Captain Pitcher, U. S. A.

The story of Bull Run's battle field is now borne to our ears.
Its wail has gone to the hearts of a throbbing people. The
hearts of the men beat high to carry the flag into the South-
land. This part of the Seventh's history I have seen fit to make
brief; being anxious to lead the reader on as fast as possible to
the days when the deep intonations of battle were heard. Days
when the dogs of war barked loudly in tones of thunder around
where the old Seventh's flag ofttimes stood encircled by a barricade of steel.

Chapter II.

[July 25, 1861–February 2, 1862]

The commencement of the three years' service.—Roster of Officers.—Camp at Mound City, Ills.—Camp at Cairo, Ills.—Leaving Cairo.—Ascending the Mississippi.—Landing at Sulphur Springs.—Camp at Ironton.—Pilot Knob.—Expedition through Missouri.—Camp at Cape Girardeau.—Descending the Mississippi.—Landing at Fort Holt.—March to Elliott's Mills.—Battle of Belmont.—Return to Fort Holt.—Expedition to Blandville and Elliott's Mills.—Preparation to leave Fort Holt.

The Seventh Regiment Illinois Volunteer Infantry now commences its three years' service with the following roster of officers:

Colonel.—John Cook
Lieutenant Colonel.—A. J. Babcock, late Capt. Co. "I."
Major.—Richard Rowett, late Capt. Co. "K."
Adjutant.—Leroy R. Waller
Quartermaster.—William Brown
Surgeon.—Richard L. Metcalf.
First Assistant Surgeon.—James Hamilton.
Chaplain.—Jesse P. Davis.

COMPANY A.
Captain.—Samuel G. Ward.
First Lieutenant.—Jonathan Kimbal.
Second Lieutenant.—William Renwick.

COMPANY B.
Captain.—James Monroe.
First Lieutenant.—Hector Perrin.
Second Lieutenant.—O. D. Ells.

COMPANY C.
Captain.—Samuel E. Lawyer.
First Lieutenant.—Leroy R. Waller.
Second Lieutenant.—Edward R. Roberts.

COMPANY D.

Captain.—Benj. M. Munn.
First Lieutenant.—Ira A. Church.
Second Lieutenant.—James M. Munn.

COMPANY E.

Captain.—Geo. H. Estabrook.
First Lieutenant.—John A. Smith.
Second Lieutenant.—H. N. Estabrook.

COMPANY F.

Captain.—Jas. T. Cummings.
First Lieutenant.—Wm. Mathie.
Second Lieutenant.—A. D. Knowlton.

COMPANY G.

Captain.—Henry W. Allen.
First Lieutenant.—Geo. W. Tipton.
Second Lieutenant.—Adam E. Vrooman

COMPANY H.

Captain.—Clifford Ward Holden.
First Lieutenant.—Leo W. Myers.
Second Lieutenant.—Jacob L. Ring.

COMPANY I.

Captain.—Noah Mendell.
First Lieutenant.—E. S. Johnson.
Second Lieutenant.—Thomas N. Francis.

COMPANY K.

Captain.—George Hunter.
First Lieutenant.—Joseph Rowett.
Second Lieutenant.—Thomas B. Rood.

After remaining in Camp at Mound City, Illinois, a few days, we proceeded down the Ohio as far as Cairo, where again the regiment goes into Camp Defiance. And whilst here, from morning until night, the officers' voices are heard in command on the drill ground, bringing the regiment up to a high standard, preparing them that they may play well their part in the coming drama.

Remaining in Camp Defiance two weeks, we take passage on board the steamer "New Uncle Sam," and are soon passing up the Mississippi river, accompanied by other steamers, loaded with troops from Bird's Point and Cairo.[8] It is rumored that we will land at some point and enter Missouri. The Seventh are now standing on the deck of the steamer as she moves proudly up the river, and as we look over into Missouri, where wicked men have assailed the flag and freedom, our hearts beat high, and we long to be there, that we may unfurl our flag and give it freedom to wave on that side the river as well as on this.

After a pleasant trip the regiment lands at Sulphur Springs, Missouri, and in a measure the wishes of the men are gratified, for they are now on rebel soil. From this point we proceed by rail to Ironton, and upon our arrival there, we are met by General Prentiss, who makes the regiment a speech, telling them that they have been ordered there to help him drive Jeff. Thompson from Missouri.[9] We go into camp in the vicinity of Ironton. The scenery around here is grand. Pilot Knob looms up peerlessly, close to where we are camped. The Seventh boys are often seen on its summits (standing as it were amid the clouds) looking down in the valley. While here the regiment is uniformed—and the Seventh's boys will remember those striped uniforms which made them look like convicts late from Jefferson City.

On the 1st of September we received marching orders. All is commotion to-night—many an interrogation is made relating to this thing and that.

On the morning of the 2nd, with every man a knapsack, haversack and canteen—and these filled to overflowing, the Seventh, for the first time in its history, took up the line of march, under command of Major Rowett, Colonel Cook being in command of the brigade, and Lieutenant Colonel Babcock absent in Illinois.[10] The spirits of the men run high—they expected every moment to be rushed into battle; but how sadly were they disappointed. For days and nights we followed Prentiss in the pursuit of Jeff. Thompson; marching over rocks and hills, passing through Booneville, Fredrickton and Jackson, to Cape Girardeau, where we go into camp in the field to the rear of the town, thus ending our bloodless Missouri expedition. No Jeff. Thompson—no rebels could be found, all having made their exit far away over the mountains. Though it was a hard march, causing the weary, foot-sore soldiers to fall oft times by the way, the Seventh as a whole, enjoyed it well, and they will not soon forget the bountiful barn-yards they so frequently made descents upon, leaving nothing behind but geese- and chicken-heads to rehearse the story. I was much amused one evening by hearing an officer tell some of the men that over beyond that hill, about one mile, was a barn full of chickens, "and the first soldier who molested them he would buck and gag."[11] By a quick wink of the eye, the boys were made to understand him, and around the camp-fires these men sat that night eating their supper and laughing most heartily, for we noticed that they were masticating some old fat hens. Of course the officer's orders were against all depredations, but orders were sometimes accompanied with a wink, which the men always watched for. If none accompanied the orders they always understood what was meant.

September 21st.—Lieutenant Colonel Babcock arrives back and assumes command of the regiment. The same evening, Major Rowett leaves for Illinois on leave of absence.

September 22d.—Articles of war read to-day; the law laid down, &c.

Battalion and company drill is now the order of the day. Colonel Babcock seems ambitious to make the Seventh a star in the battalion and company evolutions.

September 26th.—National fast by proclamation of the President. Church service 3 P.M., by Chaplain Davis. Delivers a fine sermon, which is attentively listened to by the members of the Seventh. This evening at 9 o'clock Lieutenant Vrooman died of typhoid fever; another victim given at liberty's shrine.

September 27th.—Lieutenant Vrooman is buried to-day, with military honors. Colonel Boyle, with the Eleventh Missouri, turned out and joined in doing honor to the fallen soldier.[12] Thus another soldier's mound has been reared—another waymark for the pilgrims of freedom has been built.

September 30th.—Major Rowett returned from Illinois to-day. Official notice informs us this evening that Captain Plummer, U. S. A., has been appointed Colonel of the Eleventh Missouri, and ordered to relieve Colonel Cook and assume command of the post.[13]

October 1st.—This morning Colonel Cook leaves for Springfield on a leave of absence.

October 3d.—This evening at 10 o'clock Lieutenant Colonel Babcock receives orders to report to post headquarters. Reporting, he receives orders to proceed the following day to Fort Holt, Kentucky, with his regiment, and relieve the Seventeenth Illinois.

October 4th.—At 10 A.M., we strike our tents; 12 M., we march in a thunder storm to the river, and embark on the steamer Aleck Scott. Leave the Cape at 6 P.M., run down the river fifteen miles and anchor for the night.

October 5th.—Weigh anchor at daylight, and soon after proceeding on our way, we run on to a sandbar, where we remain three and a-half hours. Extricating ourselves, we move on and arrive at Fort Holt at 3 P.M.[14]

October 6th.—This morning, as the morning gun was fired from Fort Prentiss, at Cairo, through some carelessness of the gunner, a solid shot was fired which came across the Ohio river and over the Seventh's camp, performing general havoc among the tree-tops. No damage done, save what was done in scaring the men within its range. The ball is now on exhibition at Colonel Babcock's tent as a war trophy.

October 15th.—To-day the line officers are formed into a company and drilled by Colonel Babcock in the company movements. They make a fine company, and the Colonel seems to enjoy the drill.

October 19th.—To-day Colonel Cook arrives on the steamer J. H. Dickey, and assumes command of the post.

October 23d.—To-day the regiment receives orders to clear off a new camping ground and build houses.

October 24th.—A member of company D, private James M. Sparrow, died today. Thus one by one the Union's defenders are passing away. Peace to their ashes.

October 25th.—The axes are now being swung in the Kentucky woods. The work on the houses goes on briskly. We remain at Fort Holt, working at our houses and performing the regular routine of camp duties until the evening of the sixth of November, when we receive orders to hold ourselves in readiness to move at a moment's notice, in light marching order. On the morning of the seventh we move from the Fort, marching down the river towards Columbus, Kentucky. While passing down along the shore, we behold transports descending, loaded down with troops, and we come to the conclusion that there is something in the wind. Proceeding as far as Elliott's Mills, we receive orders to halt and remain here until further orders. Colonel Babcock having been absent at St. Louis, on business for the regiment, returns this afternoon. About two o'clock we hear something that sounds very much like thunder. It is the cannon's deep, harsh tones, telling us that a battle is raging. It is the first time such sounds have ever fallen upon our ears. We are expecting every minute to receive orders to move forward. There is now a death-like silence where the Seventh stands. All are anticipating that ere the sun's rays fade from the Mississippi they will see blood flow. But it seems that our time has not yet come. Remaining here until the day is well nigh gone, a messenger arrives telling us that Grant to-day has fought the great battle of Belmont; that he has been repulsed; that the Seventh is in danger of attack from an overwhelming force now marching towards us from Columbus. We immediately re-cross Mayfield creek, and take the backward track for Fort Holt, where we arrive at 2 o'clock the next morning.[15]

November 8th.—To-day a flag of truce, accompanied by Colonel Cook, goes down the river to the battle field of Belmont to look after the fallen dead. Sixty-four were all that were found.

November 13.—This morning the steamer Aleck Scott proceeds down the river loaded with the Belmont prisoners, accompanied by federal officers from Cairo, Fort Holt and Bird's Point, for the purpose of consummating an exchange. They are met by the rebel steamer Prince, about half way from Cairo to Columbus, with the Union prisoners, accompanied by a party of Confederate officers, regalied in their most dashing colors. Meeting under a flag of truce, the steamers are soon lashed together, and Generals Grant and Polk commence the conference relating to an exchange. The Union officers are in the meantime invited on board the rebel steamer, and are soon mingling promiscuously among the "Southern Empire men." Friendly, social exchanges were made, but in the language of Tom. Carlyle, "they had their share of wind." With their gaudy glitter they paced the Prince's deck and vauntingly declared the old Union should die; that they would never surrender to the United States government. The exchange having been consummated, the Aleck Scott and

Prince commenced moving in opposite directions, one northward and the other southward. Cheer after cheer rolled from each steamer as they separated. Ere long these men will engage in the carnival of blood. How sad to know that these fostered men, beneath the shadow of the flag, should thus assail the country that gave them birth. The Seventh's officers, Colonel Cook, Lieutenant Colonel Babcock, Major Rowett, Captains Monroe, Mendell, Holden, Allen and Hunter, Lieutenants Johnson, Church, Ring, Smith, Roberts, and others, are now landed at Fort Holt from the steamer Aleck Scott, much elated with their trip to Dixie. From what we can learn, they have been "funny fellows" to-day, but this is neither here nor there. These officers, with their glittering gold, their dangling swords, their feathery plumes and manly faces, carried with them an impression that will forsooth be the cause of forbodings to the traitors. We imagine that they will have unpleasant dreams to-night.

November 16th.—Paymaster Major Sherman arrives to-day, and in the afternoon commences to pay the regiment; pays the field officers and staff, and non-commissioned staff, and companies A, D, F and H, and adjourns for the night.

November 18th.—To-day the Paymaster finishes paying the regiment. The men are now flush with the "collaterals" and in consequence the sutlers and swindlers are trying to play their hands.

November 19th.—This morning at 9 o'clock a heavy thunder storm blows across the breast of the river, during which an alarm of a rebel attack is given, which calls the Seventh forth in line of battle. Also an alarm at Bird's Point, but all prove to be false alarms.

November 20th.—To-day the camp is alarmed by the firing of the picket guards. Nothing hostile, however, is discovered. All is quiet this evening.

November 25th.—Colonel Cook left Fort Holt to-day for Springfield, and in his absence Lieutenant Colonel Babcock commands the post, and Major Rowett the regiment.

November 29th.—Colonel Cook returned and resumed command of the post. The work on the houses still progressing finely. The sound of the axe and the rattle of the saw are heard in every direction.

December 1st.—To-day a rebel gunboat steamed up from Columbus and fired a few shots into Fort Holt. Our big gun below the camp of the Twenty-eighth Illinois returned the fire with a vim, after which the rebel machine drifts back to its own congenial clime, having accomplished nothing save a little fright.[16]

December 11th.—To-day the companies move into their new houses. Evening.—We are now nicely quartered in good substantial houses, strong enough to turn shot and shell. We remain quietly housed at Fort Holt until the thirteenth of January, 1862, when we receive marching orders. All is confusion now, preparing for a forward movement.

January 14th.—Early this morning the Seventh takes up the line of march for Blandville, Kentucky, to join McClernand's Division, already marched on before us. Upon our arrival there, we find that he has left with his command, moving in the direction of Columbus. We hasten on, and join him in the evening after he has gone into camp. Everything seems to indicate that Grant means action. The camp fires are now seen burning away on the fields as far as the eye can reach.[17]

The men have all sunk to rest upon the earth, save the weary sentinel who is pacing quietly over his lonely path.

Though the heroes seem to sleep soundly, they may be dreaming of the clash of men, and the clang of steel, of the groans of the dying and the shouts of the victors. The Seventh boys are now all still. How nobly they all look as their eyes are closed, with the shadow of the pale moon playing upon their faces. We are wont to feel sad when we look around here and know that in this war for the Union some of those who lie here will go down as victims on the alter of human freedom.

January 15th.—This morning we wait for the arrival of General Smith's command. After their arrival, we move forward.[18] Soon it commences to rain, and through mud and rain we march all day. Taking a circuitous route through woods and swamps, we arrive at Elliott's Mills in the evening, and go into camp on the opposite bank of Mayfield Creek.[19]

January 16th.—This morning it is still raining very hard. We find it difficult to keep the camp fires burning. Our camp is in the Mayfield Creek bottom. The water is standing all around us. The creek is rising very high, and it is still raining.

Our subsistence is now running short, and Mayfield Creek between us and Fort Holt, our nearest depot of supplies. Mud! mud! everywhere, the situation looks critical.

January 17th.—Affairs look billious this morning. Still raining, the camp fires burning dimly. The soldiers wet and chilled. All day a party are at work moving the baggage train across the creek. Everything looks dreary; nothing cheering, nothing comfortable. No rest for the soldier to-night.

January 18th.—This morning all looks gloomy. The hopes of attacking Columbus have vanished. We await orders to return to Fort Holt. This evening the quartermaster arrives with supplies, which are in great demand. The boys are more cheerful to-night.

January 19th.—This morning we receive orders to pack up and move back to Fort Holt. We cross the creek on an old flatboat bridge. The roads are terrible. We find it a very fatiguing tramp. We arrive at Fort Holt in the evening, almost exhausted by the hard march. All seem glad to again be ushered into their comfortable quarters.[20]

For some days the effect of the forced march in mud and rain, through the swamps of Kentucky are felt by the Seventh. The remaining part of the month we remain quietly at Fort Holt, though sometimes it seemed that the rapid rise of the Ohio would compel us to evacuate, but the waters subsided without submerging us. From the twenty-fifth on until the first of February, I can note nothing but the regular routine of camp duties. On the first we receive orders to hold ourselves in readiness to move with camp and garrison equipage. This order means that we will move in a day or two. All are in confusion and many are the conjectures relative to our destination.

February 2d.—Sunday morning we are busily engaged packing up to leave the fort. Steamers are numerous in this vicinity now. Every day troops are passing up the Ohio river, and it is rumored that they head for Tennessee. Some grand expedition on foot, as everything seems to indicate. We may follow soon. Where we will go, we cannot tell; only that our faces are being turned southward. I look around the camp to-night; I see strong men, full of life and hope. They may go down there ne'er to return again. Liberty will claim them, but in the years to come there will be a disenthralled race who will pass their graves and drop tears to their memory.

Chapter III.

[February 3, 1862–February 11, 1862]

Leaving Fort Holt—Ascending the Ohio and the Tennessee—Landing before Fort Henry—The March to the Rear—The Mud—The Fall of Fort Henry—The accident met with by Company I—Our camp at Fort Henry.

Monday Morning, February 3d, 1862.—The regiment takes passage on board the steamer City of Memphis, for parts unknown. Being nearly all day loading the camp and garrison equipage, the steamer does not move until 5 o'clock, P.M.

We now steer up the Ohio river; pass Paducah at midnight. The fourth dawns beautifully, finding us moving up the Tennessee river. Rumor has it that Fort Henry is our destination. The drums are now beating, colors flying and hearts beating high, for the face of the Seventh is Dixieward. The gun boats are leading the way, and five steamers follow in the wake of the Memphis. 'Tis evening now. We see in the dim distance Fort Henry's walls and the flaunting stars and bars. We disembark four miles from the Fort and go into camp on the bank of the river. Some one remarks that there is mud here, and so say we, and the most terrible mud. As the soldiers move through the camp this evening, their cry is: "No bottom!"[21]

Wednesday, 5th.—This morning a fog hangs over the surrounding hills. About ten thousand troops are concentrated here. The gun-boats are anchored in the river, waiting for the land forces. A large number of troops are landing on the other side of the river. Everything this evening looks warlike.

Thursday, 6th.—It is raining this morning; has been all night. There may be poetry in war, but there is no poetry in Camp Halleck (the name given to this camp by general orders).[22] Mud predominates and the camp fires burn dimly. Soon the rain ceases and the clouds vanish; the sky becomes clear, and the sun sheds forth refreshing light, which is very welcome to the wet Seventh. But ere it is noon we have marching orders. The gun-boats, terrible looking monsters, are now steaming up towards Fort Henry. The army is put in motion.

We look away; and around the hills and up the ravines we see the beautiful starry banners flying. It is our fate to be one of the rear regiments, and while waiting for the assembly to beat, the regiment ascends a hill close by, from where we first behold a rebel camp. We see the ensign of treason floating defiantly over the Fort. Mad, mad, men! that they would thus insult the mother that gave them birth. But ah! they are now being circumvented. The gunboats still keep steaming up towards the Fort. We predict that ere the sun sinks to rest, that banner, the representative of a wicked people, will be struck down, and that upon her staff the old Union's flag will flutter in the wind, and cast around Fort Henry her flashing light. Up a winding ravine we pass, over the hills we climb. The troops are aiming to get to the rear of the Fort, ere the bombardment commences. The roads are cut up terribly. The artillery mires down upon the hills; the Seventh lifts them out. We are now away on the Tennessee bluffs. Looking up the river we see a smoke; we hear a sullen roar. What means it all? It is a smoke and a roar from the gun-boat Essex. The ball is now open. In quick succession the mad machines of war give vent to their death-dealing elements. The troops seem eager for the fray, but it is evident the way the artillery is miring down, that it will only be a naval battle. Shot and shell, like living monsters, are now flying over and into Fort Henry. Moving on, the imposing scene is lost to our view; but like the rumble and roar of distant thunder, the echoes roll over the bluffs and cliffs of the Tennessee. All day we keep winding around through the woods, seeking to get to the rear of the Fort. Towards evening a messenger comes riding back and his voice rings out "Fort Henry's flag is down and the rebels are flying." It being impossible for the advanced troops to get to the rear in time to cut off the retreat, they now move up and take possession of the works. We go into camp in the woods for one mile from the rebel works. Having been ordered to leave our knapsacks with the wagons this morning, we have in consequence no blankets nor overcoats to-night. It is cold. The soldiers are suffering; a bleak winter wind is blowing around them, but a rebel flag went down to-day, and the soldiers' hearts are glad, glad because in its stead floats the old Union's loved banner.[23]

Friday, 7th.—This morning the soldiers stand in groups, shivering around the camp fires. A chilling north wind whistles fiercely through these forests of pine. Last night an accident happened Company I, by the falling of part of a tree, wounding Captain Mendell, First Sergeant John E. Sullivan, and Sergeant Luke Norton. The latter's arm was broken; the Captain is hurt very badly, but we hope not seriously, for we will need the Captain in the coming battles. We move camp to-day inside the fortifications. Loud huzzas rend the air as the soldiers behold the old flag waving over the Fort. Our quarters to-night are close by the Fort in rebel barracks. We now have our blankets and overcoats. The cold winds do not reach us; we are comfortable and happy.

Saturday, 8th.—This morning we are still at the Fort. This place looks as though it had passed through a terrible storm. We will now take a stroll over the works. They have been furrowed by sweeping shell. Dark and wild must have been the storm around here, ere the flag was lowered. It seems as though nothing of human construction could have survived it. Thirty remained at the guns. We walk a little farther, and oh! what a spectral sight! What a mangled mass, what a dark picture! They are fallen rebel soldiers. The thirty who remained in the Fort and worked the guns in those hours of darkness, have been excavated from the rubbish. It is sad to think how they fell; how they died fighting against the old flag—against the country which fostered their fathers and them in the lap of human freedom. I will turn from this scene; it is too heart rending. I will wend my way to the bivouac fires. This evening the few captives of Fort Henry are forwarded to Cairo. Among the number are General Tighlman and his Assistant Adjutant General.[24]

Sunday, 9th.—This morning troops are landing. Everywhere around Fort Henry, inside and outside the fortifications, the camp fires are burning. About twenty thousand troops throng the woods. General Grant is evidently preparing for some great work.

Monday and Tuesday, 10th and 11th.—Troops are landing all the while, from Illinois, Indiana, and Ohio. The great northwest seem to be flocking in. The Seventh move their camp back in the woods and pitch their tents on high ground. We are more comfortable now; not so much crowded. We are out where the free winds blow. It is rumored that General Grant designs moving upon the rebels in their stronghold at Fort Donelson. We may advance soon. Ere another sun shall have been far on its journey, the army perhaps will be tramping, and while it is drifting on its path, may the God of heaven who smiled upon Europe's great battle fields, smile upon the army of the Republic as she flings her banners to the wind and battles for the world's last hope, for liberty, fidelity and truth.

Chapter IV.

[February 12, 1862–April 5, 1862]

Our March to Fort Donelson—The Battle of Fort Donelson—The Surrender—
Our Losses—Our Camp at Clarksville—Our Trip up the Cumberland to
Nashville—Return to Clarksville—Decending the Cumberland—Ascending
the Tennessee—The Fleet—Landing at Pittsburg Landing—Our Camp
there—Rumors of the Enemy's Advance.

Wednesday Morning, 12th.—There is a clear blue sky over
head. Aids and orderlies are moving hither and thither;
drums are beating and bugles are blowing as if to say, "Up
boys and be ready, for Grant is on his restless steed." The
army is soon in motion; the banners are fluttering, and pennons flying. We look away through the woods and behold their
beautiful light streaming around stalwart men. It is early
when our brigade (the 3d) commanded by our Colonel, "John
Cook," moves from camp in the woods near Fort Henry. The
Seventh at the appointed time takes up the line of march, under the command of Lieutenant Colonel Babcock. The regiment is in fine spirits; the hearts of the men beat high. In
their mind's eye they weave wreaths of fame. They seem to
foresee themselves crowned with glory. But do they dream
that they will see blood flow at their feet; that some of their
number will go down in glory ere the sun makes many more
circuits around the world?

A great many regiments have moved on before us. At ten
minutes past one o'clock we hear the report of artillery. It
comes from the gun-boats on the Cumberland. We move on
briskly, and go into camp two miles from Fort Donelson. the
siege of this rebel Gibralter has already commenced. The
gun-boats keep muttering. Echoes come from the river like
echoes from wrathful thunder. But by and by the regiment
falls asleep on their bed of leaves, and all night long we hear
in our dreams the bolts of war, and behold the surge of men
in terrible battle.[25]

Thursday, 13th.—This is a beautiful still morning, though its stillness is occasionally interrupted by the heavy cannonading on the cumberland. After hastily eating our breakfast, we are ordered into line.

Soon Colonel Babcock gives the command "forward!" Going a short distance we are ordered to "halt!" "unsling knapsacks!" "draw overcoats!" We throw them in the fence corners, and move forward on double-quick time. Soon we are in the fray. While marching over a hill and down towards a ravine, the Seventh encounters a masked battery. It is our first encounter—our initiation. But oh, how fierce! we are only seventy-five yards from the battery's wrathful front. Grape and canister fall thick and fast. There is a little hesitation, but with their gallant Colonel and enthusiastic Major, the men stand the tempest. Colonel Babcock, with his quick perception, discovers at once the situation of his regiment, and with the ready aid of Major Rowett, succeeds in making a flank movement, passing from the rebel battery's immediate front to a more congenial locality. In this, our first engagement, one noble soldier has fallen. It seems almost a miracle that more did not fall. But only one went down—the gallant Captain Noah E. Mendell, of company I.

The principal fighting to-day has been done by the sharpshooters. There is a lull now. Nothing is heard save an occasional shot from the gun-boats. Darkness has come and we bivouac for the night; soon it commences to rain; then changes from a cold rain to sleet and snow. Oh! how cold the winter winds blow. We dare not build any camp fires, for Grant's edict has wisely gone forth, forbidding it. The soldiers suffer to-night. Some of them have no blankets. During the latter part of the night, Colonel Babcock, with his men, could have been seen pacing up and down a hill to keep from freezing. Oh! what a long cheerless night; and with what anxiousness the soldiers wait for the morning's dawn.

Friday, 14th.—Never was morning light more welcome than this morning's light is to the army of the Tennessee, for with it comes the camp fires. Everywhere, on the hills and in the ravines, their cheering light is seen. But the soldiers are still suffering. Their blankets are frozen, their clothes are wet.

They stand everywhere shivering around the camp fires. It is still raining and sleeting, (having changed from sleet to snow). The loyal hearts would start tears of love, could they see how this mighty army is thus standing down on the banks of the Cumberland, with not a murmur heard to escape them. Imagining myself not one of these, but imagining myself disinterested, that I may be freed from accusations of egotism, I would say that manhood stands here—men of fidelity; men of unexampled devotion to the country, the flag and freedom. But how sad the fact to know that there are some who would know it not. Though it is cold, and the winds blow, and the soldiers are suffering, it is not long until the firing commences. We are now in range of the rebel batteries. The cannon balls are flying over our heads, snapping off the tree tops, and performing general havoc in the woods.

We are now remaining at "a stand," in rear of the fort, and while here we hear heavy cannonading in the direction of the Cumberland. It is the gun-boats feeling Fort Donelson's strength. The sharp-shooters are doing their work. They greatly annoy the enemy by keeping them from their guns. No general fighting to-day, but the siege goes bravely on.

It is night now. It bids fair to be one of winter's cold, rayless nights; no moon, no stars are seen. Dark, threatening clouds fling their curtains adown the sky, telling the boys in blue that they will suffer.

Saturday, 15th.—It snowed again last night, but this morning the sky is clear; the clouds have disappeared, and the sunlight is seen again on the Cumberland hills. How cheeringly does it fall around the weary soldiers. It is indeed a blessing sent from heaven, for Grant and his army. But hark! we hear the rattle of musketry. It comes from the right wing. Soon we learn that Lawman's, McArthur's and Oglesby's brigades are engaged.[26] The battle is now raging furiously. Our regiment is ordered to hasten to the left. Down the ravines, over the hills and across the abattis, the Seventh, led by the brave Colonel Babcock, and cheered by the gallant Rowett, go thundering on to where the wild battle storm rages. Arriving at the scene of action, we find the Second Iowa and an Indiana regiment in position near the enemy's works, breasting manfully a rebel battery playing upon them from a hill inside the outer works. Rushing into the conflict, Colonel Babcock forms the regiment under the galling fire. At this moment the veteran General Smith, moving through the fearful storm, draws rein to his charger in front of the Seventh, and says to Colonel Babcock, "I never saw a regiment make such grand movements under such a fire in all my military life as your's has just made. Colonel, I thank God for your command at this moment. Charge that rebel battery! charge it with your steel and silence its work of death!" The Seventh's bayonets are soon up and bristling. The battle is now raging furiously. The general casts his eyes towards the west, and beholding the sun fast sinking towards the horizon's bar, he turns to Colonel Babcock and says, "I countermand the order given you to charge that battery. It is now too late; I will leave that work for you to do to-morrow." The direful death-dealing elements are still flying thick and fast. The Seventh is now baring its bosom against the angry storm. Its colors are planted and flying over the works. Simultaneously with the Second Iowa the Seventh Illinois pass over the outer works, but they go no farther; the rebel batteries' deadly sweeps check them. The gallant Iowa boys claim the honor of being the first to scale Fort Donelson's walls. They claim it rightly, too, and history will award to them the honor of being a little ahead of the Seventh Illinois. As it is said the brave are always generous, the Seventh Illinois will demonstrate it by giving the Iowa boys the credit of what they claim, feeling assured at the same time that they will give the Seventh Illinois the credit of being with them very soon after they scaled the defenses, when together we drove the rebels back in confusion. Night now comes on, putting a stop to the carnival of blood. It is dark now, though as we look around we can see, faintly, the bodies of the gallant dead. It is indeed heart rending to see how many noble men have perished, and to see how many are wounded and how many are dying. Blood from thousands has flowed to-day, and as the sun went down it shed its light upon the field, adding beauty and hallowed glory to the crimson life blood flowing from the Anglo Saxon's heart, down through rippling rills and gurgling brooks to where the beautiful Cumberland flows.[27]

Sunday, 16th.—This morning we still occupy the position gained last evening. There is no firing this morning. Why this quiet? Why this stillness? The enemy may be preparing for a more determined resistance. But no, there is a truce! Grant is now holding communication with the rebel General Buckner. Buckner gives terms upon which he will surrender. Grant says, *"No, I demand an unconditional surrender. I propose to move immediately upon your works."*[28] He waits for an answer. All are in suspense now. Go with me to yonder elevation; look eastward; the sun is far on its journey, while over the broad land church bells are ringing, and while the loyal people are breathing a prayer to heaven for the army and navy, fifty thousand warriors are being drawn up in line of battle. Away yonder in the woods, we see the General moving, followed by his staff, and in the language of Campbell in his description of the battle of the Baltic,

> "As their war steeds went surging on their path,
> There was silence deep as death,
> And the boldest held his breath
> For a time."[29]

But hark! what mean those shouts that come rolling down the line? "Fort Donelson is ours!" The rebel flag has been lowered, and afar we see the white flag waving. An unconditional surrender has been made of the whole rebel force and munitions of war. With colors flying and drums beating, we pass into Fort Donelson. Our quarters to-night are those lately occupied by the rebels. The Seventh feels good, knowing that they have helped to gain a brilliant victory, adding new glory to the old flag.

Monday, 17th.—This morning the boys in blue are everywhere in and around Fort Donelson, scattered among the boys in gray, rehearsing the scenes they have witnessed, and the trials through which they have passed. Although the Seventh was in the thickest of the battle, as their riddled colors show, their loss is comparatively small. The casualties in the two days' battle around Fort Donelson are as follows:

Company A.—Thomas Crayon, wounded.

Company B.—Private Thomas J. Parish, wounded in left hand; private Edward P. Mann, wounded.

Company C.—John Bruit, wounded in thigh.

Company D.—First Lieutenant James Munn, wounded in face.

Company F.—John Dell, wounded; Rosewell C. Staples, wounded.

Company G.—Jno. H. Dougherty, wounded in arm.

Company H.—Private John D. Turner, wounded in head.

Company I.—Captain Noah E. Mendell, killed; Ole Porter, killed; Corporal William Boring, wounded, leg amputated.

Company K.—John W. Hopper, killed by cannon shot; Corporal Thomas Kirby, wounded severely; Corporal Wallace Smith, wounded slightly; John Rhodes, wounded severely; Julius Wolf, wounded slightly; Dilivan B. Daniels, wounded severely; Winfry Mitchell, wounded slightly; Charles Huffman, wounded severely, leg amputated; Jacob Hoen, wounded slightly. Sum total of casualties, 20.[30]

In looking over the list we notice that company K, the gallant Captain Hunter's company, sustained nearly half the loss in the regiment. Noble old Carlinville company, under its brave leader, made a fearful swing on these fortified hills. We will add no more; their list of casualties speaks for itself. It tells the story more plainly than pen can write it. Though our loss is light, we miss those who have fallen, and those who have been wounded. Among the most distinguished who fell in these wintry days of battle before Fort Donelson will ever appear the name of the brave Captain Noah E. Mendell, of company I. In view of the accident that befell him near Fort Henry, his friends remonstrated with him, and besought him to remain at the rear, but when order was given "Forward to Fort Donelson," he determined not to be thwarted by anything. Evading the surgeon, who forbade his going, alleging, as was the case, that he was unfit for duty, he pressed on, saying to his gallant First Lieutenant, Edward S. Johnson: "Ed, you take command of the company; I will follow you as long as I have strength."[31] When he heard the drums beating, and the loud huzzas away on those hills, his heart beat high, and its silent language was, men tell me not to stay; I will go where that old flag goes to-day. Being unable from the injuries received near Fort Henry, to buckle his sword belt around his waist, he buckled it around his neck and followed close in the rear of his company, cheering his men and telling them to stand by their brave, youthful leader, Lieutenant Johnson, who was then commanding the company. But how soon are his hopes dashed down. A whizzing grape comes crashing through the woods and singles him as its victim, entering his head just beneath the right ear. coming out immediately through the center of his left. His death was instantaneous, and he fell with his sword still above his head, with his face lit up with the smile of triumph—a glorious death and such as all brave and patriotic soldiers like him would wish to die—face to face with the enemies of his country. Captain Mendell was born in Blairsville, Pennsylvania, November 9th, 1837, and consequently was in his twenty-fifth year at the time of his death, February 13th, 1862. When the call was made for three months' volunteers he was among the first to offer his services, together with a majority of Captain John Cook's (State Militia) company, denominated the Springfield Zouave Grays, of which he was long a respected member. Upon Captain Cook's promotion to Colonel, Mendell rose to Second Lieutenant, in which capacity he served during the three months' service, at the close of which he was unanimously chosen Captain for the three years' service. He was the only brother of Captain G. H. Mendell, of the United States Topographical Engineers, professor at West Point, whom with a loving father and sister, he leaves to mourn his early death. He is silently sleeping now. May he sleep well, and may the noble men of his company, should they in coming years pass his grave, tread lightly there and shed a silent tear to his memory; and may every soldier of the Seventh do likewise, remembering that there sleeps the gallant Captain Noah E. Mendell, the first brave soldier of the Seventh who fell in the war for the Union, and the first in Grant's army who fell a victim upon the Union altar before the battlements of Fort Donelson.

Preparations are now being made to send his remains home to be buried in Springfield cemetery. As a martyr, we give him to the loyal people of Springfield, and the Seventh, especially his noble company, appeals to them in the language of the poetess:

> "Lay him where the clover blooms,
>   Let the gallant soldier rest
> Where the twilight dews will fall
>   On his youthful breast.
>
> "Lay him where the evening sun
>   Gives to him her parting ray;
> Where the violet droops her head
>   At the closing day.
>
> "Lay him where the midnight star
>   Sheds o'er him her gentle light;
> Where the wood bird's plaintive strain
>   Serenades the night.
>
> "Lay him where the stars and stripes
>   Will o'er him ever wave;
> Where no foe can touch the realm,
>   For which he died to save.
>
> "Lay him where bright angel wings
>   will guard his happy sleep;
> Until the Saviour's voice shall call,
>   May their faithful vigil keep."

Company D has lost for a time their loved and brave-hearted Lieutenant Munn. True to the flag and its fostered principles, he fought valiantly until wounded, when he was compelled to leave the field. We remember when he went bleeding from the hill, when we were making the assault on Saturday evening. He was foremost in the fray, fighting bravely until the battle was waning, when one of the deadly messengers selected him as its prey, inflicting a frightful wound in his face. Heroic soldier! We fear he will battle no more in the cause of human right.[32]

The wounded are now being sent north, and while there, may they receive from the loyal people tokens of gratitude, that will make them feel glad that they stood on the banks of the Cumberland, when the winter winds blew, and when the battle king made his deadly march, causing shot and shell to make a dirge-like music where they stood. We cannot pass without alluding to the noble ones who passed through the battle untouched; who bore the flag through tempest and storm and planted its staff firmly in the ramparts. But how can we distinguish any when all were brave; when all stood so nobly during those fierce hours of battle?

Lieutenant Colonel A. J. Babcock deserves the praise of all. Cool and calm as a placid brook, with a heart that prompted to daring deeds, he led his men through the terrible storm, and as they followed him there was power felt on those hills. He displayed a tact and skill in handling the regiment, forming it at one time under a galling fire, which elicited the commendation of the General commanding. We will not soon forget how often his voice rang out in inspiring tones, and how the Seventh went surging on with him, and how her flag was oft-times seen, reflecting its light where smoke and red-hot flame belched forth from brazen fronts.

Major Rowett also deserves the plaudits of all. Enthusiastic, but not rash, he was found where all the brave were found. None but could admire his dash—so free, so courageous—as he moved with the regiment on those hills with defiance, facing danger and cheering his men on to victory. Says he, since the battle: "I never felt so happy in all my life as when before that rebel battery the first day; happy because I there discovered that I had a heart to face the cannon's mouth, which I did not feel certain of having until then." Many of the Seventh can speak likewise; can testify that they feel glad in their hearts that they have been tried and not found wanting.

Among the brigade commanders none were more conspicuous when the battle was at its highest than our Colonel, John Cook. Amid the terrible storm that rolled from the cannon's angry front he stood. Though death and carnage followed in its wake, making little streams beneath his feet, he faltered not, but with that veteran soldier and brave general, Smith, he moved until the sun went down and the battle storm was hushed.

Tuesday, 18th.—This morning a fatigue party is detailed from the Seventh to help bury the dead on the battle field, and those who died from wounds received in battle, who are now lying in every house in Dover (a small village on the banks of the Cumberland inside the fortifications). All day yesterday the fatigue parties were engaged burying the noble slain. War is indeed a mad machine, terrible in its work.

> "Silently extended ont he gory main,
> The fallen warriors mid the carnage lay;
> No hand was there to ease the racking pain,
> And staunch the life blood ebbing fast away."

But when the old flag comes home to Tennessee, over the Union soldiers' graves will be built up all that their posterity shall desire of order and government.

Wednesday, 19th.—This morning it is raining very hard. A large number of troops have found shelter in the rebel barracks, but some are still out in the woods without blankets. (For once the Seventh is more fortunate.) But they are cheerful and their spirits run high when, they look at the old flag and see where and how far into Tennessee they have borne it.

Thursday, 20th.—To-day we receive orders to hold ourselves in readiness to move at a moment's notice. Lieutenant Colonel Babcock having, from exposure and care in the late battle become prostrated upon a soldier's sick bed, leaves the regiment to-day on a hospital steamer for Paducah, Kentucky. All regret to see him leave, for we can illy spare an officer who has stood by the regiment so faithfully in hours of gloom and darkness. The regiment is now commanded by Major Rowett, and our faith is, that he, like the brave Babcock, will lead us through storm and tempest to victory and glory.

Friday, 21st.—To-day we are marched on board the steamer Tigress, and soon are moving up the Cumberland river. The weather is pleasant. The scenery along the river, the cliffs, the vales and the hills, crowned with beautiful cedars, are imposing. The negroes flock to the shore and their hearts seem to bound as they behold their deliverers coming up the river with the old Union's banner proudly waving.[33]

Saturday morning we land at Clarksville, Tennessee, forty miles above Fort Donelson. After landing, the regiment is quartered in an old tobacco factory, which seems to please those who smoke, for there is a superabundance of the weed stored here. Says one: "This will save our 'collaterals.'" We remain in camp here until the twenty-seventh; during this time we are unable to note anything of much interest, but the Seventh will long remember Clarksville; their comfortable quarters and pleasant life while there; also the citizens, especially the ladies of rebel proclivities, who were ofttimes heard chanting their songs—songs that made music in the wind that swept along the Cumberland's shore. But ah! it was music for a desperate cause.[34]

Friday, 28th.—This morning we are lying on the river at Nashville, Tennessee, having arrived here last night from Clarksville, on the steamer Diana. From the deck of the steamer we behold waving from Tennessee's capitol dome "old glory," which was presented to General Nelson by one of Tennessee's patriot sires, upon his advent into the city; a banner that was presented when rebels were dominant, and the angry passions of wicked men surged around its devoted lover's head; but now it can wave unmolested, for the free winds chant their requiem over there.[35]

Saturday, March 1st.—We leave Nashville; descend the river, and return to Clarksville, where we are again quartered in the old tobacco factory. We still find Clarksville a very congenial locality, notwithstanding the citizens' hearts are with the South in its struggle for "Empire." We remain here until Friday, when the Seventh for the second time leaves Clarksville and the old tobacco factory. Marching on board the steamer E. H. Fairchild, we are soon descending the Cumberland. As we pass Fort Donelson, we are reminded that over on those hills, and in those ravines brave men sleep—sleep as martyrs for freedom. As we glide quietly down beneath the shadow of the projecting cliffs, we imagine that a voice comes from those hills and ravines, saying to us in the language of the poet:

"Ye harvesters, rally from mountain and valley,
  And reap the fields we have won;
We sowed for endless years of peace,
  We harrowed and watered well;
Our dying deeds are the scattered seeds,
  Shall they perish where they fell?"

Saturday, 8th.—This morning we are on the Ohio, and it is not long until we join the fleet that came before us from the Cumberland. Presently we make a turn and pass into the waters of the Tennessee river.

Tuesday, 18th.—This morning we are at a stand in the river at Pittsburg Landing. The fleet is large—about one hundred steamers throng the river. As far as the eye can reach, up and down, their smokestacks can be seen looming up. The Seventh has now been on the Fairchild for eleven days. They have been crowded, and part of the time the weather has been very inclement. The expedition thus far has been one of exciting interest. All along the river, where the old flag was seen to flash its light, loyal ones flocked to the shores, and as they beheld the proud steamers moving up the Tennessee, with that golden treasure on their masts, and from the decks the bayonets gleaming, they wept tears of joy, for they knew that with them would come freedom and protection.

Wednesday, 19th.—This morning it is raining, having rained all night. It is an unwelcome compliment to the fleet. The troops are landing to-day at Pittsburg Landing. The Seventh is still compelled to remain crowded and jammed upon the Fairchild. The men are all anxious to get on to terra firma. It is very unhealthy here—so crowded. The water in the river where so many steamboats are anchored, is not, (so the surgeons say,) a very genuine article, and in consequence a large number of the boys are on the sick list.

Thursday, 20th.—The troops are still landing. It seems that this point is to be Grant's base. But when we will get on the *base* is concerning the Seventh more particularly now than anything else. Only some place to breathe, that is all that is at present demanded.

Friday, 21st.—This morning, after having patiently waited their time, the Seventh is marched from the Fairchild and camped in the woods back from the landing. It is indeed refreshing and invigorating to get out where the fresh winds blow. Those of the Seventh who were fanatical on steamboat riding don't seem inclined to expatiate much upon its beauties after their thirteen day's ride and life on the Fairchild. None are found to cast a tear of regret on leaving their repulsive berths.

Saturday, 22d.—The fires are burning brightly in our camp this morning. All seem to have more genial looking faces than when on the steamboat. This evening we have dress parade, and as usual a large number of officers and soldiers from the surrounding camps assemble on our parade ground. What is the attraction? Why so many congregated here? inquires a general officer riding by. Those of the army of the Tennessee assembled tell him it is because the Seventh can drill.

Saturday, April 5th.—Nothing of note has occurred to relieve the monotony of camp life. There is now a large army concentrated here. Far away on the hills and in the ravines the tents and the soldiers are seen. Up to this time we have had considerable rain. The roads and by-ways into the camps are cut up terribly. It is with difficulty that the Seventh keeps above mud and water. Vague rumors are afloat this evening to the effect that Albert Sidney Johnson is moving towards the Tennessee with his entire command; however, not much credit is attached to it. But we may anticipate days of desperate strife—days of fire and carnage in Tennessee, for no doubt there has been or is being a concentration of the rebel armies under Johnson and Beauregard, with headquarters at Corinth, Mississippi, twenty-five miles from Pittsburg Landing. Their hopes are no doubt beating high for revenge upon Grant's army, in consideration of the blow wielded against them, in those stormy days of battle around Fort Donelson.[36]

Chapter V.

[April 6, 1862–April 29, 1862]

The battle of Shiloh—The first day—The attack—The first position of the Seventh—The advanced position of the Seventh—Their danger—Their retreat—Their new line—The fearful tempest—The lull—Grant's last line Sunday evening—The victors of that last great line—The arrival of Buell—The night—The rain—The silent sleepers—The second day—The two armies fighting hand to hand—The enemy's retreat—The falling of the curtain—The Seventh's camp upon the field—The fallen—List of casualties—The record—The Seventh's wounded—The living—Burying the dead—Our camp at Shiloh after the battle—Marching orders.

Sunday, the 6th of April, 1862.—It is now morning—a beautiful Sabbath morning. The dews have gone to heaven and the stars have gone to God; the sky is all inlaid with crimson, far away to the east. From behind the eastern hills the sun is peering; it is moving on its path. But ere it has long illumed the sky, war's dread tocsin is heard; the sullen roar of artillery breaks upon our ears, telling to us that the storm-king of battle would ride upon the banks of the Tennessee to-day. The army of the Tennessee springs to arms to meet the advancing columns of Albert Sidney Johnson.[37] The pennons are now flying. Major Rowett and the Seventh are quickly buckled for the conflict. Her old, tattered and shot-riven flag goes flying through the woods, and the regiment is soon in the conflict. Their position is now behind a rail fence. Oh! the angry tempest that rolls around here! Belching cannons, shotted to the muzzle, are now plowing deep lanes in the Union ranks. How can we describe the sound of a storm of grape and canister, cutting their hellish paths through serried ranks of human beings. It is impossible. Many are the storms flying around the Seventh now. Thicker and faster they come, but those noble men who bore that riddled flag over Fort Donelson's walls, struggle on. Many have breathed quickly, and, trampled under their comrades' feet, have rolled in bloody agonies and now lie in quiet eternal slumber. The mighty armies are now struggling—struggling desperately for the life or death of a nation.

Fiercer and fiercer rages the battle. The great Grant is moving on the field with a mighty power. But fearful odds are against us, and the army of the Tennessee is compelled to yield position after position. The Seventh has been forced to yield many points to-day; at one time being so far in the advance, we were left without support, and had it not been for the quick perception of our gallant Major, we would have been cut off and captured. Forming columns by divisions, we retreated from our critical position, and were compelled to fall back across an open field. It was a trying time. The harsh, fierce barking of the dogs of war made the earth tremble, as if in the midst of a convulsion. But there was no confusion in the Seventh—no panic there. Led by the brave Rowett, they moved firmly, as if to say, that shot-pierced flag, tattered and torn, shall not go down to-day. Major Rowett, with the aid of Captain Monroe, acting Major now form a new line with the Seventh. War's ruthless machine is moving with a relentless force.

It is now past noon. Confusion reigns; brave men are falling like rain drops. All seems dark—seems that the Union army will be crushed by this wild sweep of treason. But on the crippled army of the Tennessee struggles; they still keep the flag up. It is now four o'clock. Step by step the army is being driven back towards the river. The old Union banner seems to be drooping in the wrathful storm, but by an almost superhuman effort the tide is checked. For a while there is a lull in the battle, but only to make preparations for the last desperate assault—an assault in which the enemy expect to see the old flag come down to their feet.

Buell is said to be approaching; he is hourly expected. Grant is now seen moving with a care-worn countenance. He moves amid the carnage to form his last grand line one-fourth mile from the Tennessee, where the advance is now driven. Grant's last line is formed. It is a line of iron, a line of steel, a wall of stout hearts, as firm, as powerful as Napoleon under like reverses ever formed in the days of his imperial power. It seems almost impossible for such a line to be formed at this hour—so compact. On every available spot of earth an iron-lipped monster frowns. It is a trying moment, for Grant knows and his army knows that should this line be broken, the battle would be lost and the proud flag would be compelled to fall. At half-past four o'clock Grant dashes through the woods. His voice rings out: "They come! they come! Army of the Tennessee stand firm!"[38] A breathless silence pervades these serried ranks, until broken by the deafening crash of artillery. The last desperate struggle on Sunday evening now commences. One hundred brazen guns are carrying terror and death across Shiloh's plain. The Seventh is at its place; every officer and soldier is at his post; Rowett and Monroe are at their stations, now on foot; (Rowett's horse killed in former charge; Monroe's disabled.) All the company officers are in their places, cheering and encouraging their gallant men, and as we gaze upon the bristling bayonets that are gleaming along the Seventh's line, we know that every brawny arm that is beneath them will be bared to shield the old flag. The infantry are clashing now, but this line of stout hearts stands firm. The traitor hosts grow desperate; the earth trembles; the sun is hid behind the wrathful smoke, but amid all the deafening battle elements of the darkened field, the flag and its defenders stand. Down beneath its shadow brave men are falling to close their eyes in glory. The storm still increases in its sweeping power. About five o'clock the issue becomes doubtful; each seems to hold the balance, and like Napoleon at Waterloo, who prayed that *night* or Blucher would come, so we prayed that *night* or the army of Ohio would come. About this time, Albert Sidney Johnson poured out his life-blood upon the altar of a vain ambition. At that fatal hour the enemy's lines waver, and the sun goes down with the army of the Tennessee standing victorious on their last great line.[39]

Night comes, and with it Buell comes, but only in time to witness the closing scene on Sunday evening. We thanked God for the arrival of the army of the Ohio, but we never thanked God for Don Carlos Buell when he rode across the Tennessee and spoke lightly of the great Grant, who has successfully stemmed the wildest storm of battle that ever rolled upon the American continent.[40]

The sable curtains have now fallen, closing to our eyes the terrible scene. Soon it commences to rain. Dark, dark night for the army of the Tennessee. Many brave men are sleeping silently. They have fought their last battle. Fearful, desolating war has done a desperate work. Noble men have thrown themselves into the dread ordeal, and passed away. The human pen will fail to picture the battle-field of Shiloh as it presented itself on Sunday night. The Seventh, tired and almost exhausted, drops down on the ground, unmindful of the falling rain, to rest themselves. Ere it was noon some of the Seventh had already lain down to rest, and ere it was night others laid down, but it was an eternal rest—the soldier's last slumber. Disastrous war has wrapped its winding sheet around the cold form of many a fond mother's boy, and before many days there will be weeping in the lonely cottage homes; weeping for the loved and lost who are now sleeping beneath the tall oaks on the banks of the Tennessee. About the noble men of the Seventh who fell today, we will speak hereafter; we shall not forget them. How could we forget them, when they have played their part so well in the great tragedy?

Monday, April 7th.—Last night was a doleful night as the soldiers laid in this wilderness by the Tennessee. All night long there was a chilling rain, and the April wind sighed mournfully around the suffering, wounded warriors. Many a wounded soldier died last night. During the weary hours the insatiate archer was making silent steps.

> "One quivering motion, one convulsive throe,
> And the freed spirits took their upward flight."

Would that God would roll back the storms of war and temper the hearts of men ere any more human blood flows down like rivulets to crimson the beautiful waters of the Cumberland and Tennessee. But oh! it seems that more blood must flow; that away up yonder, in those cottage homes, where the prairie winds blow, more tears must sparkle, fall and perish; that more hearts must be broken—more hopes dashed down— more doomed

> "In their nightly dreams to hear
> The bolts of war around them rattle."

Hark! we hear a rumble and a roar. It is a rattle of musketry and the terrible knell from the cannon's mouth. We are marched to the front, where we find Nelson engaged. His hounds of war are let loose. Inroads are being made. The Seventh is filed into position and ordered to lie down. Though the enemy has given ground, they still show stubbornness. We are now in a sharp place; there is some uneasiness here. A cold chill creeps over the soldiers. How uncomfortable it is to be compelled to remain inactive when these whizzing minies come screaming through the air on their mission of death. From such places, under such circumstances, the Seventh would ever wish to be excused, for it grates harshly with the soldier, and is exceedingly distressing when he is prevented from returning compliment for compliment, as the Seventh will testify to-day. But we do not remain here long, for from this place of inactivity, we are moved to a place of action. The battle is raging furiously. The army of the Ohio and the army of the Tennessee are striking hand to hand. The tables are turning; step by step the rebels are being driven. Position after position the Seventh is now taking. The sharp, positive crack of their musketry makes a terrible din along their line. It is apparent that the rebels are retreating. Another day is waning; a day of sacrifice; a day in which has been held a high carnival of blood on Shiloh's plain. Many patriot, loyal soldiers died to-day, and as they died, many of them were seen to smile as they saw the old flag, the pride of their hearts, riding so proudly over the bloody field. Many shed a tear of joy as they beheld the beautiful streams of light falling on the crimson wings of conquest.

The rebels are now flying. Nelson is making a terrible wreck in the rear of the retreating army. Kind reader, stand with me now where the Seventh stands; look away yonder! Your eye never beheld a grander sight. It is the northwest's positive tread. They move firmly; there is harmony in their steps. Ten thousand bayonets flash in the blazing sunlight. They are moving in columns on the bloody plain. Their tramp sounds like a death knell. The band is playing "Hail to the chief." Its martial anthems seem to float as it were on golden chords through air, and as they fall around the weary soldier their hopes of glory beat high. They are retreating now; the rear of the rebel army is fast fading from Shiloh's field. Before the northwest's mighty power how they dwindle into littleness, as turrets and spires beneath the stars. They are far away now, and the great battle of Shiloh is over; the fierce wild drama is ended; the curtain falls; the sun is hid, and night has come. The Seventh goes into camp on the battle-field; their camp fires are soon burning, and those noble ones, who have fought so well, lie down, worn and weary, to rest themselves. They have passed through two days of fearful battle; amid thunder, smoke and perils they bore their tattered flag, and when the storm-king was making his most wrathful strides, it still waved in the wind and never went down, for strong arms were there and they held it up. But how painful it is to know that some comrades who were with us in the morning, are not with us now. They have fallen and died—died in the early morning of life. And why did they die? A royal herald will answer, for a country, for a home, for a name. Come walk with me now while the tired soldiers are sleeping. Who is this who lays here beneath this oak, in such agony, such convulsive throes? It is a soldier in gray; a wounded rebel who fought against the old flag to-day. But he is dying; his life is almost gone; he is dead now. Oh! how sad it makes one feel to see a soldier die, and how we pity him who has just died; pity him because he has fallen in such a desperate cause; pity him because no royal herald will ever write his name on the sacred scroll of fame.[41]

Tuesday, 8th.—Oh! what a terrible scene does Shiloh's field present this morning. It is a scene of death; its victims lay everywhere. The blood of about thirteen thousand warriors has been shed here in the last two days. My God! what a sacrifice, what a flow of blood. But liberty has claimed it for an emancipated mind, and may it water well the great tree of universal freedom, and cause it to extend its branches fosteringly over a struggling people. In these two days of battle the Seventh sustained a heavy loss. The following are the casualties:

Major R. Rowett, wounded.

Company A.—Captain Samuel G. Ward, killed; private Alden Bates, killed.[42]

Company B.—Captain Hector Perrin, wounded; private Charles Newton, killed; Michael O'Keep, killed.

Company C.—Sergeant George Mitchell, killed; Samuel Wilson, wounded.

Company D.—Private Andrew McKinnon, killed.

Company E.—Private Emanuel Keve, wounded.

Company F.—*Killed;* private Isaac Britton. *Mortally Wounded;* privates John Jackson, Chas. P. Laing, John P. Hale. *Wounded;* Wallace Partridge, John Dell, James Harrington, Hugh H. Porter, John Larkin, James Close.

Company G.—Private John Gibland, killed; Captain Henry W. Allen, wounded; private George Harris, wounded.

Company H.—Lieutenant Leo Wash. Myers, killed; private John H. Duff, killed; private Ernst H. Myers, wounded; private Charles Ward, wounded; Sergeant Laban Wheeler, wounded; private James Walker, wounded; private Geo. W. Fletcher, wounded; private Carol Hurt, wounded; private Thomas Taylor, wounded; private Charlie Halbert, wounded; private Elam Mills, wounded.

Company I.—Corporal Seth Hamilton, killed; private John Bollyjack, killed; private James Craven, killed; private James Lacy, killed; Sergeant Charles M. Fellows, wounded; private James Crowley, wounded; private John Johnson, wounded; private George Marsh, wounded; private Wm. S. Rogers, wounded; private Michael Toner, wounded; private George Vesey, wounded; private George W. Byron, wounded; private Marcus McKinnis, wounded; private Daniel J. Baker, wounded.

Company K.—Private John Nixon, killed; private Charles P. Huffman, wounded; private Jacob Howe, wounded; Sergeant J. B. Sanders, wounded; Sergeant Wm. C. Gillson, wounded; private John M. Anderson, wounded; private Thos. J. R. Grant, wounded; private Green B. Johnson, wounded; private George Reiner, wounded; private Joseph White, wounded. Total killed, 14; total wounded, 43; sum total of casualties, 57.[43]

Glorious record! Proud names! Yes, proud as any that will ever embellish our national escutcheon. Departed souls, as courageous as history can boast of. From Shiloh's dark wilderness, no nobler, no braver spirit took its flight into the skies than the spirit of Captain Ward, of Company A. He fell mortally wounded in the fiercest of the battle Sunday evening, while at the head of his company, cheering his men in to deeds of valor. Some of his company stop to carry him from the field; but while glory is beaming in the dying warrior's eye, he says to his gallant men: "There goes the flag; it will need all its noble defenders to hold it up in the terrible battle that is raging so fiercely. Boys, it is trembling now! Lay me down to die; leave me and follow the old Seventh's silken folds, and tell the boys of Company A, that ere the sun's light is hid from this field, their Captain will be no more; that I will be silently sleeping in death. Tell them to remember Captain Ward, and keep the old flag in the wind."

Fainting he falls; his features lose their glow; his eyes are closed forever to the light. Alone, he died—died in his glory. Noble sacrifices may be offered in this war for the Union, but no nobler sacrifice, no grander type of a man, of a soldier, will ever be offered in Captain Samuel G. Ward, of Company A. Captain Ward was among the first to hearken to the first call of the President in April, 1861. From a private in Company A, he was promoted by Colonel Cook to Sergeant Major of the regiment. At the end of the three months' service, Sergeant Major Ward was unanimously chosen Captain of Company A, in which position he served faithfully until liberty claimed him as a sacrifice on Shiloh's field, April 6th, 1862. Every one saw in him the elements of a rising officer; a star that was already shining, the light of which would have been seen afar had not the wild tempest blown it out so early. Though he passed away in youth's hopeful morning, ere his aspirations were reached, immortality's royal messenger will take up his name, and while soft winds chant a requiem around his grave, will say of him: "Here sleeps Captain Ward, whom liberty claimed in its great struggle on Shiloh's plain. He lived, he died, for country, home, and flag."

Lieutenant Leo Washington Myers, of Company H, died as the warriors die—nobly. He stood manfully while the bolts of war around him rattled, but he is a silent sleeper now. Amid shooting flames and curling smoke, he bravely sacrificed his life—sacrificed it as one of the martyrs of freedom. Being among the first to rush to the standard when arch treason first lifted its mad head, he was elected Second Lieutenant of Company H, and at the end of the three months' service, he was unanimously chosen First Lieutenant, in which capacity he valiantly served until his life was sealed at Shiloh, April 6th, 1862.

In the wild storm that swept over that field, no truer patriot soldier was borne down than Lieutenant Myers. As a lover of liberty he followed the flag southward and stood beneath its folds where the gulf winds blew across the plains of Mexico. With Taylor and Scott, he fought for it there. With Wallace he died for it down by the Tennesssee. Oh! how can it be that stars that gave such brilliant light should go out so soon. The providences of God are indeed mysterious.

But all died in their glory. Sergeant Mitchell, company C, Corporal Seth Hamilton, company I, privates Alden Bates, company A, John H. Duff, company H, Charles Newton, Company B, Andrew McKennon, company D, Isaac Britton, company F, John Gibland, company G, Corporal J. Nixon, company K, and many others, died crowned with laurels as bright as the midnight stars. Though they carried the musket, we will ascribe no less praise to them, for heroes they proved themselves to be. From Thermopylæ to Shiloh, the world has never produced grander types of gallantry than has been produced in these private soldiers, who fell on this battle-field. Of all the fallen of the Seventh who went down in Shiloh's two days of battle, I can only say of them as Mark Anthony said of Julias Cæsar, "Their lives were grand; the elements so mixed in them that all the world might stand up and say, they were men; they were heroes; they were soldiers."

While on the battle-field, Sergeant S. F. Flint, Company I, writes:

> Soft fall the dews of midnight and morning,
> O'er the green hills where slumber the brave,
> Fall on each nameless and desolate grave;
> And soft be the song of the slow flowing river,
> As it pours by the shores they have hallowed forever.
> In peace and off duty the soldier is sleeping,
> No more will he wake at the shrill reveille,
> As it rings through the vales of the old Tennessee;
> But the wail of the wind, and the roll of the river,
> As it thrills o'er the hills his requiem forever.

Oh! the homes in their own northern prairies and valleys,
More lonely and dark than those desolate graves,
O! The wailings that answer the winds and the waves;
O! the tears that will flow like the fall of the river,
As it swells through the dells where they slumber forever.
But lift up the old flag they died in defending,
And swear by each nameless but glorious grave,
That hallowed with triumph its free folds shall wave
O'er the hills and the vales and the bright flowing river,
O'er the whole lovely land of our fathers forever.

We will now pass to yonder hospital steamer. The Seventh's wounded lay here; among the noble company lies the gallant Captain Hector Perrin, wounded badly in the thigh. Though a son of France, he loved freedom, and being one from the school of La Fayette, he fought bravely on Shiloh's field. Among this company we find heroes, all of whom have shown and yet show that they have in them the element of steel. Patiently and silently they endure their suffering. Who ever witnessed such fortitude? The world will fail in its annals of blood to exhibit grander types. Some have lost a leg, others have frightful wounds in the face; but these are their patents of nobility. Dr. Hamilton, our popular Assistant Surgeon, as ever, has a care for the unfortunate ones. He is now, with his usual promptness, preparing to send them north.[44] Some of them will never return again; but may a grateful people open wide to them their generous hearts, and leave them not to drift through the world in storm. Returning we mingle with the living. Of the noble survivors we can only say of them, they did well; they played their part as nobly as the most gallant warriors have ever done on any battle-field. In these two days of battle Major Rowett, who is now in his tent slightly wounded, but prostrated upon his cot, worn out by excessive toil, proved himself worthy the leadership of brave men. Where danger most threatened, there he was always found. None moved amid the carnage with a more dashing force. Full of fire and life, with a reckless contempt for danger, he stemmed the wild storm. He was wounded twice and had his horse shot but nothing could check him. At the head of his regiment he was always found, and it is conceded by those who knew, that no regimental commander handled his command on Shiloh's field better than Major Rowett handled the Seventh. At no time was the regiment driven into confusion, though many times its line was broken, but each time was reformed promptly, and be it said to the credit of the regiment, not a prisoner was taken in consequence of straggling. Captain Monroe, acting Major, has won the encomiums of all. Fight and battle seem to be his element. He carries with him triumph and glory. Enthusiastic as are all the brave, his voice was ever heard cheering the men and telling them never to let the flag go down. Captains Lawyer, Hunter, Estabrook, Church, Lieutenants Ring, Smith, Roberts, Ellis, Sullivan, Sweeny and Ahern were ever foremost in the battle and ever found encouraging their men, bidding them to stand firm for the flag and freedom.[45] The color bearer, Sergeant Coles Barney, of company H, won for himself the admiration of his officers and comrades, for the gallant manner in which he bore his banner through the wild tempest.

But all were brave, and all fought valiantly. They marched in blood, and threw themselves against arch treason until the Union's proud banner waved upon a triumphant field. At times it was fearfully dark, and the flag seemed to droop, but our noble men stood around it, and while blood was ebbing, they formed a defense of steel backed by hearts that never faltered. And thus defended, their flag, the pride of the mighty millions, shed glorious light around the noble men of the Seventh.

Large parties are now at work burying the dead of both armies. Shiloh will be one vast grave-yard, but it will be destitute of marble slabs. Hundreds of Union soldiers will sleep here, and in the years to come, the patriot pilgrims will tread the earth above them, and know not that beneath sleeps Shiloh's martyrs. But should they chance to see some graves that are arched, so that they can be recognized as the graves of the lone soldiers, they will not know whether the sleepers fought for or against the old flag, and the friends of the loved and lost will not know upon which graves to throw their flowers or drop their tears.

April 9th.—There is a continual rain now falling. It seems that the battle storms of Shiloh have opened the windows of heavens. Our camp is in a wretched condition. From the 9th to the 29th of April, scarcely any sunshine is seen. During this time the odor from the battle-field is sickening, and the sick list is increasing every day. On the 16th we find the gallant Lieutenant Ring in the hospital. Being exposed so much during the battle, and ever since the battle, his physical powers have been giving way, notwithstanding his firm, determined will. We are all anxious for the recovery of his health, for the late battle tells us that company H cannot well spare him who led them so faithfully through Shiloh's dark days, after Captain Holden took sick and left the field.

We have marching orders now. We have passed through stormy days while here. The world shall never know their story. The pen will be moved to tell it, but it will never be told. We shall now enter upon another campaign. May the God of battles be with us, and nerve strong arms to hold the flag up until the song of victory and peace shall be sung by liberty's happy people! Major Rowett has been sent to a northern hospital. We regret it very much, for we shall miss him as we move southward.

Chapter VI.

[April 29, 1862–October 2, 1862]

Leaving Shiloh—The roads—Joining Sherman at Monterey—The siege of Corinth—The evacuation—Joining Pope—The march into Mississippi—The warm weather—The scarcity of water—The return to Corinth—Camp near the Mobile and Ohio Railroad—The Sixth Division Camp—Camp on Purdy road— Camp in Jack-oak Thicket—Battle of Iuka—the Iowa boys our brothers— Ordered to our old camp near Mobile and Ohio Railroad—The Second Division concentrating—Rumors of Price's advance upon Corinth.

Tuesday, April 29th, 1862.—This morning we commence early to make preparations to move from our camp at Shiloh. 9 o'clock.—We are in line, waiting for the command "forward" to be given. Colonel Babcock having returned from the hospital, is now in command of the regiment, and we all feel that he will, as in days past, lead the regiment forth to victory. But we all regret that the gallant Rowett and Ring are not with us to aid in the coming campaign. At ten o'clock the Third Brigade, consisting of the Seventh, Fiftieth and Fifty-seventh Illinois, and Twenty-second Ohio, commanded by Colonel Baldwin, of the Fifty-seventh Illinois, move forward from Pittsburg Landing, marching in the direction of Corinth, Mississippi. Owing to the condition of the roads, and the jamming together of the artillery and the army trains, we only succeed in getting about five miles from the landing, when we go into camp for the night.[46]

April 30.—This morning the whole army is in motion, except the part sticking in the mud. The Third Brigade only goes three miles, when they halt and go into camp for the remainder of the day and night. We have a good camping ground, which, with the refreshing and healthy atmosphere blowing around us, makes all seem cheerful. All seem glad that they are away from Shiloh's sickening field.

May 1st.—This morning we again take up the line of march. The army is moving slowly on, and will continue to move on until the old flag makes another victorious stand for the Union and freedom. Towards evening we increase our speed. Some one says we have been ordered to join Sherman to-night. It proves true; we hasten on and go into camp late in the evening, at Monterey, joining General Sherman's command, which has come to a stand.[47]

May 2d.—This morning we remain at Monterey, waiting for orders. We remain here all day and it seems that the army has come to a halt. This evening the Seventh is detailed for picket. The night is clear and the moon shines brightly, and the boys watch closely for any foe that may be lurking near, for we are in the enemy's country, and it is surmised that there is something threatening ahead. The soldier on picket—who can tell his thoughts at the midnight hour, when a mighty army is sleeping and depending upon his vigilance?

May 3d.—This morning we are still in camp at Monterey; it is said we are waiting for the siege guns. Our brigade is now in the advance, standing as picket-guard for the army. To-day we move a short distance from Monterey, and go into camp in the woods.

May 4th.—We are now before Corinth, the base of the rebel army under Beauregard. Pope's guns have been thundering nearly all day on the left towards Farmington. He takes Portland, on the Tennessee river, and five hundred prisoners. With our part of the army everything seems quiet this evening.[48]

May 5th.—The artillery is coming up all day. Halleck is moving slowly with his grand army. Would that Grant would be permitted to swing it; there would soon be a commotion among these tall pines. The whining and whelping would-be military masters and generals, whose wisdom is distilled out at wholesale in the bar-rooms of Northern hotels, have clamored against Grant, and since the dark days of Shiloh the army of the Tennessee, who bravely stood with him there, has been grieved to know that the government listened to those base, unmitigated lies told about him in reference to his conduct at Shiloh. We see that this contemptible and cowardly bar-room gentry charge our General with being drunk on Sunday at Shiloh. Tell it to the world, but tell it not to the army of Tennessee. If a General, drunk, can form, amid such confusion, a line so compact, so powerful, so military as was Grant's last line on Sunday evening, would to God that more Generals were made drunk that we might crush out this fratricidal war and hasten the return of peace to a stricken and throbbing people. "But mark my word, boys," old U. S. Will yet ride over these men's wicked opposition, and ere this war is over, this man wearing the old slouch hat, commanding the army before Corinth, will receive orders from General Grant; for with Grant at the head of this grand army, he would stamp armies into the earth, and plant the old flag where the gulf winds blow.[49]

Tuesday, 6th.—The latest northern papers, with flaming bulletins, are circulated in the army to-day. "All quiet on the Potomac—McClellan and Halleck before Yorktown and Corinth with mighty armies."[50] The world seems to be standing still, watching and waiting to see the triumph of freedom and self-government against the combined fronts of hell-originated treason. Would that these great leaders would move forward and let the old flag go flying on and give the reins to these impatient armies. But it is perhaps well that they are held in check.

Wednesday, 7th.—To-day Governor Yates visits the Seventh and makes them a speech, which is full of cheer, full of hope and life, right straight from Dick's big heart. He has come down to Tennessee to look after the sick and wounded Illinois soldiers. How fortunate it is for Illinois to have so good and noble a governor, during this bloody war. This afternoon our division has been reviewed; an imposing scene; such a uniformity of motion and so much vim convince the lookers on that the Second Division cannot be surpassed in the army.[51]

Thursday, 8th.—To-day our regiment moves to the front line; our pickets and those of the enemy are now close to each other. All quiet to-day. Pope is still.

Friday, 9th.—To-day we hear heavy cannonading towards Farmington. It is Pope talking. We are now close to the enemy and occasionally they fire into our pickets. Our sharp-shooters are now at work; there is a din in the woods and a brisk skirmish is going on, but nothing serious, however, develops itself.[52]

Saturday, 10th.—It is raining this morning. It is rumored that the rebels will come out from Corinth to-day. The echoes from Pope's guns are again heard coming from the left. Before noon we commence throwing up breastworks, and before night we have a strong, defensive line. It is remarkable how men will work to shield themselves from minies and shells. The most indolent all at once become active and go to work with a rush.

Sunday, 11th.—A beautiful Sabbath morning; there is quiet along the line. The army is anxious to close in upon Corinth. It is reported that the rebel army is evacuating; how true, we cannot tell. Pope still continues skirmishing; there is a continual rumble and roar along his line this evening.

Monday, 12th.—Pope still keeps thundering against the rebel defenses. Heavy details are made from the different companies to-day to help build roads through the swamps.

Tuesday, 13th.—Skirmishing still going on. In the evening we move our camp two miles forward, crossing the Mississippi line. We move with one hundred cartridges, packed away in knapsacks—a mule load. The weather is extremely warm. We again throw up a line of works—bomb proof.

Wednesday, 14th.—At our new camping ground we find water very scarce, and of a very inferior quality. To-day we have battalion drill; the regiment receives high compliments from the West Point stars who were present. The drill of the Seventh is attracting universal attention, and our commanding officer is vain enough to challenge any regiment in these woods to compete with him in the manual and battalion evolutions. Late in the evening we hear heavy cannonading on our right. It is Hurlbut shelling a swamp, to clear it of lurking rebels. Tonight we are ordered to sleep on our arms.[53]

Thursday, 15th.—To-day it is very warm and sultry. This evening we again have division drill, and as usual, the Seventh is the star. So says Davies of West Point education. Brisk skirmishing is going on this evening between the rebel pickets and our bridge builders.

Friday, 16th.—This morning the Seventh boys obtain some northern papers, which they relish very much. In the afternoon we again have division drill. We shall never forget these exercises on the cotton fields of Mississippi. This evening the

Seventh boys conclude to have some fresh beef, hence they capture and kill a steer, a genuine work ox, used in drawing siege guns from Pittsburg Landing, but he is none the worse by that. The boys feast sumptuously to-night.

Saturday, 17th.—Water is becoming very scarce. The regiment is compelled to keep guard over their wells. Our lines are advanced one-half mile this evening.

Sunday, 18th.—This morning we form our line and commence throwing up breastworks. The men work with a gusto, and before night the Seventh has a strong line thrown up, covering its front. It is remarkable to see how, like magic, these lines go up. In a few hours we have a line fifteen miles long, strong enough (with the army of the Tennessee behind it,) to check the most powerful army in the world. Lieutenant Colonel Rowett having recovered from the injuries received at Shiloh, has returned to the regiment. All seem glad to see him with us again.

Monday, 19th.—All day we are drawn up in line of battle behind our works; the pickets continue skirmishing. In the afternoon the Seventh receives a mail, and while standing in battle line they read the little messages from home and friends; we conclude that these little "billets" cheer the soldiers, for ofttimes while reading them we see smiles playing upon their faces.

Tuesday, 20th.—Last night God smiled upon the army by opening the windows of heaven and causing the rain to fall. Nature is refreshed; water is more plenty, and the soldiers look more cheerful. The random crack of the muskets along the picket line is still heard. This evening Company H receives orders to reinforce the pickets now briskly engaged in skirmishing.

Wednesday, 21st.—This morning we are ordered into battle line; we thus advance about one mile, driving the rebel pickets before us, taking possession of a ridge which has been for the last few days contested by the pickets. On the brow of this ridge we plant our batteries in regular battle line. Soon they open, hurling grape and canister, shot and shell into the low woodland in front. The storm that rolled from these iron monsters was terrific. Simultaneous with the first direful echo, the hideous shot and shell leaped from the whole line, all the way from Sherman to Pope, and with a deadly power, plowing their hellish paths through the woods, making the earth tremble. The rebels went back.

Thursday, 22d.—All day we lay behind our entrenchments; our works of defense seem impregnable. It is now quiet along our picket line. The rebels are drawing in their advance.

Friday, 23d.—To-day our regiment is detailed to advance with the picket line and protect a fatigue party while building roads and bridges for the advance of our division. We have a brisk skirmish with the heavy rebel pickets.

This evening the Paymaster visits the Seventh, and before it is midnight the Seventh is flush with the "bonus."

Saturday, 24th.—This morning the boys are busily engaged depositing their money for expressage home, not wishing to be encumbered with any extra cash, especially when a battle seems threatening. This evening we are ordered to fall in on the color line, which is repeated several times through the night by false alarms from the pickets on St. Philips' Creek.

Sunday, 25th.—This morning everything seems quiet. It is God's holy day, and the army is resting. We anticipate no attack to-day, for the attack on Sunday at Shiloh taught the enemy a lesson.

Monday, 26th.—Nothing unusual occurred to-day. In the evening we hear a noise—three rousing cheers go up from Company H's quarters for something or somebody. For what, or for who can it be? Strange to say none seem to know; but walking that way we discover that Lieutenant Ring has returned from his sick leave of absence, received at Shiloh, and is now among his men. These cheers speak for themselves; we will make no comments.

Tuesday, 27th.—This morning we can hear the beating of drums in the rebel camp. There is not a wide space between the two hostile armies. The Seventh rests quietly behind their works to-day.

Wednesday, 28th.—The weather is still very warm. To-day we hear heavy cannonading in the direction of Sherman's line. This evening we advance towards the rebel works; our batteries gaining a position, they throw some shells into their midst.

We hold our position, and soon commence throwing up breast-works; the army keeps working on them nearly all night; the Seventh finish their space by two o'clock in the morning. We now have another strong line of defense. If Beauregard stands, we anticipate a general engagement soon. All day we hear heavy cannonading along Pope's line. Would that that restless spirit whose dogs of war are continually barking could be let loose at this very hour; we know he would go sweeping like an avalanche against the fortified walls of Corinth. But it is not deemed best, and for what reasons history will show; and if it be a mistake, the world will see it, and he who is responsible will receive the censure. To-night the Seventh is restless; the men are anxious to leap those works and carry the old flag on. Their hearts long to see it flying over yonder, but they are held in check. Somebody is cautious; perhaps somebody is fearful that his name, like the name of another, will be handled harshly in the northern hotels; perhaps fearful that somebody would say he was drunk.

Friday, 30th.—This morning we hear heavy explosions, supposed to be the enemy blowing up their magazines and ordnance stores, making preparations to evacuate. How true! There is confusion now in Halleck's grand army; they seem to surge like a lashed ocean when they are told that the rebels have evacuated Corinth; that the Union cavalry now occupy the place. We wonder if the sycophant will say of Halleck he is the Union's greatest general and liberty's most fearless champion, and allege as evidence that he was sober and stained not the earth with needless blood. We are soon moving from the right towards the left to join Pope; we come up with him at Farmington, where we are ordered to go into camp for the night.[54]

Saturday, 31st.—This morning we move from Farmington. In the afternoon we come to a halt near the Mobile and Ohio Railroad, and go into camp. It seems that the enemy has left in great confusion. The amount of property destroyed is immense. In Van Dorn's camp, we find some rebel papers; from one we extract the following letter, written by one of the chivalry's fair beauties, which, though a little diverging from our subject, may perhaps prove interesting to the reader.[55]

YANKEEVILLE, April 22d, 1862.

MY DEAR SISTER: As it may be a very long time before we again have an opportunity of writing to you, Ma has made us all promise to write you a long letter; so if a corpulent budget comes to hand (provided it is not kidnapped), you need not be surprised. You see by the dating of my letter that we have moved family, house servants and all into Yankeeville. We are only about one hundred miles farther from you than when we lived at Huntsville. The portion of the United States that we live in is decidedly one of the most out-of-the-way places I have ever seen. Although the cars seem to run regularly, there is never a breath of news to gladden our hearts. I declare I have not seen a newspaper for two weeks, and expect if I were to see one now, I should regard it as a supernatural appearance, and be frightened to death. The Rev. Mr. —— is here, and preached for us, and was not so partial to the President of the C. S. A., but what he could leave him out of his prayer when he saw it was necessary. He prayed the Lord to look down upon us in mercy as we then stood before Him, political enemies. The church was half filled with officers, brass buttons and black feathers, strange to say, looking as calm and collected after their exploits as a pan of butter-milk. I wish you could see them as they pass the gate; sometimes on horse back, forty or fifty of them together, with their long, murderous swords encased in brass, and dangling with terrific clamor against the horses' sides, which produces an effect so frightening that our faces are fear blanched with terror, and we instinctively pull our sun-bonnets over our faces and stop our ears with our fingers, that we may shut out as much as possible the humiliating noise. Do you not shudder when you think that we are in the hands of these ruffians. We expect every night that the town will be either shelled or burnt, and when I wake up in the morning I am surprised to find myself safe, and that the shells have not yet been hurled this way; then I say to myself in the most thankful and cheery way, "Good morning, dear, I'm glad to see you're all here." I miss dear little Huntsville so much, and often think of the times we used to have swinging together on the porch every night. Here the streets are so guarded that one dare not go beyond the dwelling houses, and as to singing in concert, the town is too

full of Yankeedoodles ever to attempt it. Oh! how I long to see
our dear soldiers again. Although I have no near kindred in the
army, each one of them is as dear to me as a brother. All our
girls are proud and brave, and never lose faith. They give no
quarters to the Yankees, and as one of them remarked, "He had-
n't seen a woman smile since he had been here." But how can
we smile and be gay in their presence, when our hearts are with
Charley, over the water. If you see any of my soldier friends up
your way, please tell them to come and escort us back. We cannot return without protection. There is a large party of girls
here who come with me, and who will join us. Our political ca-
noe has run aground, and the no-secession waves run so high
that it is dangerous for a party of females to brave them without some trusty arm to guard the vessel's bow. I wish I could see
you all. We ought not to be separated. Kiss my brother and take
good care of him, for men are so precious these war times.

    Your loving sister   E———.

June, 1st.—This morning we remain in camp awaiting orders to move, but we receive them not; remain here all day. We
are now camped near the rebel commissary; it is one vast heap
of ruins; sugar and flour scattered all over the ground, mo-
lasses running in streams down the railroad. Everywhere the
fields are strewn with tents, cooking utensils, army wagons,
old trunks, rebel uniforms, flint lock muskets, &c., &c. It is indeed an apt illustration of the assumed confederacy. The news
from Pope's advance is cheering this evening.

Monday, 2d.—Our regiment is still encamped near the Mobile and Ohio Railroad. It rains considerably to-day, which
makes everything look cheerful. This evening we receive orders to hold ourselves in readiness to move.

Tuesday, 3d.—For some cause unknown to the soldiers, we
do not move to-day. Good accounts from Pope continue to
come back.

Wednesday, 4th.—This morning we finally move from our
camp near the railroad, and march southward. Our destination is said to be Boonville. It seems that the entire army is in
motion. The roads are soon blockaded with the artillery and
army trains, and in consequence our regiment is delayed. We

pass Danville about dark. Marching on, we go into camp about nine o'clock P.M. The boys are very tired to-night.

Thursday, 5th.—This morning we lay in the shade until two o'clock P.M., when we move about two miles. The heat is intense; the boys seek every opportunity to shield themselves from the sun's scorching rays. We proceed no farther to-day.

Friday, 6th.—This morning we remain in the shade, having no orders to move. Some of the boys sally forth into the plantations, and it is not long until they return with a large supply of chickens, turkeys, butter and eggs.

This afternoon we move forward twelve miles; march in quick time. One by one the boys drop by the way, being unable to keep up with the command on account of the excessive heat.

Saturday, 7th.—This morning we do not move. The regiment is soon busy building bower houses to shield them from the sun.

Saturday, 8th.—To-day Halleck's vast army is resting beneath the shady forests of Mississippi. The boys keep close under their houses; the weather is very warm; the water is very scarce, hence the soldiers are suffering.

Monday, 9th.—This morning we still remain undisturbed in our bower camp. Troops are hourly passing us, moving southward. The roads are very dusty; water is becoming scarcer; what we have is of an inferior quality; we need rain very much.

Tuesday, 10th.—To-day we remain in camp. It is rumored to-night that the troops in our rear are moving back towards Corinth.

Wednesday, 11th.—This morning the army is breaking camp, and taking the backward track. We look for our turn to come soon, and it finally comes; we take up the weary march; the roads are very dusty; the heat is intense; the troops almost suffocate. This grand army is suffering to-day in Mississippi, but they move on; they murmur not. We hope soon to go into camp and rest for a while. Night comes, and the army lies down to sleep.

Thursday, 12th.—This morning we are soon on the march, moving in the direction of Corinth. Oh! how hot and dusty; we seem to be moving through one vast hot cloud of dust, and what adds more to the suffering of the soldier, is the scarcity of water. We come to a halt, with orders to rest for the night, for the soldiers are weary.

Friday, 13th.—This morning about three o'clock we move. It is more comfortable marching to-day; we march briskly until we come up with the Second Brigade and our baggage train, when we stop to eat our breakfast. We do not stop long; we soon move on through the heat and dust, and in the evening go into camp at our former camping ground, near the Mobile and Ohio Railroad.

Saturday, 14th.—To-day we remain in camp; everything seems quiet, the boys look cheerful. Close by, in a winding ravine gushes a stream of sparkling water, which God, the Eternal, brews for all his children. It is beautiful, and the boys in blue kneel often there.

Sunday, 15th.—We have divine service to-day. The men pay due deference to the preaching of the gospel, though they are engaged in working war's mad machine, a machine which is said to be demoralizing in its work. The weather still continues very hot, even warmer than it has heretofore been. "Keep us in the shade," is the universal cry among the men.

Monday, 16th.—This morning a large detail is made from the regiment to prepare a new and permanent camping ground for the summer. It rains to-day, making all nature look smiling and healthy.

Tuesday, 17th.—This morning after the rain, the world around seems all beauty; the south winds blow soothingly around the Union soldiers in Mississippi.

Wednesday, 18th.—To-day we move our camp; we now have a pleasant situation. The signs of the times are changing. Direct communication is now open from Corinth to the Mississippi River.

Thursday, 19th.—This morning is still and beautiful. From the distant fields come the sound of the bugle's sharp notes. The artillery is going pell mell, practicing in the evolutions. Drill, drill, seems to be the order of the day, coming from every quarter. During our stay in camp here, nothing of much interest occurs; now and then an occasional something turns up to relieve the dull monotony of camp life. On the third of July, Colonel Babcock returns back to his regiment form his sick leave; we are all glad to see him among us again. On the Fourth we have a soldier's celebration, a barbacue and a grand dinner furnished by the officers of the regiment; we are also favored on the occasion with a good, whole-souled speech from General Oglesby, and all this on the ground where but a short time before Van Dorn's and Sterling Price's battle flags stood.[56] But they stand a little farther south now, and in their stead stands another flag, and around it stand soldiers who wear a uniform different from the uniform worn by those who stood around the other flag; the former battles for slavery, the latter for freedom; the former for the annihilation of the first independence, the latter for its maintainance. On this annual anniversary, beneath the heat of Mississippi sun, these boys renew their allegiance, and swear by the memory of the loved and lost to bear their bristling steel for the first independence that spoke into existence are public, which in its infancy seemed a paragon let down from heaven to inspire the pilgrims of freedom. On the eleventh our regiment receives a new stand of colors. The colors we carried through the battles of Fort Donelson and Shiloh are now so mutilated that we are unable to carry them any longer. They will be sent to springfield to be laid away in their glory, and while they thus rest from battle and storm, back with Illinois' great loyal people, may they ever remember as they gaze upon its hallowed ribbons, the noble ones who went down while its rents and scars were being made; whose lamps of life flickered out while wrathful storms were sweeping along the shores of the Cumberland and the Tennessee, and over the fields of Mississippi; remember that while it was swung in its glory the noble hearts of Captains Mendell and Ward, Lieutenants Myers and Estabrook, Sergeants Wheeler and Mitchell, Corporals William Boring, Seth Hamilton and Nixon, Privates Charles Newton, John Fifer, Andrew McKennon, John Teft, Richard Lamherdt, Isaac Britton, John H. Duff, John Gibland, Ole Porter, Peter Miller, John H. Hopper and others ceased their loyal throbbings forever. They loved that old banner, made so hallowed on fields of blood. It was the pride of their hearts; for it they lived, for it they died. Those shot-riven folds will speak to the loyal people in a silent language, telling them a thrilling story—a story, the letters of which have been written in blood. We send them back to the good people from whence they came, hoping

that the story they tell will find an entrance into their loyal
hearts and cause it to start to tear to the memory of those who
went down beneath its folds.

On the twenty-eighth we strike tents, and move into the
camp lately occupied by the Sixth Division. During our camp
here the regiment is on picket every other day. We find the locality very unhealthy.

On the seventh of August the regiment is ordered to advance a short distance and clear off a new camping ground. In
the evening we notice some of the Seventh boys escorting in
from the picket line a squad of guerrillas. They are taken to
Corinth that they may have their names registered and obtain
lodgings at the Military Hotel.

On the ninth we move to our new and fresh camping ground,
near battery C. Captain Hackney will remember the day we
moved, for if we remember correctly the ague shook him like an
earthquake, but the soldiers's medicine proved a sure remedy.[57]
What a god-send! While here our camp and picket duties are
heavy. Lieutenant Ring is now detached from his company, having been detailed as Police Officer of Corinth. General Ord has
indeed made a good selection, but has damaged Company H.[58]
Contrabands are coming in daily. While in this camp some of
the boys bring in one of these exiles from bondage, to enlist as a
company cook, followed by his master, who enters complaint.
The General being strictly averse to the "peculiar institution,"
makes disposition of the case by compelling the old man to take
the oath of allegiance and make his exit from the lines.[59]

On Monday, the 25th, we strike our tents and move from our
camp. The weather is warm and sultry. We pass through
Corinth, marching in platoons; it is very dusty, and the boys almost famish for water. We go into camp two miles north of
Corinth to stand as outposts for the army surrounding, and
the garrison in Corinth.

The 26th we are busily engaged cleaning off our camp
ground; we have no water here; are compelled to haul it from a
distance. To-day we send six trains and a guard for water; they
return, but with no water. There is no alternative but to haul it
from beyond Corinth, about four miles distant. During our camp
here on the Purdy road, we live like kings; the result of the

sharp trading of the boys with the citizens who are daily seen in our camp with fruit, milk, chickens and eggs. We dare say our men traded with many a rebel spy, and the information gained by them resulted in making additions to the already long list of names of those who are now sleeping silently in the south-land. There was a mistake somewhere; somebody committed an error; where that mistake, and who that somebody was, we are not prepared to say. The world, perhaps, will never know.

September 15th.—Company A, Captain McGuire, Company G, Lieutenant Sayles, are detached from the regiment to take charge of a battery.[60] To-day rumor has it that the rebel army under Price is moving upon Corinth. If they come, of course we will meet and extend to them our hospitality. It is also reported that there is fighting going on at Iuka, Mississippi, about thirty miles from Corinth; there may be some truth in it. If so, ere long we may be hurled into battle.

On the 20th we receive dispatches informing us that Rosecrans is engaged in battle with Price at Iuka. We are expecting every minute to move. It is now towards evening; we know that our men are struggling to-day; we know not the result; we fear that the battle has been desperate, but we hope that the old flag has not been caused to droop.[61]

Sunday, 21st.—It is reported to-day that Price has been beaten, and is now making a flank movement towards Corinth. Soon we are ordered to Corinth, and there we lay in line of battle all day; but no Price comes, and we return to camp in the evening. Dispatches from Rosecrans inform us this evening that he has routed Price. Praises for Rosecrans and the noble Fifth Iowa come from every one. The Illinois soldiers can ever find it in their hearts to speak words of praise about their brothers from Iowa, especially when like the Fifth who maintained such a desperate bayonet charge to save their colors from falling into the hands of the rebels. Right here we would say that the Seventh Illinois Veteran Volunteer Infantry will not soon forget the Seventh and Second Iowa, starting in the service together, fighting side by side in the assault on Fort Donelson, together carrying their flag in the thickest of the battle, camping side by side on the weary march. They seemed to each other as brothers, for brothers they were, fighting in one common cause to keep the old flag on its staff, and to-day there are men in the Seventh that would fling their coats for a fight, should they hear any one speak disparagingly of the Seventh and Second Iowa infantry. They are camped now some where around Corinth, but we do not know exactly where; however, we remember them, and we imagine when the war is over, and when peace comes back to her people, should a soldier from the Seventh Illinois Infantry meet one from the Seventh or Second Iowa Infantry, who fought with him at Donelson, it will be a congenial meeting, and if he does not treat him as a gentleman it may be marked down as a fact that he does not understand the business.

Tuesday, 23d.—We move our camp from the Purdy road to the Pittsburg road to give way for the Sixteenth Wisconsin. We encamp in a beautiful place in the woods, or a dense thicket of Jack Oaks. We are inclined to think that it would be difficult for the rebels to find us here. Yesterday we received some new recruits in our regiment, brought down from Springfield, Illinois, by Capt. Estabrook, which greatly improves the appearance of the regiment.

Wednesday, 24th.—This morning we are busily engaged in cleaning off our new camping ground. It has been suggested that the Seventh take the contract to clear off Tishomingo county. We have already cleaned off nearly enough camping ground to camp the old Second Division, this being the sixth camp the Seventh has prepared in the last six months; but, as one of our officers remarked to-day, the Seventh stands flat-footed for anything, whether it be cleaning off camping grounds, doing guard duty, running, or stealing, and it is now whispered around confidentially that in the latter the Seventh might be safe in claiming a little accomplishment.

Thursday, 25th.—To-day, in every direction, we can see the Seventh boys reading the papers (for by the way, the Seventh is a reading regiment,) and from every quarter comes bitter denunciations against the enemies of Pope, and laudations upon Abraham Lincoln for having the backbone and the wisdom to issue at this turbulent and threatening period the great emancipation proclamation. We hail this as one of the most powerful blows against rebellion; the freedom of the slave paving the way for the advance of free thought.[62]

Monday, 29th.—All is quiet; a dull monotony reigns in camp. It is rumored that the command will move from Corinth ere long. All seem anxious for that hour to come—seem tired of this inactive life. General Rosecrans has command of the forces here. In the evening he visits our camp; seems greatly pleased with our dress parade, and the efficiency of the regiment in the manual of arms.

Wednesday, October 1st.—This morning we receive marching orders; about noon we strike tents and move out, all in a glee, as it is rumored that we are going to have a fight ere long with Price and his boasted legions. We march as far as our old camp in the Second Division, near the Mobile and Ohio Railroad, (this being the third time we have pitched our tents here since the evacuation of Corinth).

Thursday, 2d.—Troops are moving to-day in almost every direction. It seems that the old Second Division is collecting together for some forward movement. This evening the command receives marching orders; ordered to have prepared two day's cooked rations in haversacks, also to move with two hundred rounds of cartridges to the man, forty in the cartridge box, and the remaining one hundred and sixty to be hauled in the wagons. These orders to the Seventh, we are inclined to think, mean business. There is certainly a storm coming. God only knows how soon the terrible din will be heard; only know how soon there will be a rattle of musketry and clash of steel; when more blood will flow, more hearts will bleed, and more tears will fall. If such days come again, throwing around these stout hearts war's fierce realities, may the spirit of the great Jehovah control the wrathful storms and nerve the Union soldier, that he may not falter.

PROMOTIONS.

Up to this date the following promotions have been made in the regiment, for meritorious services performed in battle at Fort Donelson:

Colonel John Cook to be Brigadier General.

Lieutenant Colonel A. J. Babcock to be Colonel, vice Cook, promoted.

Major R. Rowett to be Lieutenant Colonel, vice Babcock, promoted.

Captain Monroe to be Major, vice Rowett, promoted.

Adjutant B. F. Smith promoted to Captain and A. A. G., on General Cook's staff.

Second Lieutenant Newton Francis to be First Lieutenant of Company I, vice Johnson, promoted.

First Lieutenant Newton Francis to be Adjutant, vice Smith promoted.

First Sergeant Thomas McGuire to be Second Lieutenant of Company A, vice Renick, resigned.

Second Lieutenant Thomas McGuire to be First Lieutenant of Company A, vice Kimball, resigned.

First Sergeant Ben. Sweeney to be Second Lieutenant of Company A, vice McGuire, promoted.

First Lieutenant Hector Perrin to be Captain of Company B, vice Monroe, promoted.

Second Lieutenant O. D. Ells to be First Lieutenant of Company B, vice Perrin, promoted.

First Lieutenant Edward S. Johnson to be Captain of Company I, vice Mendell, killed.

First Sergeant John E. Sullivan to be Second Lieutenant of Company I, vice Francis, promoted.

Second Lieutenant John E. Sullivan to be First Lieutenant of Company I, vice Francis promoted.

First Sergeant Joseph S. Fisher to be Second Lieutenant of Company I, vice Sullivan, promoted.[63]

For meritorious service performed at Shiloh:

Sergeant George W. Wheeler to be Captain of Company A, vice Ward, killed.

Second Lieutenant J. L. Ring to be First Lieutenant of Company H, vice Myers, killed.

First Sergeant Thomas J. Pegram to be Second Lieutenant of Company H, vice Ring, promoted.

Chapter VII.

[October 3, 1862–December 17, 1862]

The battle of Corinth, first day—Orders to move—Rumor of Price and Van Dorn advancing—Marched to the outer works—The Seventh's position in the works—The contest on the hill—The flanking of the Seventh—Its safe retreat—The charge of the Second Division—The Second Division fighting the whole rebel army—Ordered into camp for the night near the college—Movements during the night—Second day—Position in the morning—Early firing from a rebel battery—The regiment's position behind the temporary works—The attack—The fierceness of the battle—The falling back of the troops—The re-action—The victory—The casualties—The camp on the field—The pursuit—The camp at Rookerville, Mississippi—The march back to Corinth—Our camp at Corinth—The Second Division—The Cincinnati Commercial's Correspondent—Captain Holden's resignation.

Friday, October 3d, 1862.—This morning ere it is light, the drums are heard, which tell us that something is demanded of the Seventh—a march and a fight forsooth. Orders for a march we have already received, but orders for a battle may be forthcoming, for these come unexpected sometimes. Rumor, which is ever busy, is circulating many things; one is that Price and Van Dorn, being dissatisfied with Iuka, are now threatening Corinth. But every one seems to be ignorant of anything hostile any where in Northern Mississippi. The Seventh is soon ordered into line, and with everything buckled and in trim, we take up the line of march towards Corinth. After going a short distance, we are ordered to move in double-quick time. This leads us to think that there is something coming this way, that will give us battle music, but who will play it, we know not. We are soon in Corinth; everything is in commotion; troops are moving, and aids and orderlies dashing everywhere. Soon we are informed that Colonel Olive, with the Fifteenth Michigan, has been driven in from Chewalla, an out-post on the Memphis and Charleston Railroad, nine miles south of Corinth.[64] An orderly is now seen dashing up the Chewalla road. He comes from Colonel Olive, and informs the General that the Fifteenth Michigan is pressed, and if not reinforced, will be unable to maintain its position now on the hill, on the line of the old rebel works, crossing the Chewalla road, two and a-half miles from Corinth. Colonel Babcock is ordered forward on double-quick time with the Seventh, to reinforce him. Arriving at the scene of action, we find McArthur in command on the hill. Reporting to him, Colonel Babcock is ordered to take his position in the rebel works, forty rods to the right of the Fifteenth Michigan; the artillery being immediately to our left. Colonel Babcock now sends forward Company H, deployed on a skirmish line along a ravine beyond the abattis. Soon we hear sharp firing down there; with a sweeping power the rebels are hurled against them, compelling them to fall back, and as they come over the works, they carry with them Lieutenant Ring, wounded and bleeding, which is a serious loss to the company. It is sad to think that after he had obtained permission from the General in the morning to return to his company, that he should thus fall in the commencement of the battle; that the company should thus be deprived of its brave leader. But such are the fortunes of war; the brave spirited heroes are generally the first to go down. Before Lieutenant Ring is carried from the field, he says to his men, "I may never be with you any more," and exhorts them to stand firm for the old flag and do it and their homes honor, as they had always done on every battle-field. How sad it makes us feel to see our brave ones fall; to see our leading spirits leave us when we can illy spare them. The brave Ring is now borne back in his glory.

We will now turn to the situation. By this time it is discovered that Price and Van Dorn are in our immediate front with their entire commands, numbering about twenty-five thousand men, which tells us plainly that there will be a work of blood to-day in these woods. We now look across the abattis and behold the angry legions of the south moving towards our front in terrible array. The battery on our left, the Fifteenth Michigan, and the Fifty-seventh on the left of the Fifteenth, now open a terrific fire. At this juncture we discover a large body of rebels emerging from the timber in solid column, about forty rods to our right, moving directly across the unprotected works. The Seventh turns its fire towards them and checks them for a few minutes. This column's fire soon turns the Seventh's right flank. The enemy in our front having been repulsed by the Seventh, soon rally and are on to the breach again, receiving our fire with a remarkable indifference. Up to this time the battery and the force on our left have been making the woods ring with their terrible thunder, but they are silent now; their cannons are still; their musketry is hushed. What means it all? Owing to the dense undergrowth in the woods we are hid from them. Colonel Babcock has not received any word from McArthur since taking his position here. The battle still rages in our immediate front. Colonel Babcock cast his eye to the rear; he looks down a ravine and beholds the Chewalla road swarming with rebels. The fact soon flashes upon his mind that McArthur, with his force, has been driven from the hill, leaving the Seventh isolated and alone. The rebels are now pressing us in the front, a column moving past us to our right, another rebel force on the Chewalla road to our left and rear, rebels in our front, rebels on our right and rear, rebels on our left and rear; soon their right and left columns will meet; soon we will be surrounded if we remain here. Colonel Babcock's observing eye sees the situation of the regiment in an instant. The command is given, "By the right of companies to the rear." Will we get back? Will we save ourselves by moving direct to the rear? We may; this is our only hope. The regiment moves steadily; no confusion, no panic; how like clock-work they move. We succeed in getting back ere the rebel columns meet. We find Colonel Olive's command and the regiments composing the Third Brigade, in line of battle one-half mile from the hill, where they had been driven. The Third Brigade is now formed on the Chewalla road; the Seventh on the right, with the left resting on the road, and in their order the Fiftieth and Fifty-seventh on the left of the road; and as soon as the Seventh is formed, Colonel Babcock reports to General McArthur, who had assumed command of that part of the line. By his direction we move by the left flank east of the Chewalla road, forming a new line of battle facing north. Companies I and C, under the command of the gallant Captain Johnson are now deployed forward on a skirmish line covering the front of the Third Brigade. The positions of the regiments in the Third Brigade are as follows: The Fifty-seventh on the right, and in their order the Seventh and the Fiftieth. Thus is the position of the Second Division, commanded by General Davies: The First Brigade, commanded by General Hackleman, in the center; the Second Brigade, commanded by General Oglesby, on the right; and the Third Brigade, commanded by Colonel Baldwin, on the left.[65]

There is a lull now; the rebels seem hesitating. The heat is intense; no water; the men are famishing; some of the Seventh fall in their tracks, fainting and exhausted under the scorching sun. While the men are thus suffering, we advance; the Fifty-seventh takes the lead, the Seventh follows, then the Fiftieth. Through the woods they swept with the power of a terrible whirlwind. For one-half mile they surge with a relentless force, making a fearful inroad among the rebels, but at this juncture fresh rebel troops are hurled against our flanks, compelling us to give way. That was a trying hour; the storm raged furiously; the woods were wrapped in smoke and flame. We fall back to our former position, and crossing the railroad, move back a short distance, where we find the Sixth Division drawn up in line of battle. General McArthur now directs Colonel Babcock to take his regiment to the rear of the Division and let it rest.

The Sixth Division advances and engages the enemy and for fifteen minutes the storm rages wildly. Generals Hackleman and Oglesby charge from the white house, near Corinth. General Hackleman falls a martyr—goes down in the sweeping tempest, and at the same time General Oglesby is badly wounded; thus we lose from the Union army two brave and noble men.

Night now lets fall her dark mantle, and the great storm is hushed. General Davies' Division made a fearful swing to-day. During the long weary hours while his men were famishing and dying, he fought the whole rebel army and held it in check. Where was Rosecrans, with Hamilton and Stanly, when the Second Division was struggling as warriors have but few times struggled on this continent? They may have been where duty called. We trust they were. It may have been necessary for the Second Division to alone stem the angry current, and to-night we feel glad that we never let the old flag go down, but kept her up to gladden the hearts of many brave men as their life blood ebbed away on this field of fearful carnage.[66]

We are ordered into camp one-half mile southeast of Corinth, near the college, but we do not remain here long until Colonel Babcock receives orders to report with the regiment to Corinth. Though the men are weary, they are soon in line. On arriving near the town, we are ordered to halt, and as soon as done the battle worn men drop down upon the ground to rest themselves; but their eyes are scarcely closed, when again the command "fall in" is given, and we move to another position, and thus during the long weary night we are kept moving from one place to another; and, in consequence, there is no sleep for the tired and almost exhausted Seventh.

Saturday, 4th.—At two o'clock this morning the Second Division is huddled promiscuously around the headquarters of General Rosecrans, on the north side of Corinth. About three o'clock, a sheet of fire is seen to burst from a rebel battery planted during the night in the woods near the Purdy road; all morning it continues to send forth its glaring light; the air is full of bursting shell; the heavens seem all ablaze; the stars for a moment seem eclipsed. The light from the morning king is now flashing against the bayonets of the two hostile armies. Smoke and wrathful messengers still continue to leap from the woods where the rebel monster frowns, and as its storm comes sweeping on its track, death follows in its wake, for some brave men are seen to fall, breathe quickly, and die. Our big guns at batteries Williams and Robinett now open upon this rebel battery with a roar that is hideous; sending echoes across the fields and through the surrounding woods that sound unearthly. This battery is soon disabled, and rebel heels are seen to fly heavenward, thus putting a stop to its deadly sweeps.

About eight o'clock the regiment is moved forward and placed in a position behind some temporary works constructed during the night. The position of the Second Division resembles an ox yoke, minus the bows; the First Brigade and Powell's battery forming the right curve, with the bulge facing the enemy north and northwest;[67] the Second Brigade forming the center, facing northwest, and the Third Brigade forming the left curve, facing north and west. The position of the Third

Brigade, commanded by Colonel Dubois, U. S. A., is as follows:[68] The Seventh Illinois on the right with its right resting on the Purdy road, and in their order the Fiftieth and Fifty-seventh Illinois. Soon after taking our position in the great yoke of bayonets, Colonel Babcock is ordered to move forward, deploy his regiment and support Berge's sharp-shooters.[69] We soon discovered the enemy crossing the railroad in large force. Upon making the discovery we are ordered to return to our position in the "yoke." The enemy is now evidently making preparations to take Corinth, if possible, at the point of the bayonet.

While there is a lull in consequence of these preparations, we will review the situation. Here, marshaled upon Corinth's fields, can be seen thousands of determined warriors supporting their bristling steel, waiting to engage in the work of blood. There is silence along the Seventh's line, and we all feel that it will prove to be a line of stout hearts. The gallant Colonel Babcock and Lieutenant Colonel Rowett are at their posts. The commanders of companies, Captains Lawyer, Hunter, Johnson, Knowlton, McGuire, Perrin, Clark, and Lieutenants Estabrook, Pegram, Smith, Sullivan, Sweeny, Raymond, Ahern, Atchison and Gillson are resting upon their drawn swords.[70] They will soon wield them and we know that they will be wielded so as to reflect glory and honor upon those who swing them. The story of the terrible days of the past assure us as much. The sun is now far up in the sky, but it is evident that ere it sinks to rest many a noble soldier will have laid himself down for a quiet, eternal sleep. We look across the fields; the ghastly stars and bars are seen peering from the woods; the drunken Arkansas legions under the command of General Caball are surging towards the Third Brigade's front, four regiments deep in columns of attack.[71] The redoubt on the right is now taken; the right is giving way in confusion; there is a gap in the line to our right on the Purdy road; the attack on the left being slight, the Fifty-seventh is removed therefrom and thrown into this breach. At this period a battery in our rear on an elevation overlooking Corinth opens upon General Caball's charging column. The shot from this battery falling short, Sergeant Wheeler, of Company H of the Seventh, is thereby killed.[72] The battle now rages furiously; many noble men are falling victims; streams of blood are flowing; the death archer is at work. The charging column is overwhelming; the Seventh is now driven from the temporary works; the yoke is broken; the regiment is retreating slowly; they are contesting manfully every inch of the ground. Falling back a short distance, Colonel Babcock and Lieutenant Colonel Rowett, with the ready assistance of the officers of the line, succeed in rallying the regiment, forming a line at a small house on the out-skirts of Corinth, where the Seventh stands like a pillar of fire. Volley after volley they are now sending into the Arkansas hosts. They seem determined though they die to keep the old flag in the wind. On, the storm king of battle rides. Reckless shot and shell are making deep furrows in the earth. The air is full of whistling minies; things look fearful. We stand amid the dead and dying. Smoke from iron mouths rolls everywhere; everything seems to be wrapped in flames. How can our thinned and almost famished Seventh stem this mad storm? For a few moments, the regiment's determined front staggers the enemy and throws them into confusion, but they have re-formed, and are now coming across the open field in terrible array. The regiment that has thus far stood up so manfully is now made to waver— the flag is seen to tremble. At this trying moment an aid comes dashing down the line (we believe it was Capt. Lovell) crying out, "Oh, noble Seventh! noble Seventh! stand the storm, it won't last long!"[73] The battery on the hill in the rear still continues its firing. The Seventh being unable to stand against the overwhelming and sweeping rebel force, and being exposed to the fierce storms of this (our own) battery on the hill, again falls back and forms out of the line of its fire. In this retreat the gallant and brave Lieutenant Estabrook of Company E was killed. The battle all along the entire line is now raging desperately. The earth is trembling around Fort Robinett, wrathful thunder is rolling from her brazen guns. The battle smoke seems to roll against the sky. General Rogers and his Texan legions have thrown themselves into the ordeal there, but like grass before the mower's scythe his mad rangers are falling victims to a wicked ambition.[74] We now turn our eyes, casting them along the Second Division's crippled line. They are fighting desperately against fearful odds, hotly contesting every inch of ground on the streets of Corinth. The regiments are broken up in small squads, commanded by Lieutenants and Sergeants. Colonel Babcock and Lieutenant Colonel Rowett, with a part of the Regiment are now standing heroically with their trembling flag; the remaining part of the Regiment being disconnected from the colors, is engaged in heated contest on other parts of the field. Confusion reigns; darkness seems to be throwing her sable wings around the struggling Second Division. The main drift of the battle has been against them. General Davies, with the gallant Captains Lovell and Hanna, Colonel Dubois, Colonel Babcock, Lieutenant Colonel Rowett, and the brave officers of the line, have been laboring hard to check the adverse tide.[75]

The sun is now passing down towards the western horizon. Will the battle be lost? will this brave army be crushed? will the flag be lowered? will the loyal people be compelled to bow their heads and drop tears over another ill-fated field? No! Such a story shall not go to the hearts of the loyal people. We look away; we behold the right wing swinging around, hurling volley after volley into the flanks of the enemy. There is a reaction now; the Second Division rallies again, and led by General Davies, fights with renewed vigor. The rebel lines are seen to waver; our big guns are now mowing them down by hundreds. Seeing this wavering of the rebels, the men are encouraged. Colonel Babcock, with the Seventh, moves firmly and with power. The Fiftieth are making a glorious charge; a smile of triumph seems to be playing on every face. The enemy are being driven; foot by foot they are falling back from Corinth's field. The Union's proud banner is again advancing; loud shouts from our lines are making a din in the air. The dying heroes, as they pass away, leave ringing in our ears, "Follow the flag!" "Keep it up!" "Don't let it fall!" Oh! what hearts! what glory! what manhood! A rebel retreat is ordered. The shouts of victory make the welkin ring. The old Seventh's flag in its shreds and ribbons seems to shed a halo of glory around its exultant and happy defenders.

Sergeant Newell and Corporal Bordwell, color bearers, deserve honorable mention for their gallantry in carrying our flag through this terrible battle.[76] No braver soldiers ever moved on a battle-field. No one ever looked to the rear to see the Seventh's colors; but on the front line in the fiercest of the battle, their noble bearers were ever seen standing with them. They unfurled them in the battle wind and never let them go down. They seemed to be the pride of their hearts, and their faces looked sad when the fortunes of battle compelled them to carry them back. In the wide universe there is nothing so beautiful to behold as a brave man fighting for his country's flag; nothing more beautiful than to see fearless spirits like Sergeant Newell and Corporal Bordwell, bearing the proud banner of freedom through smoke and flame.[77]

Night has now come, and the worn and almost exhausted Seventh lie down upon the blood-stained field to obtain some rest. Though we are all weary and tired, we feel glad in our hearts that the old flag has been honored to-day, and while we thus feel happy we feel sad when we look around us and see that comrades and officers who were with us yesterday morning and this morning are with us no more. The following is the Seventh's casualties in the two days' battle:

STAFF.—First Lieutenant William Brown, Quartermaster, mortally wounded; T. N. Francis, Adjutant, wounded in foot; Fred W. Cross, Fife Major, wounded through mouth, severely.

COMPANY B.—John Fifer, killed; Wentworth D. Wolf, taken prisoner; John Devine, corporal, wounded in the face; W. Graham, corporal, wounded in left shoulder; L. D. Porter, private, wounded in left hand, finger off; Wm. Auld, wounded in left hand, severely; Wm. Nelson, wounded in left hand slightly.

COMPANY C.—E. R. Roberts, First Lieutenant, wounded in hand, finger off; W. H. Ferguson, Second Lieutenant, wounded in right arm, severely; Clark B. Alford, private, killed; G. W. Baldwin, private, wounded in right arm; Edgar Campbell, private, wounded in right hand; J. Hamilton, private, wounded in hand, slightly; J Kopf, private, wounded in arm, slightly; William Shell, taken prisoner.

COMPANY D.—Sergeant F. Bradshaw, taken prisoner; Corporal T. Raymond, taken prisoner; T. M. Reeves, private, taken prisoner; W. H. Harris, private, taken prisoner; Michael Greely, private, taken prisoner; Michael Walsh, private, wounded slightly.

COMPANY E.—Henry N. Estabrook, Second Lieutenant, killed; John Tefft, private, killed; Jasper Eveland, private, wounded, leg amputated; William Robinson, private, wounded in hip; Albion P. Gossard, private, wounded in arm; Thomas H. Watt, private, wounded in shoulder, severely; John B. Forbes, private, wounded in hip, severely; Joseph Lancaster, private, wounded in head, severely; Edwin R. Jones, private, wounded in head, severely; Martin V. Miller, sergeant, taken prisoner; John J. Frost, private, taken prisoner.

COMPANY F.—James Adams, private, killed; Bernard Keely, private, mortally wounded; R. C. Staples, private, wounded; Hans Hanson, private, wounded; Joshua S. March, private, taken prisoner.

COMPANY G.—William Hawks, private, wounded, finger off; D. C. Munson, corporal, wounded in thigh, severely.

COMPANY H.—Jacob L. Ring, First Lieutenant, wounded in breast, severely; Laban Wheeler, sergeant, killed; W. T. Taylor, private, wounded in hip, severely; Edmond H. Cook, private, wounded in foot, slightly; John D. Turner, corporal, taken prisoner; James M. Halbert, private, taken prisoner; John Fowler, private, taken prisoner; William T. Omay, private, taken prisoner.

COMPANY I.—John H. Shankland, first sergeant, wounded in chin, slightly; David Walker, private, wounded in ankle; Robert Walker, private, wounded in right shoulder; George Heisey, private, wounded in arm severely; Patrick Crowley, private, wounded in right foot, severely; John Mow, private, wounded in left leg, severely; Michael O'Connor, private, wounded in left hand; John W. Campbell, sergeant, taken prisoner; Peter Miller, private, taken prisoner; Wm. E. Norton, private, taken prisoner; Daniel J. Baker, private, taken prisoner.

COMPANY K.—Felix Lane, private, wounded slightly in the face; Richard Taylor, private, wounded slightly in the back; George Palmer, private, taken prisoner; David Lewis, private, taken prisoner; Mike Connerty, private, taken prisoner. Total number killed, 6; total number wounded, 43; total number taken prisoners, 21; sum total of losses, 70.[78]

As we look over this roll of honor, we think of those noble hearts that have ceased their pulsations forever, and of those now bleeding, mangled and torn, lying in the Corinth hospitals. In the years to come, when the tocsin of war shall have been hushed and the country is at peace, may America's great loyal people drop tears to the memory of those fallen heroes, and throw a fostering arm around her maimed and crippled warriors whose glorious nobility will be traced back to the most sanguinary battle-fields of the nineteenth century. As we cast our eyes around us, we are wont to say, oh! had we the picture emblazoned upon canvass, with all its horrifying details and gloomy shadows; could the loyal people but discern the ardor, the industry, the exertion, the valor, the iron arm of strength that was raised in these two days on Corinth's bloody field; could they but feel the glow of patriotism that warmed the hearts and brightened the eyes of those noble ones, who went down to-day on this crimson field; could they but feel the inspiration of the hour when life was nothing and the country all, they would then know the importance of the hour and believe in the providence of God, who will guide the ship of state into a prosperous haven. The Seventh is now sleeping; they are weary; their loss has been heavy. Terrible were the shafts of war hurled against them. When the battle's smoke vanished away, we all bowed our heads in silence, when we remembered that the gallant officer and christian soldier, Lieutenant Henry N. Estabrook, of Company E, was with us no more, but was sleeping the eternal sleep on Corinth's field of glory.

History tells of many brave spirits; its pages are teeming with plaudits for its daring heroes. But the historian has never moved his pen to eulogize a truer manhood and a purer spirit than was embodied in the life and character of Lieutenant Estabrook. Possessing an excellence of character, a gentlemanly demeanor, and high-toned manhood, he won for himself the esteem of his men and fellow officers. Though he was engaged in working war's mad machine, it never cast a shadow upon his Christian character. His mind was ever dwelling upon things that were high, grand and noble; spurning that which was groveling and ignoble as beneath the dignity of a Christian gentleman. We saw him when he fell; when the Union army's center was giving way, and while waving his sword, and cheering his gallant men, he went down beneath the old Union's swaying flag, and as his life-blood ebbed away upon the altar of the world's last hope, a smile was seen to play upon his face; it was a smile of triumph, a smile of sunshine and of glory, and the indistinct language of his soul was, "Lo, peace is here." And his spirit fled from his field of blood and death, home to God. A truer man, a better commanding officer, a braver soldier than Lieutenant Estabrook has never been stricken down on America's great battle-fields. No purer spirit ever fluttered for entrance at the windows of heaven. Though he is dead, his name will ever live in the memory of the Seventh, and especially in the memory of his noble company, who stood with him until he fell a martyr to freedom. The faithful historian will write his name among the crowned ones of immortality. And from the warrior's grand calendar no ribbon, nor belt, nor jeweled cross will ever bear a prouder name than that of Lieutenant Henry N. Estabrook.

Lieutenant Brown, regimental quartermaster, deserves honorable mention. He was mortally wounded on the first day, while endeavoring to get water to his famishing and suffering regiment. Stemming danger and death, with a noble determination to work his way to where the smoke of battle rolled around the Seventh, he fell amid the raging tempest, fell in the performance of his duty to his country and his men. Brave soldiers who went down in this great battle, you have won for yourselves a name. Peace to your ashes. May the patriot pilgrims who in the years to come pass this way, drop tears of grateful remembrance over your last resting place, and may they feel that you have gathered laurels, eternal and bright as a pyramid of stars. Everyone, officers and men, played well their part in this great battle. Ever found where duty called, each one is worthy of honorable mention—hence we will leave Corinth without particularizing any one of the gallant survivors.

Sunday, 5th.—This morning, Rosecrans with his victorious army is soon in motion, thundering in the rear of the retreating and shattered foe. Early in the morning we pass over the battle-field of Friday. The dead lie everywhere. They have all turned black; the scene is revolting and sickening. The heart sinks within as the eye falls upon the dreadful, gloomy picture. Oh, terrible war! in thy wrath what art thou doing in this land? What sable pictures art thou making for this nation's

historic page? The columns move slowly; the roads are blockaded by wagons and artillery—there is impatience in the
army; it is eager to dash on in its power and make a charge
against the rear of the retreating army. The heat is intense;
the water is scarce; the troops suffer. We succeed in getting
about eight miles, and go into camp near Chewalla, Tennessee.
Rosecrans' victorious army is weary to-night—but it complains
not. Its steps are firm, and there is power felt where they fall.
Many prisoners have been taken to-day and sent to the rear.
This evening Ben Hesket, of the quartermaster's department,
ever on the alert, furnishes the regiment with a fine steer, and
it is not long until it is served up in the very latest style, and
around the blazing camp fires the Seventh sit and satisfy the
inner man. By and by the camp fires go out, and the sturdy
Seventh sinks to rest upon the bosom of mother earth. No
sound breaks the stillness except the measured tramp of the
sentry as he paces to and fro upon his solitary beat. We will
now pass where these warriors lie sleeping. The beams of the
moon as it rides among the stars are resting upon their up-
turned faces. Something tells us that we see here the impress
of nobility. They may be dreaming now; the roaring tempest,
the rush of men, the clang of steel, the groans of the vanquished, and the shouts of the triumphant, may be heard by
them while the stars over them their nightly vigils keep.

Monday, 6th—This morning about three o'clock General
Rosecrans comes riding up to Gen. Davies' headquarters,
(which is near the Seventh's camp,) calling out—"General!
General! It is time for reveille. Get the Second in motion as
soon as possible," and on he goes dashing to the front. Long before day we are moving. All day news from the front is cheering, the rebels are abandoning everything and fleeing to the
swamps and woods. Hurlbut engages them at the Hatchie
river, disputing their passage by fighting a desperate battle,
which throws the whipped rebels in still greater confusion, but
turning they succeed in crossing six miles above the Hatchie
bridge. In the afternoon we halt, make some coffee and eat our
breakfast; rather late, "but better late than not at all." After
which our regiment, with a section of artillery, makes a scout
in the Tuscumbia bottom. Finding nothing but a few straggling

rebels we return, and on the way Colonel Rowett halts the regiment and puts it into a sweet potato patch, commanding the men to go to work or he would buck and gag them. The boys dig with a gusto and their haversacks are soon filled, when the regiment moves on and takes its position in the division, and after moving across the Tuscumbia we go into camp upon its banks, and after enjoying a bountiful supper on sweet potatoes, we lie down to rest.

Tuesday, 7th.—This morning we again move early. We cross the Hatchie to-day, entering the great Mississippi pineries. We find it a barren wilderness. All day we keep sending prisoners to the rear. Nothing but a wreck is seen on the war path. The road is lined with old, broken wagons, tents, cooking utensils and blown up caissons. The exhausted rebels fall by the way, hundreds are being picked up and are found in a pitiful condition, being half starved; but none are found who fell in love with Corinth, and by the way they don't like to talk about this subject, or at least they don't seem inclined to introduce it. About dark we go into camp—the boys make a raid upon a flock of sheep close by, and the Seventh have mutton chops for supper. It is over now and they are cheerful, and many a soldier sits round the camp fires enjoying hugely his pipe and "legal tender." We know by experience that it is an earthly heaven for a soldier and his comrade to sit by the camp fire's glimmering embers, and while from each other's pipe the spiral festoons are forming in air to talk of home and the halcyon days that have flown. And then, going to sleep, dream of glory, and wreaths, telling of fame that will not vanish, but wreaths that are a fadeless as the stars in the canopy above.

Wednesday, 8th.—At three, A.M., the Seventh is moving, but owing to the intense heat, we move slowly. In the evening we camp at Rookersville. The regiment feasts to-night on chickens, geese and sweet potatoes. The whole country is being foraged of everything that affords subsistence. News from the front informs us that the fleet-footed rebels are far away.[79] We are now fifty miles from Corinth. Our advance is at Ripley. We are told this evening that the mail agent will return to Corinth in the morning and forward a northern mail, and many a weary soldier is now sitting around the camp-fires writing to the loved ones.

Thursday, 9th.—This morning we remain at Rookersville, and the probability is that we will remain here all day. This is indeed a wrecked country, being almost brought to a state of starvation. To-day, Frank Morse, commissary sergeant, takes some meat to a suffering family in Rookersville, when the lady replies, "Oh, dear! this is Yankee meat; I don't know whether I can eat Yankee meat or not, I fear it is contaminated!"[80] Thus the South's ignorant classes have been deluded by wicked and unprincipled men. This evening some of the magnanimous Seventh boys give bread to children who are crying for something to eat. How sad a sight it is to see innocence suffering. Oh! wicked men! why did you fling these dark curtains around this people? Why did you whelm this fair sunny south in cruel, desolating war, and cause your beautiful innocent ones to cry for bread?

Friday, 10th.—This morning the army begins to countermarch. They have done their work—have routed the rebel army in Mississippi. The morning has been cloudy. At noon it commences to rain. At one, P.M., our division moves on the backward track towards Corinth. The road is muddy. We march briskly, and succeed in making nine miles. Go into camp near Jonesborough. To-night it is dark and gloomy. A drizzling rain is falling. But the fence rails are plenty, and the camp fires are made comfortable. The Seventh succeed in getting some straw from a stable close by, and upon this straw under their rubber blankets—notwithstanding a stormy wind is blowing and a rain falling—we sleep soundly.

Saturday, 11th—This morning we move early. Instead of dust we now have mud. To-day we cross the Hatchie, where General Hurlbut confronted the enemy on his retreat. By the roadside we see the graves of many brave Union soldiers. May the waters of the beautiful Hatchie never disturb their quiet repose; but may they move on their winding way, and over the projecting rocks chant requiems to the memory of the noble sleepers by her side, who fell there in liberty's great struggle. We pass on through the pine forests and cross the Tuscumbia and go into camp four miles beyond. Being much worn and fatigued from hard marching, rest seems sweet to the soldiers to-night.

Saturday, 12th.—This morning we are soon in line and moving. The regiment marches briskly. The men seem anxious to get back to Corinth, which is now only twelve miles distant. We pass the battle-ground, where the old Second Division so gallantly stemmed the storm on the third of October. The fields present one vast graveyard. We pass through Corinth at two P.M., and arrive in camp at three o'clock, all tired and foot-sore. We had a hard tramp down in Mississippi; but it is over now, and all seem glad to know that they went down there with the old flag and saw it swung in threatening grandeur, along the rear of the shattered rebel army. After washing our-selves and getting on clean shirts (discarding those that can now "go it alone") and after eating our supper prepared by the convalescents, we feel happy, and looking around us we see many smiles playing upon the soldiers' faces, as they recount to each other the incidents of the last ten days—incidents that will be sung in song and rehearsed in story because of their glory and their terror. Since returning to Corinth we have been perusing the journal of a rebel officer who was taken prisoner in the charge upon Fort Robinett, from which we take the following extract:

"Saturday, October 4th.—An eventful day. At four o'clock A.M., our brigade was ordered to the left, about a quarter of a mile, and halted where we deployed forward a skirmish line which kept up a constant fire. A battery in front of the right of our regi-ment opened briskly and the enemy replied in the same manner. The cannonading was heavy for an hour and a half. Our regi-ment laid down and stood it nobly. The shell flew thick and fast, cutting off large limbs and filling the air with fragments. Many burst within twenty feet of me. It was extremely unpleasant— and I prayed for forgiveness of my sins, and made up my mind to go through the tempest. Colonel Sawyer called for volunteers to assist the Second Texas skirmishers. I volunteered and took my company. Captain Perkins and Lieutenant Munson being taken sick directly after the severe bombardment, I led the company all the time. I went skirmishing at seven-and-a-half and re-turned at nine-and-a-half. Two of Captain Foster's men were killed, but none of ours. The enemy fired very fast. We got behind trees and logs, and the way bullets did fly was unpleasant to see. I think twenty must have passed within a few feet of me humming prettily. Shells tore off large limbs, and splinters struck my tree several times. We could only move from tree to tree by bending low to the ground while moving. Oh! how anxiously I watched for the bursting of the shells when the heavy roar proclaimed their coming. At nine-and-a-half o'clock I had my skirmishers relieved by Captain Rouser's company. Sent my men to their places, and went behind a log with Major Furger. At ten o'clock the fight opened in earnest; this was on the right. In a few moments the left went into action in splendid style. At fifteen minutes past ten Colonel Rogers came by us only saying, "Alabama forces!" Our regiment with the brigade rose unmindful of shell or shot and moved forward, marching about two hundred and fifty yards, and rising the crest of a hill, the whole of Corinth with its enormous fortifications burst upon our view. The United States flag was floating over the forts and in the town. We were now met by as perfect storm of grape, canister, cannon and minie balls. Oh! God, I never saw the like. The men fell like grass. Giving one tremendous cheer we dashed to the bottom of the hill on which the fortifications are situated. Here we found every foot of ground covered with large trees and brush. Looking to the right or left I saw several brigades charging at the same time—what a sight! I saw men running at full speed, stop suddenly and fall on their faces, with their brains scattered all around; others with legs or arms cut off. I gave myself to God, and got ahead of my company. The ground was literally strewed with mangled corpses. One ball passed through my pants and cut twigs close by me. It seemed that by holding out my hand I could have caught a dozen bullets. We pushed forward, marching as it were into the mouths of the cannon. I rushed to the ditch of the fort— I jumped into it, and half way up the sloping wall; the enemy were only two or three feet from me on the other side, but could not shoot us for fear of being shot themselves. Our men were in the same predicament. Only five or six were on the wall, and thirty or forty in and around the ditch. Catesby, my companion, is on the wall beside me. A man within two feet of me put his head cautiously up to shoot into the fort, but suddenly dropped his musket, and his brains were dashed in a stream over my fine coat, which I had in my arms. Several were killed and rolled down the embankment. This was done by a regiment of Yankees. Some of our men cried "put down the flag," when it was lowered or shot into the ditch. Oh! we were butchered like dogs—for we were not supported. Some one placed a white handkerchief on Sergeant Buck's musket, and he took it to a port hole, but the Yankees snatched it off and took him prisoner. The men were falling ten at a time. The ditch being full, and finding that we had no chance, we, the survivors, tried to save ourselves as best we could. I was so far up I could not get off quickly; I do not recollect seeing Catesby after this, but think he got off before. I trust in God he has. I and Captain Foster started together, and the air was literally filled with hissing balls. I got about twenty steps as quick as I could, about a dozen being killed in the distance. I fell down and crawled behind a large stump. Just then I saw poor Foster throw up his hands and saying "Oh! my God!" jumped about two feet off the ground and fell on his face. The top of his head seemed to cave in, and the blood spirted straight up several feet. I could see men falling as they attempted to run; some with their heads blown to pieces and others with the blood streaming from their backs. Oh! it was horrible. One poor fellow being almost on me, told me his name, and asked me to take his pocketbook, and if I escaped to give it to his mother and tell her that he died like a brave man. I asked him if he was a christian; he said he was. I asked him to pray, which he did with the cannons thundering a deadly accompaniment. Poor fellow, I forgot his request in the excitement. His legs were literally cut to pieces. As our men retreated the enemy poured into us a terrific fire. I was hardly thirty feet from the mouths of the cannons. Minie balls filled the stump I was behind, and the shells burst within three or four feet from me; one was so near it struck me and burnt my face with powder. The grape-shot knocked large pieces from my stump; it was gradually wearing away. I endured the horrors of death here for one-half hour. Our troops formed in line and advanced a second time to the charge with cheers, but began firing when about half way, and I had to endure it all. I feigned death. I was between our own and the enemy's fire. In the first charge our men did not fire a gun, but charged across the ditch and up to the very mouths of the cannons. But our boys were shot down like hogs; they could not stand the storms that came from the Yankees' thundering guns. I had no chance whatever. All around me were surrendering. I could do no better than follow suit; but thank God I am unhurt; nothing but a merciful providence saved me.[81]

This is a rebel soldier's discourse about the great battle of Corinth and especially the charging of Fort Robinett. Let the loyal people look at the above pen picture, and there see how terrible was the war for the Union, and with what mad desperation the rebels struggled for dominion.

Monday, 13th.—This morning the Seventh is busy cleaning and scouring up the guns, which is the soldier's first duty after a battle is over. Troops keep coming in from the front all day. Orders are now issued to the effect that the Division is to be newly brigaded, and in consequence we move our camp this evening close to General McArthur's headquarters. We do not pitch our tents, but spread them down upon the ground and sleep upon them during the night.

Tuesday, 14th.—This morning our camp is staked off, and we take our position and stake our tents. Our brigade now consists of the Seventh, Fiftieth and Fifty-seventh Illinois, and the Twenty-second and Eighty-first Ohio, commanded by Colonel A. J. Babcock, of the Seventh.[82] There is a commotion in the Second Division. The Cincinnati Commercial, with W. D. B.'s lying communication, villifying and basely misrepresenting the heroic Second Division, who so bravely stemmed the current of battle on Corinth's sanguinary field, has been circulated.[83] The heroes of Belmont, Fort Donelson and Shiloh rage to-night, and adding still more to this correspondent's villification, comes the congratulatory address of General Rosecrans, with the following remarkable passage: "I desire especially to offer my thanks to General Davies and his Division, whose magnificent fighting on the third more than atones for all that was lacking on the fourth."[84] As a defense, we will simply transcribe the circular of "Justice," written by a soldier of the Second Division, which gives a clear exposition of facts relative to the history of the Second Division in the two day's battle at Corinth:

"They did fail to do what they should have done, namely: there were captured by the whole army of Rosecrans, two thousand two hundred and sixty-eight prisoners, and the Second Division (Davies'), captured only one thousand four hundred and sixty of that number, mostly on the fourth; they should have captured the whole. Then again the whole army captured fourteen stand of colors; Davies' Division captured ten of these on the fourth; they should have taken all! They fought Van Dorn and Price's army on the third, alone, and whipped them. This was right. On the fourth they fought with others and whipped the enemy; they should have done it alone and would have done so but for the giving may of troops on the right flank—names I will not mention. Now, the Second Division well know they should have done all these things alone, and they must throw themselves upon the clemency of a forgiving country. The throbbing patriot's heart will have some sympathy, and the facts will atone for the short-comings of the Second Division when they are told that they went into action on the third with two thousand nine hundred and twenty-five officers and men, the balance of the Division being detailed in and about Corinth. Loss, seventy-five officers; total loss, one thousand and four. Forgive these "lacking and erring boys of the Northwest, for next time they will try and do better."

We remain in this camp, uninterrupted until November the 2d, when we are ordered inside the fortifications, the greater portion of the troops having left on an expedition southward. It is said our Division will remain and garrison Corinth for awhile. Our regiment is now camped close to Corinth, on the old battle field of October the 4th, and the probability is that we will remain here for some time, and in view of these indications, the Seventh is soon at work fixing up its quarter, building chimneys and fire places; and making general preparations for the approaching cold weather. The Seventh having its complement of mechanics, it is not long until the quarters are made quite comfortable, and as we look along the officers' line this evening we behold a neat row of chimneys, the work of the genial and accommodating "General Grant" of Company K. Of course the officers will all vote the General their hearty thanks.

November, 14th.—To-day the resignation of Captain C. W. Holden of Company "H" takes effect. The remainder of this month we remain quietly in camp.

December 1st.—To-day Lieutenant J. L. Ring having recovered from his wound received in the battle of Corinth, returns to the Regiment and assumes command of his company. During these days we find nothing to note; everything is quiet until December 17th when the military is discovered to be unusually active, aids and orderlies moving to and fro giving orders and carrying dispatches. Being so long quiet in camp we surmise we will move soon. So may it be; for all are eager to march forth again upon the war path.[85]

Chapter VIII.

[December 18, 1862–April 7, 1863]

The march into West Tennessee—Arrival at Purdy—Arrival at Lexington—Arrival at Pinch—The rebels withdraw from Jackson—The march to Henderson—Take the cars for Corinth—Our line of communications cut—Foraging—The close of 1862—The new year—Lincoln's proclamation—The railroad still cut—Arrival of the mail by Pony express—Rations running short—The troops compelled to subsist on corn—Communication open—Full rations—The conversation of two sentries—The non-arrival of mails—The cold weather—The comments of the soldiers on modern democracy—Arrival of the mails—Soldiers letters—Their welcome—The game cocks—Trip to Hamburg landing—The heavy duty of the regiment—Corinth a Gibralter—Meeting of Illinois officers in Music Hall, Corinth—The passing of resolutions relative to the vigorous prosecution of the war—The office of Chaplain—Trip to Davenport Mills—Resignation of Colonel Babcock—Celebration of the first anniversary of the battle of Shiloh.

December 18th, 1862.—To-day, 10 o'clock P.M., move from Corinth in the direction of Purdy, Tennessee. The whole available force from the garrison under the command of General G. M. Dodge, is on the move. We march briskly. It seems to be a forced march. The night is dark; no moon shoots forth its arrows of light. The Seventh soon becomes sleepy and tired, and many of the men fall by the way perfectly exhausted. Three o'clock in the morning we come to a halt. Those who are not too much exhausted build camp fires and prepare their breakfast, but the majority of the men being so weary, drop down upon the ground and are soon slumbering. At the early dawn of day all are aroused and the Seventh's weary men are compelled to move forward without any breakfast. We arrive at Purdy, Tennessee, by noon, where we halt, eat our dinners, and steal a few hours for sleep. This is a beautiful inland town, situated in West Tennessee, thirty miles northwest from Corinth, and four miles from the Mobile and Ohio Railroad. The drums now beat, and again the regiment is formed in line. Rumors are now rife that there is a fight on hand somewhere in West Tennessee. We move forward twelve miles, but finding no enemy, we go into camp for the night. The soldier is weary this evening, foot-sore and hungry.

Saturday, 20th.—This morning we move forward at 9 o'clock, and march briskly all day. By the road-side many a weary, foot-sore soldier falls. We are now in the rear of Jackson, Tennessee, a town on the Mobile & Ohio Railroad, which the rebels, it is said, are trying to circumvent.

Sunday, 21st.—We are this morning fifty miles from Corinth in an enemy's country. Our command numbers about two thousand. We are running some risk in moving so far away from support, but our leader has in his composition the "sand" and the "steel," and in him we trust. We move from camp on quick time, the spirits of the men are up; all anticipate a fray with Forrest and his West Tennessee raiders.[86] By noon we arrive at Lexington, but find no enemy as we expected. We halt here and eat our dinner, after which we move on and go into camp for the night at Pinch.

Monday, 22d.—This morning General Dodge discovers that the enemy has evaded him by withdrawing hastily from Jackson and his advance. The command being nearly all foot-sore from hard marching, the General finding it impossible to pursue the enemy any farther, takes the head of the column, and leads towards Henderson, Tennessee, a station on the Mobile & Ohio Railroad, twenty-five miles distant. We make a hard day's march, and go into camp for the night, five miles from Henderson. Notwithstanding the soldiers are weary and foot-sore, they will forage—will trespass upon plantations—will enter smoke-houses—make raids upon hen-roosts, and demonstrations in barn-yards, much to the discomfiture of the presumingly innocent natives, whose maledictions are no doubt falling fast upon the heads of the "invaders." From the superabundance of chickens and geese heads strewn around in the Seventh's camp, we are forced to conclude that they have just cause for giving vent to their aggravated feelings.[87]

Tuesday, 23d.—This morning we cross Beach river, and march into Henderson. We are told that from here we will proceed by rail to Corinth. Never was news so gladly received as was this by the Seventh's weary members. The First Brigade, General Sweeny, receive transportation immediately for Corinth, thirty miles distant. And it falls to our lot to remain at Henderson until the train returns. It returns at 2 o'clock and we are soon rolling over the road towards Corinth. At 5 o'clock P.M. we enter our old camp. The railroads running from Corinth to Memphis and Columbus are now cut, closing our communications with the government, and in consequence the command has only half rations issued to them.

Every day is now dawning with Corinth isolated as it were from the rest of the world, with no mail, no news, and only half rations, but the soldiers are in fine spirits, and seem to feel indifferent concerning the situation. Forrest and his raiders seem to have full sway in the direction of Memphis and Columbus. We miss the engine's shrill whistle, and above all we miss its ponderous load. But as we look among these stalwart men this evening, we are inclined to think that the enemy's present mode of warfare, though a legitimate one, will not annihilate this army. The voice of the Seventh is, we will smile to see them starve us, though we are in an almost destitute country.[88]

Tuesday, 30th.—This morning Companies H and I, under the command of Captain Johnson, are sent on a foraging expedition, taking with them the Division train. They go within six miles of Purdy, making a general sweep of everything that would in any way serve to satisfy the "inner" of both man and mule.

Wednesday morning they start back with the train loaded down with corn, hogs, sheep, chickens, and geese, and arrive in camp about noon. The Seventh is well supplied, having plenty to eat now though they are minus the half rations due from the government, and we conclude to-night "that Mr. rebels are robbing Paul to pay Peter."

Another year is now closing—another child of time passing away. Soon turbulent and boisterous sixty-two's death-kneel will be sounded, and while she is slowly dying, we trace its history, and behold that great events have transpired since it first walked forth. America has been in commotion, a great people engaged in civil strife. The force of law and the power of republican freedom have been arrayed against ignorance, rebellion, and mad ambition. May this force and power in its mighty

march sweep from this land every vestage of marshaled opposition ere the death doom of another year is spoken. Would
that this year of war would roll out and a year of peace come
in; that no more hecatombs of loyal dead might be reared in
the southland; but that harmony, quiet and fraternal love
might reign where the beautiful magnolia and citron bloom.

Thursday, January 1st, 1863.—The new year dawns peace-
fully, but not with a nation at peace. 1862 has been a year of
blood, and 1863 may be likewise, for the loyal soldiers, with
their bayonets, stand beneath the Union's battle-flag, all over
this land, eager to follow it down where treason lifts its hydra-
head ready to engage in the carnival of blood. To-day we are
reminded that Lincoln's great proclamation takes effect. A
chained race is declared free. The Seventh's boys are now dis-
cussing the expediency of this proclamation. We discover that
it has its advocates and its opposers among the members of
the Seventh, some being fanatical in its praise, and others bitter in its denunciation, but the time will come when all will
view this proclamation as the most powerful blow against the
slave-holder's rebellion.

January 5th.—This morning a pleasing smile is seen to play
upon every face after receiving the intelligence that a mail will
arrive from the north to-day. Every one seems anxious to hear
from home—from the army before Richmond—from
Burnside—from Congress, and of the great things talked of
there.[89] In fact we are anxious to hear of what is going on generally in the free outside world. We have now been cut off from
communications for two weeks; if not opened soon half rations
will all be consumed. About twilight this evening we hear the
cars coming and shouts from the camps rend the air, but oh! it
is not a through train, only from Jackson. Although disappointed in not receiving supplies, the weary, anxious, waiting
hearts are gladdened by the arrival of the mail, which was con-
veyed part of the way by Pony express. It is indeed interesting
to see with what eagerness the soldiers crowd around the
"P.O." The mail is now distributed, and the soldiers can be seen
in every direction perusing the home missives. All feel cheerful
after reading these words that come from the loyal hearts of
the loved ones at home.

Wednesday, 7th.—Last night a train arrived from Memphis bringing provisions, but not sufficient to relieve us from half rations. Things look gloomy in and around Corinth. The troops are compelled to subsist in part on corn obtained by the foraging parties. The Seventh is now shelling corn for the purpose of making hominy. Should the rebels make a raid now upon Corinth (for which the soldiers all hope and pray) we dare say they would be met in a becoming manner, and somebody would be made sick—we are strongly of the opinion that it would not be the Union soldiers.

Thursday, January 8th—The troops still on half rations, and a very small half at that. A few more days, and we anticipate that we shall be nearly starved out. Still no news comes this way from the armies; but we hope the tide of battle is rolling with the old flag aloft.

Friday, 9th.—This morning the boys are busy shelling corn to make hominy, and while we walk through the camp of the Seventh we are reminded of the stories told of our revolutionary fathers, in their struggle for independence.

Saturday, 10th.—To-day some of the Seventh boys return from a foraging expedition in West Tennessee, bringing in some hogs, sheep, chickens and geese, making quite a welcome addition to our scanty supplies. The boys are again becoming very anxious for a mail. How long will they yet be compelled to wait? But no doubt there are more anxious hearts in our far off northern homes.

Sunday, 11th, dawns, and with it comes full rations. The trains are now running from Memphis to Grand Junction, and thence to Jackson, and to Corinth. In this way we receive supplies, and how welcomely they are received by the hungry troops in and around Corinth. May the troops guarding the railroads be more vigilant in the future, and never more pull down the old flag and hoist the flag of truce!

Monday, 12th.—To-day supplies continue to arrive by the way of Grand Junction and Jackson; but no mail arrives. How anxious and lonely the soldiers are becoming here in this secluded part of the world, without any mail or any news from the north. But we have a good time for abstraction, and a good time for the study of human nature. Man cannot find a more extensive scope for its study than here in the camp and field. If man has faults he will show them; if he has virtues they will shine like the beauty and splendor of the noon-day sun; and those manly virtues that go to beautify the character of man, are seen shedding their light all around us. But we believe that here, more than in any other place, man can be persuaded of the truthfulness of the doctrine of human depravity; and at the same time can he be persuaded of the beauty of human redemption.

Tuesday, 13th.—This morning is beautiful and pleasant, much like a happy June morning in Illinois. In the evening we have brigade drill; the boys do not relish it much just now, not having had full rations long enough.

The garrison troops are now foraging on an extensive scale; parties are sent out daily, who rake the country of everything in the subsistence line. "Confiscation and extermination" is our motto. Anything to weaken this inhuman rebellion.

Wednesday, 14th.—A cold drizzly rain has been falling all day. The sentry will have a dreary time to-night for the howling winds are piercing. It is now dark and the ground is all saturated with water (shivering winds, and chill whistlings.) Hollow coughs and long sighs are heard as the sentinels pace their lonely beats. Quiet tramping is now heard, and amid the dense darkness two comrades meet. We see where they stand by the falling of the sparks from their pipes. They are talking now about the news from Stone River, and the Rappahannock, and of the flow of blood that has made red their brewing waters.[90] They stop—they are silent—but again the stillness is broken; says one, "John, I received by the last mail a letter from home, and they tell me that they trail the flag up there— that they shoot down the furloughed soldiers, and insult our wounded comrades, that our father's lives have been threatened because they have hearts that go out and take in the army and navy, because they have sons who wear the blue, fighting for the flag and union." As these sentries turned on their way, we imagine that on that dreary path along where the winter winds kept sighing mournfully, tears fell, and their hearts were sad, because they knew that in the north, around their father's homes, where once they looked in the innocence of childhood, could be found so many who would smile to see the old flag go down and Liberty's cradle rock no more.

Thursday, 15th.—This morning the lowering clouds shut out the sun's genial rays, as if to prolong the night. It is cold and stormy. It has ceased raining, and is now snowing. We shall receive no news—all is lonely. "A kingdom for a mail"—for one ray of light from the civilized world. Hark! the Locomotive is sending its signal, but its sound is soon lost in the shouts from the soldiers—alas! it brings no mail, but sad disappointment.

Friday, 16th.—This morning the boys are seen wending their way to the timber to chop wood. It is very cold, and the boys are kept busy getting fuel. It snows all day, and except those detailed to get wood, the boys keep close around the camp fires, busily engaged at something. Some talking of home and friends, some about the armies, and others about the Emancipation Proclamation. Some are perusing old Waverlys, and others amusing themselves with Harper's cuts, one has a volume of Shakespeare with his mind following intently the dramatic play of Edward the "three times."[91] We are wondering now, how the leaders of northern democracy would feel could they hear the comments made, and the anathemas heaped upon their devoted heads by the soldiers, sitting around the winter camp-fires to-night in Mississippi. We are of the opinion that they would not consider themselves very much flattered.

Saturday, 17th.—Still cold and blustery. No mail—no papers—no light. All dark, there is certainly something wrong.

Sunday, 18th.—This morning we find the clouds have disappeared, and the sun is shining brightly on the carpet of snow that mantles the earth, but it is cold, and the soldiers are compelled to keep close around the camp fires. Such weather was never known in this climate, and the citizens say that it is caused by the Yankee's superhuman agency. This evening it is all mud—the snow did not tarry long. And yet the cry goes forth from the "P.O." "no mail"—"no papers." Oh! cruel fates!

Tuesday, 20th.—The troops still continue foraging, and in consequence the country has well nigh become impoverished, almost everything in the line of subsistence having been confiscated. But occasionally a hog, goose, or chicken ventures from some hiding place and falls a prey to the "inveterate Yankees." Good news! the P.M. informs us that the train has brought the mail.[92] At last it is distributed, and how eagerly the soldiers peruse the little white sheets. Could our friends but know how much good a letter does a soldier, they would drift to him "like dew-drops from heaven"—that is, letters of cheering words. They make us better soldiers too. We get the blues sometimes, and feel like going to the dogs. Perhaps we are worn out with duty, are all wet and muddy and the wind changes right into our eyes; and then the coffee is bad; and the crackers are worse, and all this when we are as hungry as wolves. But the mail-boy comes, and hands us a letter—a good long letter from home, or some one else, we won't say who—we are not tired now; the fire has ceased smoking; the coffee is pronounced good; the old musty crackers are decidedly better, and everything glides on smoothly with us.

Wednesday, 21st.—This morning all nature looks lovely. The silver-tinged landscape presents a scene of beauty. The soft south breezes are intoxicating. The mail comes regularly now, and with full supplies the soldiers are happy.

Thursday, 22d.—Our camp now puts one in mind of an Illinois farm-yard, roosters crowing and hens cackling all over camp. The roosters the boys are training for game-cocks.

Friday, 23d.—"Hello, Hampton, I'll bet you ten dollars that my rooster can whip yours!" cries a soldier across the way, "Well, done!" replies Hampton of Company K, and a crowd of soldiers assembles, sprinkled considerably with "shoulder straps"—the fight commences; they show pluck—show that they have been well trained, but Hampton's rooster gets vanquished, so decide the judges. Thus the weary hours are killed in the camp of the Seventh.[93]

Saturday, 24th.—It is raining to-day. The soldiers keep in their tents, some reading, some writing. All peaceful and quiet this evening.

Sunday, 25th.—Still raining; how dreary the hours, and how slowly they pass away; what a dull monotony reigns in camp, and the cry is for something to dispel it. The soldier's prayer is for action; yes, give us action, for action gives vigor to life, and value to being. Let us bear the old flag on.

Monday, 26th.—This morning our regiment together with the 27th Ohio, 81st Ohio, 7th Iowa and the 52nd Illinois are ordered to escort a forage train to Hamburg Landing and return. The 27th Ohio takes the advance and the Seventh the rear. We find the roads in a desperate condition, the mud about knee deep, and soon it begins to rain. We arrive at Hamburg about dark— mud, mud, and rain, rain; how terribly dark. The regiment is ordered to take shelter in the surrounding houses and stables— the horses being turned out to grope their way in the elemental storm. The boys tear down fences to make fires to dry their drenched clothes. The houses and stables for the regiment are limited and in consequence they are densely crowded. No sleep for the soldier to-night—no place to rest his weary body.

Tuesday, 27th.—This morning the fires are made to burn more brilliantly by an addition of boards. The boys hasten to make their coffee and eat their breakfast, that they may be ready to move with the train, which is now loaded, and headed towards Corinth. The train soon commences to move out. It is the Seventh's lot as usual to follow in the rear. Oh! what a time—mud, mud, no end to mud, slash, slash, go the wagons, and down go the mules in the mud over their ears. The seventh extricate them; it is very fatiguing to follow in the rear. The men soon become tired, but on they go determined to see Corinth to-night. Night overtakes us five miles from camp. The Regiment scatters, every man for himself. The teams are left in the mud, and as the demoralized Seventh went lunging on their way they could hear for miles back the high keyed notes from the M. D.'s, whose curses and epithets were falling thick and fast upon the poor meek long-eared race.[94] Oh! what untiring energy! Ungenerous would be the one who would speak disparagingly of the services of this race in this struggle. We imagine that in the future the faithful chroniclers will say, "here's to the mule that with patience and fortitude performed well its part in the war for the Union." The Seventh arrive in camp between the hours of 7 and 10 o'clock P.M., every one looking most lovely.

January 28th.—Corinth now presents a more lively appearance—communications regular—mail prompt—papers circulated, and perused eagerly by the soldiers. All are anxious to hear of some change at the seat of war. "Has the old Potomac

Army become demoralized," is the inquiry frequently heard now among the Western soldiers. But we hope not—hope that yet it will make the successful tramp "on to Richmond."[95]

Thursday, 29th.—The duties of the regiments now stationed at Corinth, are very arduous. Almost every day a regiment or two are called upon to make a trip either to the Tennessee river for forage, or to the Davenport Mills for lumber to construct fortifications. Corinth is becoming quite a Gibraltar. The freedmen are all the while kept busy upon these works. This evening the officers of the Illinois regiments meet in Music Hall to give expression to their views upon modern democracy, and their bitter detestation of the treasonable element that is becoming so prevalent in Illinois. The following are the views of the Illinois soldiers on copperheads and defunct democracy. The object is to show to Governor Yates and to all our friends at home that we are still in favor of a vigorous prosecution of the war, and that we will uphold our President and our Governor in all their efforts to crush the rebellion and restore the Union. On motion a committee to draft resolutions was appointed, consisting of the following officers: Colonel Chetlain 12th Illinois Infantry commanding post; Colonel M. M. Bane, 50th Illinois Infantry commanding Third brigade, Lieutenant Colonel Wilcox 52d Illinois Infantry, Colonel Burk, 65th Illinois sharp-shooters, Colonel A. J. Babcock, 7th Illinois Infantry, Colonel Merser 9th Illinois Infantry, commanding Second brigade, Lieutenant Colonel Morrill, 54th Illinois Infantry.[96] The committee submitted the following resolution which were unanimously adopted:

> *Whereas,* Our government is now engaged in a struggle for the perpetuation of every right dear to us as American citizens, and requires the united efforts of all good, true and loyal men in its behalf: and whereas, we behold with deep regret the bitter partizan spirit that is becoming dangerously vindictive and malicious in our state, the tendency of which is to frustrate the plans of the federal and state authorities in their efforts to suppress this infamous rebellion; therefore,
>
> *Resolved,* That having pledged ourselves with our most cherished interests in the service of our common country in this

hour of national peril, we ask our friends at home to lay aside all petty jealousies and party animosities, and as one man stand by us in upholding the president in his war measures, in maintaining the authority and the dignity of the government, and in unfurling again the glorious emblem of our nationality over every city and town of rebeldom.

Resolved, That we tender to Governor Yates and Adjutant General Fuller our warmest thanks for their untiring zeal in organizing, arming and equipping the army Illinois has sent to the field, and for their timely attention to the wants of our sick and wounded soldiers, and we assure them of our steady and warm support in their efforts to maintain for Illinois the proud position of pre-eminent loyalty which she now occupies.

Resolved, That we have watched the traitorous conduct of those members of the Illinois Legislature who misrepresent their constituents—who have been proposing a cessation of the war, avowedly to arrange terms for peace, but really to give time for the exhausted rebels to recover strength and renew their plottings to divest Governor Yates of the right and authority vested in him by our state constitution and laws, and to them we calmly and firmly say, beware of the terrible retribution that is falling upon your coadjutors at the south, and that as your crime is ten-fold blacker it will swiftly smite you with ten-fold more horrors, should you persist in your damnable work of treason.

Resolved, That in tending our thanks to Governor Yates, and assuring him of our hearty support in his efforts to crush this inhuman rebellion, we are deeply and feelingly in "earnest." We have left to the protection of the laws he is to enforce, all that is dear to man—our wives, our children, our parents, our homes,— and should the loathsome treason of the madmen who are trying to wrest from him a portion of his just authority render it necessary in his opinion for us to return and crush out treason there, we will promptly obey a proper order so to do, for we despise a sneaking, whining traitor in the rear much more than an open rebel in front.

Resolved, That we hold in contempt, and will execrate any man who in this struggle for national life, offers factious opposition to either the federal or state government in their efforts or measures for the vigorous prosecution of the war for the suppression of this godless rebellion.

Resolved, That we are opposed to all propositions for a cessation of hostilities, or a compromise other than those propositions which the government has constantly offered; "Return to loyalty—to the laws and common level with the other states of the Union, under the constitution as our fathers made it."

LIEUT. COL. PHILLIPS, 9th Illinois,

President.

T.N. LETTON, Adjutant 50th Illinois[97]

Secretary.

Friday, 30th.—Everything seems quiet to-day. The soldiers seem well satisfied with the resolutions adopted last night in Music Hall. This evening they are submitted to the men for their decision thereon. The Seventh being drawn up in line adopt them with a vim, saying amen to every word. All the Illinois Regiments adopt them without one dissenting voice, except ten men belonging to the 52d Illinois Infantry.

Saturday, 31st.—This morning our new chaplain arrives, the Rev. Mr. Perkins. It is indeed a happy arrival for we have been without one for a long time. This office is now a very difficult one to fill as the soldiers have become so reckless that should the angel Gabriel receive a commission as chaplain to the Seventh, he would give it up as a bad bargain. War is atheistic, heathenish, devilish; qualify it as you may with all that civilization and christianity can do, it is yet the mightiest reaping machine in the harvest of hell. We do not say that God has nothing to do with its running, for we believe that hidden behind the veil of human wrath he directs every move to his own glory; but he who drives this terrible instrument is very apt to become like it, being barred as we are from civilization and the refining and ennobling influence of female society.

Sunday, February 1st.—To-day our chaplain preaches for the first time to the Seventh; having not heard a sermon for a long time, the boys listen with considerable attention as he preaches a very interesting sermon, and from the remarks we conclude that after all the Seventh have not become hardened to the gospel.[98]

Tuesday, 3d.—This morning it is very cold, and a fierce north wind is blowing. The Seventh are aroused early, and having last night received marching orders, we are soon in line with three days rations. The Second Iowa takes the advance, the division and post teams follow, the Twenty-ninth Ohio the center, the Seventh Illinois the rear. We go to the Davenport Mills, about twenty miles away to the south-east in the north Mississippi pineries to get lumber. In the evening we load up in order to get an early start in the morning for Corinth. Loaded up, the troops go into camp; soon the camp fires are blazing; pine boards burn briskly. After making our coffee we lie down by the fire to sleep, but no sleep for the soldiers; the wind blows too coldly, and we find it difficult to keep warm, for we burn on one side and freeze on the other.

Wednesday, 4th.—Early this morning, long ere it is light, the soldier is up with his can bucket making his coffee—how it refreshes him this cold morning. The light of day is now approaching and is being hailed with a welcome, for the night has been long and weary. After finishing our breakfast we are ordered into line; and for once since the battle of Corinth, the Seventh takes the advance, the Twenty-seventh the center, and the Second Iowa the rear. We march briskly this morning, it being cold and frosty, and by twelve o'clock being considerably ahead of the train, we are halted long enough to eat our dinner, after which we move on; we find it difficult marching to-day, the roads being frozen. This afternoon the boys soon begin to limp, and some are compelled to drop back to the wagons. We find this country a deserted wilderness, and what few inhabitants we see, starvation seems to stare in the face; famine seems to follow both friend and foe. When within three miles of Corinth, clouds that have been gathering begin to spit snow. Onward the Seventh goes arriving in camp about three o'clock in the midst of a snow storm.

Thursday, 5th.—This morning, Oh! how cold! howling winds and drifting snow. It is indeed a fair representation of the sunny south. Nothing unusual occurs to-day. The soldiers hover closely around the camp fires.

Friday, 6th.—This morning the boys are compelled to wend their way to the woods to obtain fuel. It remains extremely cold. Hark! what do we hear? Marching orders with three days rations, says one. Back to the Davenport Mills, can it be possible? Yes! cries the orderly, we will start at 1 o'clock. Twenty miles to go to night, and load one hundred teams with lumber; rather a hard task says one, but we suppose it is honest. The drums beat; and with our equipments, rations, &c., strapped to our backs, we move out from Corinth. We are soon joined by the Ninth Illinois and Sixty-sixth Indiana; the Ninth takes the advance, the Sixty-sixth the center, and the Seventh the rear. After going a short distance we get into the wagons and ride; the roads are desperate; but on we go slash! slash! through the wilderness of pines. Along the road we meet families, men, women and little children wending their way to Corinth to seek protection under the old flag. We arrive at the mills at 1 o'clock A.M. After stacking our guns we proceed to make some coffee, and after drinking it we all lie down to obtain a few hours of sleep, but soon "rub dub, rub dub" goes the drum, the soldiers give a groan and then commence railing out upon the drummer for waking them so soon, but there is no use of whining—up we must get and that *"instanter,"* as we are promised the advance back to Corinth. The teams are now all loaded. The Seventh feel slighted in not being called upon for their services. The teams are soon moving, the Seventh taking the advance; but before going far we are halted by the Colonel of the Sixty-sixth Indiana, commanding forces, and informed that he had promised the Sixty-sixth the advance. Captain Lawyer is then ordered to march with the Seventh in the center. We move on briskly and arrive in camp 5 o'clock P.M.

Sunday, 8th.—This morning the boys remain in their bunks unmindful of reveille, showing a determination to obtain some sleep and rest after the two days, trip to the mills. No news came with this evening's mail and everything seems quiet and dull in and around Corinth. During the latter part of this month, (February) nothing of note occurs, and also during the month of March a dull monotony prevails in the camp of the Seventh.[99] Colonel Babcock having been for some time president of the Military Commission in session at Corinth, for reasons best known to himself resigns his colonelcy of the Seventh regiment and leaves the service; and we all regret to see him leave for he has been to us a good, brave and faithful officer. The following testimonial from his companions in arms will speak for itself.

Whereas, Colonel Andrew J. Babcock has resigned his commission as Colonel of the Seventh regiment of Illinois Infantry Volunteers, and we the officers and men of the Seventh having been long under his command, both appreciate his worth and deeply regret his separation from us, therefore be it

Resolved, That in Colonel A. J. Babcock the state of Illinois and the army of the United States have lost a brave, competent and meritorious officer.

Resolved, That we, who have for nearly two years been associated with him in his duties, in the garrison and in the field, through many toilsome marches and in the hard fought battles of Donelson and Corinth, bear witness that he has proved himself a most daring, discreet and loyal leader; and that in the execution of his office, as well as his personal bearing, he has won not only the confidence and respect but also the esteem and affection of all his command.

Resolved, That as Colonel Babcock from the first organization of the first regiment of Illinois—from the opening of the war to the present date, has proved himself before us, as a commander most efficient—as a man and a brother in arms at once just, genial and generous, we sincerely hope and trust that his affairs may again permit the government to avail itself of his invaluable services in the field; and should such be the case, it will be our highest happiness to be again associated with him in the service of our common country.

R. L. METCALF, *Pres.,*
Surgeon Seventh Ill. Inft.,
J. S. ROBINSON, *Secretary,*
Adjutant.[100]

As the Colonel leaves us we remember those wintry days of battle on the Cumberland hills before Fort Donelson, and how with the private soldiers he endured the battle's privations there; and how amid smoke and flame he led the Seventh on to glorious victory. We also remember how he moved upon

Corinth's bloody field and proved himself a leader true, when darkness and gloom seemed to mantle the Seventh's brave soldiers. May he on his return to civil life receive tokens of gratitude from Illinois' grateful people.

April 6th.—We remember to-day, that one year ago we stood upon Shiloh's plain, and stemmed the wild tide of battle that rolled there. To-day preparations are being made by the officers and soldiers of the post to celebrate the closing hours of that great battle.

April 7th.—In compliance with orders from headquarters the 3d brigade commanded by Colonel Bane, is marched and put into position in front of Division Head-quarters, where a large flag-staff has been erected and preparation made for speaking, &c. One o'clock P.M. all the infantry regiments, battalions of cavalry and artillery are on the ground, and after they are arranged and in position, General Dodge gives the command, attention! and reads in a loud and clear voice the order of the day: 1st music, 2d raising of the flag, 3d salute, 4th music. After the salute and the martial notes had died away, General Dodge said, "Fellow officers and soldiers of the 2d division, we have assembled here to celebrate an eventful day— the day on which Shiloh's great battle closed. Brave men, you remember it well, and I am glad in my heart that you were there and performed so well your part. But I cannot talk to you, my heart is too full, and for your further entertainment I will introduce (though he needs no introduction,) the gallant Colonel M. M. Bane, the popular commander of the 3d brigade, whose empty sleeve will tell you quickly that he has a right to speak." Colonel Bane takes the stand and delivers a good speech, full of enthusiasm and soul, which is often interrupted by loud bursts of applause. After Colonel Bane closes, the division is formed and marched in review, and then the regiments are conducted to their respective camps, long to remember their first anniversary of the battle of Shiloh.

Chapter IX.

[April 14, 1863–May 10, 1863]

Marching orders—Leaving Corinth—The column headed towards the Tuscumbia Valley—Camp at Burnsville—Iuka, Mississippi—Camp near Bear River—Our advance disputed—Crossing Bear river—Skirmish with the enemy—The regiment falling back—Camp near Bear River—Colonel Rowett after the sheep—Plans for ambushing the rebels—The failure—Arrival of reinforcements—Foraging—The arrival of Col. Straight—Some bold movement contemplated—The Alabama cavalry and the Kansas Jayhawkers on the war-path—Arrival at Tuscumbia, Alabama—The springs—The Seventh ordered to South Florence, Tennessee river—The soldier's way-side dream—Flags of truce—Battle of Town creek—Crossing Town creek—Following the enemy—The march back to Corinth—The destruction of property—Swimming Bear river—Arrival at Iuka—Arrival at Corinth—Receiving news concerning the fall of Richmond—The excitement.

Remaining in camp at Corinth without anything of note occurring until the evening of the 14th, we receive marching orders. The guerrilla Roddy, having been hovering around Glendale and Iuka, committing unwarranted depredations for some time, the rumors this evening, confirmed by general indications are, that General Dodge is about to start on an expedition against him, and the camps seem in a bustle all around Corinth this evening.[101]

Wednesday, 15th.—Reveille is beat early this morning and soon the Seventh is on its feet. At sunrise we report to brigade headquarters. It falls to the third brigade to take the rear, and in consequence we are slow in leaving Corinth. A heavy force under the command of General Dodge is now on the tramp, headed towards the Tuscumbia valley. We travel slowly all day, save at times when we are compelled to make brisk steps owing to the tardiness of the teams. We go into camp to-night at Burnsville, fifteen miles from Corinth. The boys are in fine spirits, eager to push forward. It is intimated that the expedition will be directed towards Decatur, Alabama. It seems evident that some bold movement is contemplated.

Thursday, 16th.—This morning the boys are soon up, eager to push forward. We eat our breakfast and are moving by six o'clock. The sun shines intensely hot to-day, and in consequence many fag by the way. We halt for our dinner at Iuka, Mississippi, which place is noted for its mineral springs, the resort of the chivalry, where in brighter days they loved to rehearse to the south's fair ones their gallant deeds; but those days have flown, and on these rocks the encased swords of the Union's warriors now make grating music. After dinner we move on, march hard all the afternoon, and at night go into camp three miles from Bear River.

Friday, 17th.—This morning as soon as it is light, we take up the line of march towards Bear River, where it is expected our advance will be disputed. We halt a few hundred yards from the river, when a battery is run into position to our rear on the hill and opened upon the enemy on the opposite bank, causing them to fall back in confusion. The troops now commence crossing the river on flat-boats, which the rebels in their haste failed to destroy. But the Seventh being impatient and eager to dash upon the enemy, they buckle their cartridge boxes around their necks, and plunging into the river they wade across; and without waiting to wring the water out of their clothes, push forward, and coming up with the enemy, are soon engaged in a brisk skirmish, driving them pell mell over the hills and through the woods into the Tuscumbia Valley. After which we go into camp six miles from Bear River.

Saturday, 18th.—This morning about nine o'clock the 3d brigade takes the backward track towards Bear River. We come to a halt about two miles from the river, and are ordered into camp for the remainder of the day and night. As usual when such movements are made, rumors are on the wing, and one says, "we are taking back water," another, that "the enemy was reinforced last night and has been trying this morning to get in our rear, between us and Bear River". If we are retreating we are doing it very slowly. As soon as our arms are stacked, Colonel Dick Rowett rides along the regiment and calls for five brave men from each company, for, says he, I am going to do something that will call for that kind of metal. Following him they dash into the mountains, and in about one hour he returns with about thirty sheep and a quantity of bacon, found hid away on the mountains by the rebel citizens. The Seventh live like kings to-night.

Sunday, 19th.—Last night it rained very hard, giving everybody and everything a general wetting. The boys are now busy pulling balls and getting their guns in order. The rebel cavalry are now seen lurking along our front. Changing position, the 3d brigade are secreted in the brush for the purpose of ambushing the rebels in case of an advance by them. The pickets have been removed and a battalion of cavalry sent out to engage them and draw them down the road towards the river; but for once the rebels were too wary for the artful Yankees. In the evening we return to the camp occupied by the Seventh the day and night before. Reinforcements arrive this evening— the Ohio brigade, and the Kansas Jayhawkers. It is rumored that the command will move forward in the morning. The boys are all in fine spirits this evening in consequence of the rumor. All are anxious to follow the old flag up the Tuscumbia valley, and drive the enemy across the mountains into Georgia.

Monday, 20th.—This morning the soldiers are on their feet and moving around the blazing campfires, busily cooking their breakfast, and their cooking utensils are quite novel. A flat stone for a frying-pan, and a sharp stick for a fork (we use no knives.) After eating our breakfast, we commence building sheds with pine twigs, to shield ourselves from the sun's warm rays. The command does not move as was rumored last night. No demonstrations to-day, all quiet.

Tuesday, 21st.—Reinforcements still continue to come, and we still remain quiet. Why we do not move we cannot tell. Perhaps the General is waiting for all expected reinforcements to arrive. Captain Smith with Company E is sent on a foraging expedition to Dickenson's plantation, coming back in the evening well supplied. This evening the Seventh seem in a gleeful mood. Around every camp fire they are now singing "Bonnie blue flag,"—"Rally round the flag, boys," making the mountain gorges re-echo with patriotic songs. No discord here; no discontent manifest—all seem united in the great work of saving the Union.

Wednesday, 22d.—This morning the command is ordered to be kept together, ready to move at a moment's notice; what is contemplated or whither our destination, is a mystery to the soldiers. To-day Colonel Straight arrives from Murfreesboro with a brigade of mounted infantry.[102] Each day indicates that some bold movement is contemplated. Another day is closing and yet the command still remains at a stand.

Thursday, 23d.—This morning the command "forward" is given to the impatient men, and they march briskly, their steps are firm. To-day we witness war's desolating scourge on the plantations. The devouring elements of fire are doing their work. The Alabama Union cavalry and the Kansas Jayhawkers are on the war-path: their day has come—their day of retribution.[103]

Friday, 14th.—This morning at the first tap of the drum we are up, and soon on the move. About noon we arrive at Tuscumbia; the enemy having all retreated before the Union army's advance. This is a beautiful town in Northern Alabama, noted for its beautiful springs of water, that leap from the rocks like gushing and swelling fountains. How well do the weary soldiers love to kneel down by these flowing streams after their hard day's march, and drink of their refreshing waters. After arriving at Tuscumbia, the Seventh is ordered to South Florence on the Tennessee River, six miles distant. We arrive about four o'clock, finding Lieutenant Colonel Phillips, with his Ninth Illinois mounted infantry, occupying the place. Soon after our arrival, a flag of truce is sent across the river to Florence, demanding the surrender of the city. On its return we are informed that the rebels have all fled and that no satisfaction could be obtained relative to the surrender, the civil authorities refusing to act. We go into camp to-night on the banks of the Tennessee.

Saturday, 25th.—This morning another flag of truce is sent across the river under the command of Captain Ring of the Seventh, and after remaining a few hours in Florence he returns, reporting the place surrendered and free from armed rebels. The boys are now enjoying themselves bathing in the river.

Sunday, 26th.—This morning the dark overhanging clouds are threatening rain. The Seventh are ordered to quarter themselves in the few scattering houses yet remaining in South Florence. Hark! the drum beats for an assembly. The Seventh are ordered to their camping ground on the hill. Colonel Rowett calling the regiment to attention, informs them of the wanton destruction of property out on the plantations, and orders the First Sergeant to call the roll, who reports all present or accounted for, and as usual the Seventh is clear. Though no one would ever suspect any of the Seventh guilty of pillaging houses or stealing, yet a general order is applicable to all—hence the roll call by the first sergeants of the regiment. After this the soldiers return to their houses where they remain comfortable during the night.

Monday, 17th.—This morning we move from South Florence, having been ordered to join the main column at Leighton, ten miles from Tuscumbia on the road leading towards Decatur. The roads are very muddy, but we march briskly and strike the road in advance of the column, when we halt to await its advance. Coming up we take our position in the brigade and move forward through mud and rain. About four o'clock we come up with the rebels and commence a brisk skirmish. The rebels falling back across Town Creek, we go into camp for the night about one mile from the creek. The soldiers, weary and warm, fall down upon the damp ground and are soon sleeping.

Tuesday, 28th.—To day we expect to meet the foe, who threaten to dispute our passage across Town Creek. The morning is beautiful, nature is smiling, and the sun is far up, moving on in its path of blue. The soldiers are ordered to rest themselves as much as possible, for the indications are that much will be demanded of them ere the sun sinks to rest. Looking beneath a tall pine our eyes rest upon a soldier leaning against its base, with his musket on his arm. His head is bowed, and his eyes are closed. We imagine that he is dreaming,—that shadows of light are flitting through his spirit's chamber. He now arises, and we discover that it is our poet soldier, Sergeant S. F. Flint. Our eyes follow him as he is now seated with his pencil and paper. His genius is now at work, and soon after the artillery commences to send forth its harsh echoes over the hills and through the vales of Alabama, he produces the following:

THE SOLDIERS WAYSIDE DREAM.

The word was "rest," the dusty road was rocky, worn and steep,
And many a sun-browned soldier's face sank on his breast to sleep.
Afar the Alabama hills swept round in billowy lines,
The soft green of their bowery slopes was dotted dark with pines;

And from their tops a gentle breeze, born in the cloudless sky,
Stole through the valley where a stream was slowly warbling by;
And as it passed it brought a cloud of odor in its plumes,
Of violets and columbines, and milk-white plum tree blooms.
The coolness and the perfume o'er my weary senses crept,
And with my musket on my arm I bowed my head and slept;
No more the Alabama hills, no more the waving pines,
But still the scent of violets and red wild columbines.
I drew my breath in ecstacy, my feet were shod with joy,
I dreamed I trod the prairie sod in my beautiful Illinois,
The lark sung welcome in the grass the well known path along,
And the pulsations of my heart seemed echoes of his song.
I thought the sunlight never shone so gloriously before,
But sweeter were the smiles of love that met me at the door.
O! hold my hand while yet you may, love of my earlier years,
And wet my face, my mother, with thy proud and happy tears,
And bless me again, my father, bless me again, I pray,
I hear the bugle, I hear the drum, I have but one hour to stay.
Alas! my dreaming words were true, I woke and knew it all,
I heard the clamor of the drum, I heard the captain's call,
And over all another voice I oft had heard before—
A sound that stirs the dullest heart—the cannon's muffled roar.
No longer "rest," but "forward;" for e'er the day is done
It will tell of the fearful glory of a battle lost and won,
And ere the breath of its blackened lips has time to lift away,
My hand must be red and warm with blood, or white and cold as clay.
O! pray for me in thy gentle heart, love of my earlier years,
And mother, only weep for me those proud and happy tears,
And bless again, my father, bless me while yet you may,
My dream words may be doubly true I may have but an hour to stay.

The troops are now in line, skirmishers are deployed forward towards the creek and they soon discover the rebels in force with considerable artillery on the rise beyond the creek. While advancing, the enemy open upon them with their batteries, whereupon our batteries are placed in position and made to play with a telling effect upon the enemy. For about one hour a fierce artillery duel is kept up by the contending forces; the distance being so far between nothing serious is accomplished. Though there is a terrible clamor and a deafening thunder, the flying monsters from the rebel artillery pass harmlessly over our heads or fall a short distance before us. The division is now drawn up in battle line with the intention of effecting a crossing over the creek. While thus drawn up in line of battle, the mail messenger brings us a mail, and there, unmindful of shot and shell flying around us, we read the little love freighted missives; some almost forget that the dogs of war are barking as they peruse the lines from the home circle, for no doubt they may be thinking that perhaps these will be the last lines they will ever receive from mother or sister, for ere 'tis night they may lay themselves down to take the soldier's last sleep. The division now advances; and when within a short distance of the creek, Colonel Rowett is ordered to deploy the Seventh forward on a skirmish line to support the pioneers while building a bridge for the infantry. The artillery firing now ceases. A crossing is soon prepared and the division passes over and forms in line of battle; the skirmish line advances, followed by the division's compact and solid battle line, which moves firmly and in order presenting a grand and imposing scene on this Alabama cotton field; but it all ends with slight skirmishing. The cautious Roddy would not stand, but retreated into the mountains leaving General Dodge the undisputed possession of the beautiful Tuscumbia Valley. Tonight all the division recross Town Creek, except our regiment and the Second Iowa, which are ordered to remain on this side as an outpost. We sleep quietly to night, knowing that the enemy is far away.[104]

Wednesday, 29th.—This morning the order is to take the backward track to Corinth. As our supplies are running short the command is now on half rations. The Seventh Illinois and Second Iowa cross Town Creek and join the Division and soon we are moving. The weather is now very warm, and the roads being rocky and rough, the marching is severe, and we are compelled to denominate our regiment "the foot sore Seventh." A great many of the men's shoes are about worn out; some are barefooted, and in consequence many are limping; and as the continental army could have been tracked by the blood at Valley Forge, so can this army be tracked by the blood that makes crimson the rocks on the road leading down the Tuscumbia Valley; but on they move and no murmur is heard. How sad it is to know that modern democracy would to-day smile to see these untiring and devoted men fall and perish by the way; and how they would love to dishonor their names and rejoice to see those silken folds trailed ruthlessly in the dust. We discover to-day that General Dodge's object in remaining so long in the valley was to engage the attention of the enemy until Colonel Straight could get started on his great raid into Georgia. He is now far on his way, and we hope he may succeed in carrying the Union's battle flag far into the south-land. War is now making the most terrible sweep down the valley to the right and left; the direful element of fire is doing its devouring work, innocent ones are suffering, suffering because their brothers leaped from the cradle of freedom and struck the mother that gave them birth. Mad, mad men! would to God that they could have been stayed in their wrath, and this desolating scourge averted that is laying low many a once happy southern home. This evening we pass through Tuscumbia and go into camp three miles beyond. The regiment is very tired to night and they soon sink down to rest.

Thursday, 30th.—Five o'clock A.M., the command is moving. We march hard all day. Many men are barefooted; more soldiers are limping, but on they go with an unyielding determination to follow where the flag goes to night. We reach Bear River towards evening and find it very high; so high that it is evident that we will be detained. The pioneers are soon put to work to construct a raft. A regiment is called for to cross the river, stand picket, and guard the pioneers, but none being found the General sends back for the Seventh. After moving forward the General says to the Colonel, "Can your men swim?" Dick replies, "General, I would not have a man that could not swim." Sure enough, we find that there is no other chance to cross but to swim, and that too against a swift current. But the Seventh having never hesitated before don't hesitate now, and off they strip, placing their clothes, guns and accoutrements on a small raft, and into the river they plunge, and soon the regiment is on the opposite bank safe and sound, though one man belonging to Company H, (we will not name him) came very near drowning. Not being a good swimmer he was urged not to venture, but remembering the reply of Colonel Rowett to the General, he resolved to try it that he might not be discarded and considered unworthy his membership in the Seventh, and into the river he goes. He struggles for life but makes no headway, drifting down to the raft rope, by which he, with the aid of two of his comrades, succeeds in saving himself; and the Colonel, notwithstanding his reply to the General, concludes not to banish him, inasmuch as he had the courage to try. As soon as the regiment is over and dressed we go into camp a short distance from the river. The teams are ferried across on the constructed raft, and when we get our supper we lie down to rest. The Pioneer Corps are kept busy all night, crossing teams, troops, wagons, &c.

May 1st, 1863.—Our brigade is in the advance this morning. Notwithstanding so many are foot sore we march briskly, and arriving at Iuka about noon we halt and wait for the train and the rear to come up. Thousands of freedmen, exiles from bondage, are now following the command. They dream of freedom, and their hopes beat high; they are building castles in the air, but we imagine that they will be disappointed in their ideal of freedom. After the train and the rear come up we proceed to Burnsville, and go into camp, Oh! how weary the soldiers are to night, and no rations, only ten pounds of meal to the company is all we have, and twenty miles from Corinth— things appear somewhat bilious. What mean these shouts from the camps on the surrounding hills, that are now rending the air? We listen, and we hear a train coming up the road from Corinth. It comes loaded with supplies, and all are made to wear a pleasing smile, for now we have plenty to satisfy the cravings of the inner man; and to night for the first time since leaving our camp at Town Creek, we lie down without being too hungry to sleep.

Saturday, 2d.—This morning all are roused up early. The barefooted and footsore men receive transportation on the cars for Corinth, which thins the command considerably. The entire command reaches Corinth about 5 o'clock, and never was the ship wrecked mariner more glad to see land than was the Second Division to see Corinth.[105]

Sunday, 3d.—This morning after the boys clean up the camp and arrange things in order, they write to their friends. All have a little romance and history to write—a long march—sleepless nights—the beautiful country—the blooming groves—the gushing springs and the leaping fountains—wading creeks—fighting battles—sweeping a valley—carrying a sword in one hand and a torch in the other—staining the roads and the projecting rocks with blood—swimming a river; and a hundred other minor incidents are now being painted in pen pictures for those at home.

Monday, 4th.—All is quiet this morning; the order is to prepare for muster and inspection. The men are now busy cleaning up their guns and accoutrements. Everything seems to move smoothly along now at Corinth. The news from the north is cheering, from the fact that we are assured that the loyal people are more deeply aroused to the importance of the hour that will tell of the greatest trial through which liberty has passed for centuries.

Tuesday, 5th.—To-day northern papers are received containing Burnside's General order No. 38, for the benefit of Ohio's devilish democracy. We deem it a good cure for treason and traitors, and we all hope that it will be enforced to the letter, and that the leading light of modern democracy, C. L. Vallandigham, will become a victim to its force. All hail, Burnside! as the honest general who dares to do right—who dares to prosecute the war with an earnest determination—who dares to punish traitors in the north![106] They may tell us the war is a failure—that the great Union is declining—that the gallant dead have died in vain—that they have closed their eyes in death, dishonored men; they may say, as has been said by Miller, in the Illinois Legislative chamber,[107] that the time will come when the surviving Union soldier will be ashamed to hold up his head and say he took part in the war for the Union, but we catch the spirit of prophecy and say that the time will come when modern democracy as a party will be branded as a gigantic liar—that the time will come when the children of the soldiers and sailors who battled on land and sea for the republican idea, will, in the language of Grace Greenwood, date their rights to nobility back to grander battlefields than Agincourt or Bannockburn.[108] Many a coat of arms in the future will have one sleeve hanging empty. We may picture to ourselves a group of noble young lads, some ten years hence, thus proudly accounting for their orphanage—an orphanage which the country should see to it should not become destitute. Says one, my father fell fighting with Wallace in the Wilderness of Shiloh; says another, my father fought with Hooker, when his guns flashed flame in midnight darkness over Lookout Mountain; another, my father suffered martyrdom in Libby Prison; and another, my father was rocked to sleep beneath the waves in the iron cradle of the monitor.[109] Then there will be hapless lads who will steal away and in the bitterness of soul will say, alas, for me! I have no such gloryings; my father was a rebel who fought against the flag of the Union; and there will be another class still more unfortunate, who will utter the pitying wail, oh! my God, help me! my father was a cowardly northern copperhead, who denounced the defenders of the Union as hirelings and vandals. Yes, and the time will come when the record of modern democracy in these years of war will be sought to be buried and consigned to the "dead past," when this treasonable faction will pander to those men who saved the Union when they sought its life. They will feign to drop tears over the graves of those they murdered, and utter hypocritical words of sympathy to the widows and orphans whom they insulted when the Republic was passing through the long night of war. Soldiers of the Union, mark the prophecy.

The following extract from a communication written by a soldier of the Seventh, may not be inappropriate to these pages:

CAMP SEVENTH ILL. VOL. INFANTRY
CORINTH, MISS., MAY 1, 1863

"While sitting here in my quarters near the once beautiful but now desolate city of Corinth, I have been thinking of my country's troubles, and of the mad ambition of wicked men to ride to power over the ruins of the American Union; who are striving to subvert civil liberty, inaugurate a despotism and shut the gates of mercy upon down-trodden people. But when I look to the front where the Union armies are struggling as armies have scarcely ever struggled, struggling for the world's last and only hope, I feel hopeful, for I know all goes well there; no political strife troubles them, but all are of one mind, one aim, one faith and one hope. That mind is for the salvation of the Union—that aim is to transmit it unimpared to posterity—that faith is that this Union will be saved—saved from despotism—saved from slavery's black curse. That hope is that Omnipotence will soon smile upon these fields of blood, and sustain liberty with His heart and hand—will soon check the tide of war and stay this great sacrifice of human life, giving to us a peace—a happy, glorious, conquered peace. But when I look to its rear around the home of my childhood, and behold there so many comforting, and thereby giving aid to those who are waging the wicked war against the flag of my country, my heart is made sad, and I am prompted to exclaim oh! my country! my country! will she live? will she pass safely through this night of war? will the graves that have been made, the prayers that have been offered, and the tears that have been shed, be made, offered and shed in vain? We answer that with a united north the great republic of the west will live, and the future will see it standing peerless amid the grand galaxy of nations, fulfilling a destiny that will illumine with its magnificent splendor the whole world, and shed its blessings of peace and prosperity upon generations yet unborn.

"Loyal people, the appeal that goes up to you from this southland—that goes up from camp and grave, from hospital and prison pen, is couched in this language, Oh! stand firm; do not abandon the Union to the mad men; do not forsake liberty in its present great trial; do not cast a shade upon our last resting place; be true, oh! be true to the cause for which we gave our lives a willing sacrifice; listen not to the hair-splitting technicalities and specious sophistries of corrupt and unprincipled men. The soldiers have watched and are watching the northern traitors— their course in Congress is remembered—how they refused support to those brave men whose life-blood tinted the waters of the Potomac when rebel guns thundered over the heights of Arlington, sending echoes of treason away to Washington's tomb. We remember how they have slandered the brave men who died that this nation might not perish from the earth."

To-day we were shown a letter from one of the lights of modern democracy in Logan County, urging a soldier to desert the hireling abolition army, and not disgrace his friends any longer, telling him that the war was a failure, and for him to return to the house of his friends. The reply was made, "I am a man, and no consideration offered by modern democracy can tempt me to desert the banner of freedom. What! disgrace my friends! I to-day disown all who would, like you, urge me to barter away my manhood. You tell me the war is a failure; you evidently base your judgement upon its prolongation. This does not discourage me; I remember that it took eight years to establish the first independence, but what would twenty years be in permanently establishing a government that may in time revolutionize the civilized world? When you and your traitor friends, conscience stricken and seared with crime and sin, shall, as an apt illustration of latter-day so-called democracy, go down to the grave, over your head should be written, 'Here sleeps a modern democrat; and may the winds of heaven never kiss his solitary abode, nor the worms feed upon that flesh that will in all coming time be the scorn and derision of mankind; may he not be permitted to come forth in the resurrection morning, but may he sleep on, unmourned and forgotten forever.' In conclusion, I would urge loyal men everywhere not to listen to the clamor for peace and compromise, for that means a withdrawal of the Union armies and to give up the struggle and acknowledge the independence of the south. From the commencement of the war up to the present time, we, the soldiers of Illinois, have helped to fight the great battles for the Union—we have seen our comrades bleed and die—we have trod in their heart's blood—have passed through many sleepless nights, watching and waiting, but the war still lingers on, the south with its wild legions still struggles for dominion, and yet while shouts of victory ascend from crimson battle-fields, designing men would have us compromise, would have us concede to the murderers and assassins. Shall we do it? The loyal people say no; a voice from every battle field, and from the waters where moved the men of war, cries no. But may a morning with a conquered peace soon dawn, when we can behold our flag floating over every sea, the pride of a victorious people and the envy of the world."

Wednesday, 6th.—To-day all is quiet, save now and then a cheer caused by some rumor created for the occasion by some mischievous soldier. In the evening a chilling rain commences to fall. The night is dark, the winds keep sighing like some crushed spirit. We sit by a slow glimmering campfire and think of the happy years when the country was at peace; we think of the clouds of war that hang over a land that has been looked to as a land of promise by the chained and crushed ones of earth. We look around us and behold rows of muskets, which seem to tell us that ere long they will be pointed at the breasts of men, and why, oh! why? can it thus be that men of one common blood brothers of one common family, will engage in deadly strife and seek each other's life? But so it has ever been through all the intricate course of empires down to the present time; first a conflict of ideas, then a conflict of arms. War seems to be a nation's highest tribunal, and a fierce ordeal it is through which to arrive at justice, but nations must pass through this ordeal. The conflict between right and wrong, between liberty and slavery, have produced champions and advocates who have been unwilling to yield, hence a rush to arms to settle the controversy.

Thursday, 7th.—Nothing but a dull monotony reigns in camp to-day. The hours glide wearily along. We all hope for a change ere long, for this remaining in camp so long at one place is becoming tiresome. This evening we receive a mail which brings cheer and sunshine to many a soldier—letters that tell us of hearts beating true to the cause of freedom and Union—letters that tell us of hearts that go out for the soldiers—of hearts that are sad when battles are lost, and the flag is made to droop over the noble slain. These letters tell us that the great north will not let these sacrifices be made in vain—that they will not permit the names of the Union's defenders to be forgotten.

Friday, 8th.—The news from the armies is becoming more cheering. The political sky seems to be clearing up. The word comes again, "Onward to Richmond." We expect to hear of great battles ere long—battles that will make the loyal hearts throughout the Union leap with joy—battles that will shake the confederacy to its very center. And yet how sad it is to know that hearts that throb lightly now will before many days be cold in death—will have ceased their beating, because of the wicked ambition of men. Modern democracy will smile when the tide of war sweeps them down, but good men will drop tears to their memory, knowing that they died struggling for the advance of free thought and christian civilization; and over their graves will be written, "Defenders of the Union, and benefactors of a redeemed and disenthralled race."

Sunday, May 10th.—Since our return from the Tuscumbia Valley nothing of interest has occurred until to day; flaming bulletins are now flying everywhere exciting loud huzzas from the soldiers in and around Corinth. "Richmond fallen," "Stoneman occupying the city," "the stars and stripes floating over the ramparts," "Vallandigham arrested, &c." Everything seems perfectly wild to night, and loud acclamations rend the air for Hooker. Bonfires are burning in every direction. The excitement beggars description. Cheers are heard everywhere for Hooker, Burnside and No. 38; for the arrest of Ohio's arch traitor, the seared and corrupt hearted, sycophant, C. L. Vallandigham. May he be banished and be compelled to go creeping and whining through the back grounds of an English aristocracy, there to be execrated and condemned by all liberty loving people, for the ignoble part he played upon the American stage; and when peace shall have returned to a stricken people, should this traitor leader on the northern line return among America's loyal people, may the widow and the orphan child say, there goes the traitor Vallandigham, who, when our loved and lost were being submerged by war's crimson wave, was standing upon the American Congress floor, saying that he would sooner see them die and the flag go down than vote one dollar for the prosecution of the war. Sad, sad record for one of the republic's sons![110]

Chapter X.

[May 13, 1863–October 24, 1863]

Move from Corinth—Camp at Bethel, Tennessee—Visit of Adjutant General Thomas—The evacuation of the Mobile and Ohio Railroad—Return to Corinth—Cornyn's raid—His laconic letter to Colonel Biffle, C. S. A—His conversation with the Alabama D. D.—The Seventh mounted—The mules—Rowett's first raid—Camp on Hortan's plantation—Camp at Cotton Ridge—Camp at Henderson—The charge into Montezuma—Camp at Fort Hooker—Return to Corinth—News from Vicksburg—The raid of the rebels on the Government corral—The pursuit—Return to Corinth—Another raid into West Tennessee—Camp at Hamburg—Passing the old battle-field of Shiloh—Camp on Gravel Hill—Return to Corinth—The execution of a deserter—Preparations for another expedition—Leaving Corinth—Camp at Lexington—The arrival of Hatch and Phillips—Rowett and Hatch sweeping the country—Camp near Huntington—The little girls at Huntington—Camp near Louisville and Memphis Railroad—Arrival at Trenton—Camp at Gibson—Camp at the town mills—Grinding corn—Return to Corinth—The boldness of the guerrillas—Major Estabrook's raid—Passing through Adamsville—Jack Creek—Johnson's Mills—The guerrillas—Camp at Henderson—The attack of the guerrillas—Return to Corinth—Rowett's raid with the Seventh Illinois and Kansas Jayhawkers—Camp at Fort Hooker—Pass through Henderson—Camp at Mifflin—Killing of Sergeant Picket—At Jack Creek—Pursuing Colonel Newsom—The fight at Swallow's Bluff—Returning to Corinth—Captain Clark attacked at Purdy—Return to Corinth—Leaving for Chewalla, Tennessee—Camp at Chewalla—Returning again to Corinth and going into our old quarters—The arrival and movement of troops—Indications of an aggressive movement.

May 13th, 1863.—To-day the regiment is ordered to prepare to move from Corinth with camp and garrison equipage. In the afternoon Companies E, B and C, proceed by rail to Henderson, Tennessee, a station on the Mobile and Ohio railroad. In the evening the remaining companies load their camp and garrisons equipage on the cars, ready to start in the morning for Bethel, Tennessee, on the same road, four miles above Henderson towards Corinth. The news comes to-night that Hooker has re-crossed the Rappahannock; that Stoneman has been driven back, and that yet the rebel government holds sway in Rich-mond. So much for rumor. Hooker is dropped now and the accla-mations of the Seventh are confined to "Burnside and No. 38," and for the arrest of Vallandigham.

Thursday, 14th.—This morning we take the train for Bethel, and in about one hour we arrive at this outpost and are con-ducted to the barracks lately vacated by the Forty-third Ohio. We find the Seventh Iowa stationed here, who very cordially welcome the Seventh Illinois as their "Brother Crampers."[111] The two Sevenths soon come to a mutual conclusion that they can run this part of the line and impart general satisfaction to all concerned. It is said that smiles are not wanting for the "vandals" in these parts. In the afternoon the regiment is pa-raded to receive Adjutant General Thomas, who is expected to arrive on the afternoon train. After his arrival and reception by the troops, he addresses us for a short time upon the issues growing out of the emancipation proclamation, and then pro-ceeds on his way towards Corinth.[112]

We remain at Bethel from the fourteenth of May until June 7th, 1863. The Seventh will long remember Bethel and Hen-derson, Tennessee. How they stood picket; how they patroled the railroad; how they drilled; how they run the lines and sal-lied forth into the country; how they mingled with the chivalry and partook of their hospitality; how they sat down and talked with the beautiful, and how they listened to their music, "Bon-nie Blue Flag" and "Belmont;" how the citizens flocked to our lines; how the boys traded "Scotch snuff" to the gentle ones for chickens, butter and eggs. Yes, Bethel and Henderson will long live on memory's page.

June 7th.—The work of evacuating the Mobile and Ohio Railroad is now going on. Having been ordered to move again with camp and garrison equipage, we this morning long before it is light, take the train for Corinth. The Twelfth Illinois hav-ing been ordered to Pocahontas, Tennessee, on the Memphis and Charleston Railroad, our regiment is quartered in their barracks. The twelfth had things arranged in style, so that everything presents a good appearance; the locality is fine, having a beautiful view of the romantic looking Corinth, and the battle field of October 4th, 1862.

June 11th.—From day to day nothing but the weary routine of camp and picket duty greets us—rain or shine the same continual thing—no relaxation. But such is the soldier's life. These sleepless nights, surrounded by a chilling atmosphere, incident to the climate, watching for lurking traitors, is not an enviable life; but cheerfully the sentry paces his lonely path, and when his hours are up he rolls in his blanket upon the cold damp ground, and is soon lost in dreams, perhaps of home, perhaps of battles, the clash of steel and the roar of cannon.

Monday, 15th.—The late raid of the dashing Cornyn to Florence, Alabama, is attracting considerable attention. Though it may be diverging, we would ask the reader to indulge us in recording here Colonel Cornyn's laconic letter, written while at Florence to Colonel Biffle, commanding forces C. S. A., which is as follows:[113]

COLONEL BIFFLE:

Sir—Your pompous demand for the surrender of one squadron of cavalry (Fifteenth Illinois), occupying this place, and your cowardly retreat before you received Captain Carmichael's reply, suggested the propriety of visiting upon the traitor citizens here who tried to assist you in the capture of those gallant Illinois boys, a little legitimate revenge of my government; therefore, in the name of our glorious Union, I hereby make good the grand exordium of the declaration of independence, *i.e.,* "that all men are created free and equal," and to-day I free and take with me from this place, every colored creature who inherits with the human race everywhere the image of his Maker and an immortal soul.

FLORENCE M. CORNYN,
Colonel Commanding Cavalry Brigade.

An officer accompanying the raid, rehearsed to us to-day the following conversation held between Colonel Cornyn and the Rev. R. A. Y., one of Alabama's D. Ds., formerly of St. Louis:[114]

Y. Do you not think it horrible to shell a town occupied by women and children?

Cornyn. Do you not think it horrible for a rebel Colonel and a traitor to seek a town and its houses to make breastworks and cover for his cowardly traitors from which to shell and shoot the brave and generous patriots of this land of liberty, who are willing to meet their country's enemies in open fields every hour of the night and day?

Y. I don't.

Cornyn. You lie, d—n you! You, the offspring of some low white libertine and a debauched Indian squaw, are trying to establish a distinction in favor of yourself, a child of shame, and the negro, a race from the hand of God, bearing his image and ennobled by an immortal soul. The negro is your superior.

Y. Are my wife and children safe while your forces hold this town?

Cornyn. Yes; the brave are always generous, and my soldiers are among the brightest examples on this planet.[115]

An order comes to the Seventh this evening, to the effect that they are to be mounted on "the meek and patient mules." The guerrillas in West Tennessee will be hunted down now.[116]

Friday, 19th.—To-day we draw our mules and saddles; now look out for jayhawking. The Kansas Seventh already fear for their reputation. Dick Rowett is already jubilant, for he knows that he can give more rein to Charley now.

Sunday, 21st.—The "long ears" are issued to the different companies to-day, and in every direction the men are seen trying the virtue of their steeds. As is characteristic of this animal, they prove stubborn and spring towards the "latter end," and in consequence many of the soldiers are elevated. It is indeed amusing to see our donkeys lunge, jump, "thrust and develop." We remarked to a soldier this evening that the mule was not the patient creature it seemed, who, feeling inclined to defend the mule, and who by the way was an observing soldier, replied that "his mule was so patient that it waited three hours to get a chance to kick him." But the Seventh being a conquering regiment, soon subdue the unruly ones. The virtue of each man's mule is now being freely discussed, each soldier claiming that his mule is a superior mule. All are anxious for a scout or a raid now; all are of the opinion that the Seventh on their steeds will present quite an imposing cavalcade; we are sure they will strike terror in rebeldom when Dick leads them forth. From the twenty-first to the twenty-eighth the regiment is principally engaged in breaking mules, &c., making preparations to respond quickly to the expected blast of the bugle.

Sunday, 28th.—This morning companies F, G, H, I and K, mounted and equipped, under the command of Colonel Rowett leave Corinth. We move out on the Purdy road; our mules travel finely; at noon we halt and feed our mules out of a rebel wheat field, after which we pass on through Purdy. This town shows marks of change since we last passed through it. War's scourge has been felt here; some of the finest mansions have been laid in ruins, which is the legitimate vengeance of the loyal Tennessee cavalry. Passing on some miles farther, we are informed by our guide, Captain Aldridge, a loyal Tennesseean, that we are now two miles from Colonel Horton's one of the guerrilla leaders of West Tennessee, and that in all probability he is now at home; therefore, Colonel Rowett, with an intent if possible to capture him, makes a disposition of the companies, directing them to file around in different directions and surround his house.[117] The house is circumvented, but no Horton can be found. It is night now, and we go into camp on the plantation; a descent is made upon the corn pens, and also on the garden and chickens. These proceedings, of course, embitter the family against the soldiers. The old lady's ever ready weapon is soon plying; she talks bitterly, using the words "vandals," "ruffians," and "black abolitionists," freely. Finding that her invective tongue proves powerless, she gathers a hoe, attacks the men, and of course drives them from the yard; then commences on the mules tied to the yard fence and after beating them awhile and seeing Colonel Rowett passing through the yard, she makes an assault upon him, attacking him simultaneously with her hoe and wrathful invectives. "You the leader of these vandals, clear out of my yard." The affable Colonel soon succeeded in quieting her, and we believe he succeeded in persuading the old lady to give him his supper. After the camp fires had gone out, a company of volunteers, under the command of

Captain Clark, of Company D, are sent out, and guided by Captain Aldridge, they visit every guerrilla house in the country and succeed in capturing a Captain from Bragg's army.

June 29th.—This morning the command proceeds on to Cotton Ridge, where it is joined by Captains Clark and Aldridge, who were sent out last night on the hunt of guerrillas. From this ridge we move in the direction of the Mobile and Ohio Railroad. In the evening we strike the railroad at Henderson, but no guerrillas are found, all having fled to the woods. The command goes into camp on a plantation near Henderson. We fare sumptuously to-night; hen-roosts and potato patches at our disposal. We sleep in an old cotton gin; the cotton is strewn everywhere to make beds.

Tuesday, 30th.—This morning we take the road for Bethel, but after riding about six miles some Union citizens come riding after us at full speed, and report a company of guerrillas at Montezuma, about four miles from Henderson. The Colonel immediately countermarches the command, and hastens back, and deploys and makes a charge through the town. But no rebels; all have fled. It is now noon. Colonel Rowett divides the command into small squads, and putting them in charge of our guide, Captain Aldridge, they are sent to the rebel houses to get their dinners, and as a matter of course the boys are supplied with the requisite necessaries, though they were furnished with reluctance. After dinner Colonel Rowett proceeds toward Fort Hooker, where we arrive about dark and go into camp. Nothing found to-day. Everything in the shape of an armed rebel flees away into the brush.

July 1st, 1863.—Early this morning, we move on the Purdy road. A great many citizens are now following the command, who have been compelled to leave their homes to seek protection within the Union lines; all because of their adherence to the old Union. About dark we arrive in camp at Corinth. All agree that the mule is a good institution, for there is no complaining of feet being sore to-night. All are cheerful, and eagerly do the boys read the news from Vicksburg, which is indeed cheering.

July 4th.—Early this morning the stillness is interrupted by the national salute, for it is the eighty-seventh anniversary of the nation's birth. The day passes by pleasantly without any demonstration. During the evening it is surmised that Grant and his army have, with imposing grandeur, celebrated the day. Vague rumors are on the wing this evening that Grant to-day has made another successful swing; that Vicksburg has fallen.

July 6th.—Full reports come to-day from Vicksburg; how the news cheers the soldiers. Loud shouts are heard everywhere; the Seventh feels proud to know that their history is identified with Grant and the army of the Tennessee.[118]

July 8th.—Last night about four hundred of Roddy's command ventured to the government corral, two miles from Corinth, capturing a company of the Thirty-ninth Iowa, and drove off about six hundred mules. Cornyn, with his cavalry, is now in hot pursuit. In the evening the Seventh's bugle blows and we are soon in the saddle. We travel nearly all night on the road leading towards Iuka. The boys become very sleepy, and it is with difficulty that they remain on their mules.

Thursday, 9th.—This morning about two o'clock we come to a halt near Burnsville, Mississippi, and send a company forward to reconnoitre. During this time the remaining companies obtain some little sleep; some reclining by the road side, some in the road. Occasionally a mule steps upon a soldier, and then the poor meek creature gets a set-back. At daylight the company sent out returns without discovering anything. The bugle now blows and we move on a few miles and halt upon a blue grass common to graze the mules and eat our breakfast, after which we move on to Iuka, where we remain about one-half hour and return to Burnsville, halt, feed, and eat our supper. About dark the bugle blows and the regiment is soon in the saddle. We move on to Glendale, halt and lie down to obtain some rest.

Friday, 10th.—This morning we move on our way to Corinth; we get back to camp about nine o'clock, after a fruitless scout. The four hundred rebels made good their escape across the Tennessee with all their spoils.

Saturday, 11th.—This morning the companies send details with the mules out on the commons to graze. Of all the stubborn and aggravating beings on earth, the mule is the chiefest. It would make a saint swear to lead a mule. Whenever they discover a soldier is vexed, they draw back their ears and look so provokingly mean at him, taking all the delight imaginable in tormenting and teasing their master.

Thursday, 16th.—This morning Dick leads the Seventh forth again, heading for West Tennessee. Soon we are winding through the Mississippi forests. The weather is exceedingly warm, and oh! how dusty the roads. None can form any clear conception of the beauty of a ride in July save those who have witnessed in this month a regiment of cavalry or mounted infantry dashing along a Mississippi or Tennessee highway. Arriving at Hamburg, Tennessee river, about dark, we go into camp for the night.

Friday, 17th.—After eating our scanty breakfast of hardtack and coffee, the bugle is sounded and we saddle up and are on our way, taking the road towards Adamsville *via* Shiloh and Crump's Landing; about nine o'clock we pass a portion of the great battle-field of Shiloh, the place where the gallant General Prentiss stood so long fighting as it were against hope. A melancholy stillness pervades the whole command while passing this great battle field, for we remember that comrades sleep here. Oh! how vividly the day, the hour, the evening, comes to our minds when we saw them fall in the fierce struggle for the mastery. As we emerge from the dreary wilderness, where so many Union warriors lie sleeping, we are wont to say in the language of Tom Moore:

> "Oh how blessed a warrior sleeps,
> For whom a wondering world shall weep."[119]

At noon we arrive at Adamsville, but no rebels are found; *i.e.* hostile ones. Everything seems quiet. We halt, feed, and eat our dinners. War has also made its mark here. From appearances this has been in former times a thriving little village; but alas! how different now. Three o'clock, we pass through Purdy and move on towards Corinth; we halt on Gravel Hill and go into camp for the night. The boys soon sally forth, and after being gone awhile return with plenty of oats and roasting-ears, upon which the mules and men make their supper.

Saturday, 18th.—This morning we proceed on our way, and arrive in camp at Corinth about noon, much disappointed in not finding any rebels, the design of the expedition being to cut off Colonel Biffle and Forrest who were retreating from Colonels Hatch and Phillips. But like somebody else, we were one day too late.[120]

Tuesday, 21st.—During the time we remain in camp, all seems monotonous and dull, scarcely anything happening to relieve it. Every day the boys are seen wending their way out of camp to gather blackberries, which are very plentiful around Corinth.

Thursday, 23d.—This morning orders are issued for all the troops in and around Corinth to be paraded on the review ground by eight o'clock, A.M., to witness the execution of one Johnson, a deserter from Company A, First Alabama Union Cavalry. At the appointed time all the troops are on the ground and in position. The sun shines intensely hot, and the tramp of infantry and the galloping of horsemen keeps in the wind one dense cloud of smoke. Soon the procession with the unfortunate man appears upon the ground. They march slowly along the division line, the doomed man walking, supported by the Chaplain of the Sixty-sixth Indiana. He has the appearance of a guilty man—guilty of deserting the flag and his comrades. After the procession has passed the line, they march to the place of execution; the deserter is placed upon his coffin in a sitting position. A solemn and impressive prayer is offered by the Chaplain after which he is blindfolded. The executioners take their position, the Provost Marshal gives the command, and the man who so unhappily erred from the path of duty is launched into eternity. May his ignominious death prove a warning to all who might peradventure be tempted to do likewise.[121]

Saturday, 25th.—This evening we receive orders to prepare for another expedition. The boys are now running to and fro, getting everything in order for an expected fray.

Sunday, 26th.—This morning we are aroused early by the shrill notes of the bugle. By day-light the Tenth Missouri Cavalry, Seventh Kansas, and a battallion of the Fifteenth Illinois Cavalry report to Colonel Rowett, who assumes command and leads the column forth on the Purdy road. We pass through Purdy about 3 P.M., and proceeding about ten miles farther the command goes into camp for the night on the Lexington road.

Monday 27th.—We move early this morning; cross Jack Creek about noon—a noted guerrilla resort. As the rear was crossing, some of the flankers were fired upon by the bushwhackers, and in vain were our efforts to capture them, they having made good their escape into the brush. We move on and arrive at Lexington about four o'clock, and go into camp near the town. Everything looks dreary and desolate here; we see the effects of war's ruthless hand everywhere. The male inhabitants have nearly all cast their destiny with the South in her desperate struggle for power. Chivalry's daughters seem to rule the place, exhibiting a vaunting defiance. One boasted that no Yankee vandal had ever soiled her carpet. A cavalryman hearing her boast, soon dismounts and presently we hear the music of huge spurs and clanking sabre coming from the shaded corridor; we now hear in the front room sharp and bitter invectives; they come from fair chivalry's wrathful tongue, but the stoical and stern soldier heeds them not, but calmly and coolly he makes his exit, rides to camp, lights his pipe, sits down and rehearses to his comrades his adventure through one of chivalry's gorgeous mansions.

Tuesday, 28th.—This morning Colonel Hatch, with his cavalry brigade, arrives in Lexington. At eight o'clock A.M., the bugles are blown, and the commands move from Lexington, Colonel Hatch moving on the road towards Huntington, Colonel Rowett on the road by the way of Spring Creek, Companies H and A, under the command of Captain Ring, are detailed to guard the train, which is to follow Colonel Hatch's command. Companies and squads of soldiers are now scouring the country for horses and mules. The citizens plead their cases well, but war and the warriors are stern; they will not relent. Rowett and Hatch are now sweeping the country; innocence pleads for the avenging hand to be stayed; its tears fall at the warriors' feet, but the stern and legitimate work goes on. We know that

"The South has fallen from her former glory,
   Bowed in slavery, crime and shame;
And that God from his storehouse is sending
   This tempest of steel and flame."

The command goes into camp to-night near Huntington, on a large plantation, *i.e.* that part that is with Colonel Hatch. Mules and soldiers live high to-night.

Wednesday, 29th.—Soon after breakfast the bugle is sounded and the men are soon in their saddles; about eight o'clock we pass through Huntington; here we find a great many Union citizens who hail our advance with joy. The little girls stand by the roadside waving their beautiful little Union banners as the soldiers in blue pass along. We thought we had never seen the old flag's colors look so brilliant as they appeared to us in the hands of those little, smiling, bright eyed girls. They seemed to love them so fondly; loved them for their beauty; loved them for their virtue. "Why do you love that flag so much, little girl?" "I love it because it is the Union's flag, and because my father suffered and died for it at the hands of the traitors." With these associations connected with the Union flag, their little hearts seemed to worship it, and we thought we never beheld a more touching scene than the little girls, with their flags, standing by the roadside in Huntington, and we imagine to-night that the years will not make the memory old. We pass on through this place and halt for dinner at Macedonia. After dinner we are told that we will remain here this afternoon to wait for the arrival of Rowett's Brigade. While so doing Captain Ring gets permission from Colonel Hatch to go out scouting, &c. We succeed in capturing some fine secesh mules, and then return to camp. Colonel Rowett has now come up, and Companies A and H join the regiment. We remain in camp here to-night.

July 30th.—This morning we leave Macedonia, taking the road leading towards Trenton. We halt for dinner at Ewel's Cross Roads. Moving on we arrive at Dresden, on the Louisville and Memphis Railroad; about six o'clock we go into camp two miles from the railroad.

Friday, 31st.—After traveling briskly all morning we arrive at Trenton on the Mobile and Ohio Railroad. We notice that here too war's scourge has been felt. We press on through and take the road leading to Jackson; about three miles from Jackson we pass Hatch's command. We halt at Gibson, feed, and eat our dinner; we will remain here all day. Hatch is now moving on towards Humboldt. To-day the regiment forages extensively; horses and mules are eagerly sought after by the Seventh, and the consequence is that the regiment is becoming well mounted. Companies and squads are being sent out all day. It is impossible for us to narrate the experience of all these scouting parties, as we could only accompany one. We follow a detail of ten men this evening, traveling about six miles, and succeed in capturing two fine mules; one from a negro who was, by the direction of his master, making his way to the brush. Cuffee, "smiling approvingly," says "De massa Yankee who ride dat mule will be well fixed." It is now near sun-down and we are six miles from camp; but some forage, chickens, &c., we must have. Stopping at a plantation, we make a draw and get a sack full of pullets, a few hams, &c. It is now dark and we must hasten; but going a short distance a sable friend informs us where we can get another mule. Two men are sent to obtain the mule, and the remainder push on towards camp. We are now on a strange road; the night is dark, but on we go, and after traveling about four miles through the dense woods, we strike the Jackson road at Gibson. "Halt! who comes there?" breaks upon our ears. "Who challenges?" we reply. "Be it known that we are the invincibles, representatives from the Kansas Jayhawkers. Give us your character?" "We are raiders from Rowett's command." "Roddy's command!" Click, click in quick succession the triggers go. "D——n you, not Roddy's, but Rowett's command," cried one of our men. "All right, brother crampers, pass on." We soon arrive in camp. The boys now make preparations to skin some chickens; all anticipate a good supper, but when we come to look for the pullets they are not to be found. The truth soon flashes upon us that R. J. —— became frightened in the dense woods and threw them away. Dear reader, imagine our disappointment. It is useless to say that R. J. —— didn't rest much that night.

August 1st, 1863.—The advance is now passing our regiment. It falls to our lot to be in the rear to-day. Soon we are all in the saddle and on the road. At noon we halt on one of Tennessee's large plantations to feed and eat our dinners. The corn pens are now mounted, the garden fence is scaled, the smokehouse entered; the hams are going, the turkeys are running and chickens squalling. Passing through the yard, a fair one approaches us and enquires for the chief commander. Of course we didn't know, and no one could be found who did; but when she discovered the corn pen rapidly diminishing for the benefit of Rowett's two thousand mules, that the boys in blue were stern and determined, and that her artful persuasion proved of no avail, she seemed to resign calmly to the "fates," and commenced to talk quietly to the soldiers. She said she loved the South, her heart was with it in its struggle; that she had two brothers who were officers in the Confederate army, and that she was glad of it. But she could not bear to be called a rebel. Says she: "Call me not a rebel, but a confederate." After dinner we proceed on our way, cross the Mobile and Ohio Railroad, and camp on the road leading to Lexington.

August 2d.—This morning we move on the Lexington road and arrive at Lexington about noon. The command, with the exception of the Seventh, halt and go into camp. The Seventh moves on to the town mills, about two miles from Lexington, where we go into camp and start the mill to grinding corn, our rations having run out.

August 3d.—This morning we are ordered to remain here and keep the mill running until we have enough ground to do us until we get back to Corinth. Foraging parties are being sent out in every direction. We are now compelled to subsist wholly upon the country.

August 4th.—Early this morning we are off for Corinth. We go into camp twelve miles from Purdy. Our comrades and we now sally forth to get our supper; we soon draw up at a plantation. The lord of the manor espying our uniforms, welcomes us and extends to us his hospitality, *i.e.* a good supper, and while partaking of his bounty, the old lady stood picket for us, and when leaving, the old man, with tears in his eyes, says, "You are welcome to my house. The boys in blue are men after my own heart. I have lived too long under the protection of the old flag to now rebel against it." Returning to camp, a comrade rehearses to us his adventure; that he came across some Union ladies this evening, who cheered them as they rode up, told them of secesh neighbors, and proffered to carry up feed for their mules if they would go and take their neighbors' horses. The horses were captured. This we call true Union. God bless the loyal ladies of the South! God bless the loyal ladies throughout America for the part they are playing in the great drama! Their prayers and tears are to-day doing more to save the Union than the armies and navies can do.

August 5th.—This morning we are thirty miles from Corinth. We pass Purdy about noon, halt and feed close by, after which we move on and arrive in camp at seven P.M. All seem glad to get back to Corinth. This morning we interest ourselves in reading the letters that have accumulated during our absence. These do the soldiers good, and in consequence they are cheerful to-night.

September 3d, 1863.—For the last month nothing but a dull monotony has reigned in camp, but things are now becoming more lively. The paymaster has made his appearance; greenbacks and gray-backs are plentiful. The latter now and then dash from their hiding places in the brush upon the soldiers. Sergeant Leatherman and two men belonging to Company K, while out on a detail, were captured to-day. Companies B, C, E, and K, under the command of Captain Johnson, are now in pursuit of the guerrillas.[122]

September 4th.—All quiet this morning; the companies sent out yesterday return this evening; only captured one guerrilla.

Friday, 11th.—This morning we receive orders to get ready for a scout; to start at four, P.M. At the appointed time our regiment, a detachment of the Third Tennessee Cavalry, and one company of the Tenth Missouri Cavalry, under the command of Major Estabrook, move from Corinth in the direction of Adamsville. It is soon dark; we travel all night; at midnight our advance is halted by a squad of rebel soldiers. Their character is demanded; they reply, "A detachment from Forrest's command." "All right, advance one." The one is captured, the remainder make their escape. About three o'clock A.M., we halt and lie down to rest, weary and sleepy.

Saturday, 12th.—This morning, at the sound of the bugle all are on their feet. After eating our breakfast, we move forward and pass through Adamsville at eight o'clock A.M., and taking the road leading towards Jack Creek. The flankers and scouts now and then run into skulking squads of rebels. We go into camp six miles from Jack Creek. This evening Company I is sent on a scout to Skinner's Mill, where they encounter and drive to the bush twice their number of guerrillas. The object of this expedition is to break up Newsom's conscript arrangements in West Tennessee.[123]

Sunday, 13th.—This morning by sun-rise we are moving. The advance encounters a squad of Newsom's band at Jack Creek, which is soon put to flight. One company is now left with the teams, and the command dashes forward, but soon comes to a halt. A dust is discovered ahead. One company is dismounted and deployed forward, but no enemy is seen; all are now far away in the brush. The regiment now hastens on as fast as possible to Johnson's mill. Here, also, our advance encounters a lurking band, which quickly makes its exit. We halt here for dinner, after which the soldiers commence on the mill, and soon it is destroyed. No more guerrilla bands will ever grind their corn here. The command is now divided, and ordered to leave Johnson's mill in different directions, and after scouring the woods for miles around, the different detachments and companies concentrate, but as soon as done a squad of guerrillas dashes across the road and fire into our rear as they pass. But their buck and small shot pass harmlessly over our heads. The regiment moves on slowly and camps for the night on Forked Deer, five miles from Henderson. To-night our pickets decoy and capture a rebel Major, a conscript officer.

Monday, 14th.—To-day companies are sent in every direction, scouring the country for rebels, Company H to-day capture the noted rebel Ross, once a member of the State Legislature.[124] Some one charges him as being one of the motley crew who made such an ignoble retreat when Nelson made his appearance in the vicinity of Nashville, but as it is to his credit, he denies the accusation. In the evening the different companies and scouting parties form a junction at Henderson Station, on the Mobile and Ohio Railroad.

Tuesday, 15th.—This morning we leave Henderson. Captain Ring is ordered to take charge of the prisoners, and act as rear guard. Our captures up to this time are about thirty. After leaving Henderson, and while riding slowly along, bang! bang! bang! go about thirty guns, and the bullets whistle harmlessly over our heads and leave their impress in the trees beyond. The rear guard, consisting of twelve men from company H wheel, and about two hundred yards down the road we see coming and yelling like so many demons, about thirty guerrillas. The men stand very coolly; the Enfields now commence rattling. The guerrillas seeing the coolness, halt, wheel, and away they go into the brush. Soon a company of horsemen come dashing back from the front (a company of the Third Tennessee Cavalry). In the meantime the guerrillas ambushed, and as the Union troops went charging through the woods, they fire a volley and away they go through the woods into the swamp, making good their escape. By this volley one brave trooper was killed. "Oh! ye sons of the South, boast of your chivalry.": We leave the fallen soldier at the house of Major Aldridge, (Union) for burial. Thus we leave him as a sacrifice at liberty's shrine, in an enemy's country. Peace to the brave trooper's ashes. The bugle blows and the regiment moves on. Passing a fine peach orchard, Captain Ring gives three of his men permission to stop and get some peaches for his company. The lady of the house meets the boys, expressing a sympathy for the Union soldiers, bids the boys take all the peaches they want, invites them to remain and take dinner, and brings out some milk and proffers it to the boys. They turn to go; her object is partially accomplished; the tramp of horsemen is heard. "Guerrillas, boys!" says one, and they are off. Bang! bang! "halt, halt, you blue coated vandals!" The rear halts and wheels, and up the road we see the boys coming, the guerrillas closely pursuing, with their carbines raised to strike them on their heads. Bang! bang! go the Enfields and Captain Ring's revolver. They suddenly wheel and are soon far away. We succeeded in wounding one, so we concluded from the blood seen on the road. The column halts and again cavalry is sent back, but they accomplish nothing. The cowardly rebels sought shelter in the dense undergrowth, soon putting themselves out of harm's way. Night coming on, we go into camp between Purdy and Corinth.[125]

Wednesday, 16th.—Early this morning we are off for Corinth, moving over the old familiar highway. Oh! how dusty; the rising clouds almost hide the sun. We arrive at Corinth about noon, hungry, tired, sleepy and miserably dirty. The soldiers are soon perusing the papers, which seem to tell us that the long dark night of war is waning. The shouts from the soldiers that roll from the camp to-night are: "Hurrah for Gilmore!" and "More Greek fire for Charleston!"[126]

Saturday, 27th.—In vain do we seek for something of interest to jot down during the weary, monotonous days we remain in camp. But this evening a relief from this dull monotony comes. Orders to be ready to march in the morning; the soldiers are cheerful to-night.

Sunday, 28th.—Three o'clock this morning the shrill notes are heard; all are now in a bustle and uproar. By day-light the Kansas Seventh reports to Colonel Rowett, and by sun-rise his troopers are again moving on the old Purdy road towards West Tennessee. Nothing of note occurs through the day. We travel about thirty miles and go into camp at Fort Hooker, on the Mobile and Ohio Railroad.

Monday, 29th.—Early this morning the command is up and ready to move forward. While waiting to hear the bugle call, Sergeant Flint, with his mind ever ready, pens the following:

> My girth is tight, my stirrup strong,
>   My steed is staunch and free;
> I wait to hear the bugle clear,
>   To mount my saddle tree.
>
> No soul to say a last God-speed,
>   I give no fond adieu;
> But only this, my good-bye kiss,
>   My lady sweet, to you.
>
> The saddle and the forest camp
>   Are now my home once more;
> And hearts that long were soft grow strong,
>   The bivouac fire before.
>
> And if my breast in some wild charge
>   Should meet the deadly ball,
> My mates will spread my soldier bed,
>   And lay me where I fall.
>
> My blood will be my epitaph,
>   That marks my jacket blue;
> Read it with pride—He lived, he died,
>   For country, home and you.

The bugle now blows and we move forward on the road leading to Henderson. We pass through Henderson about noon; find
all quiet; rebels all gone; just left, so the citizens tell us. How
singular it is that they vanish so soon. After leaving Henderson
we take the road leading towards Mifflen, and when about four
miles from Henderson our advance comes upon a squad of five
rebels at a Union man's house, in the act of enforcing the con-
scription act. We succeed in capturing two of them, the remaining three making their escape to the brush. In the evening we
go into camp at Mifflen, a noted guerrilla resort, but upon our
advance none were found. Perhaps they have hid their guns
and are now playing the peaceful citizen. The camp fires are
soon burning brightly; the porkers are now making their last
earthly appeal. We eat our supper and lie down to rest. About
ten o'clock, bang! bang! go the muskets on the picket line. The
bugle is sounded, and in two minutes the Seventh is ready for a
fray; but no farther fray; it is all over with now. A squad of
Newsom's cowardly band crawled up and fired upon the pickets. One soldier, Sergeant Pickott, of Company G, was killed.
Not being on duty at the time, and being a religious young
man, he leaves his comrades and goes away a short distance to
engage in secret prayer, and while the christian soldier was
there kneeling, one of these marauding, uncivilized guerrillas,
taking advantage of his advanced position, fired upon him,
dealing a mortal wound from which he died in two hours, leaving the freed spirit to take its flight home to God.[127]

> Now his spirit has departed,
> And from eyes unused to weeping
> Fall the bitter tears unheeded,
> For another gallant soldier
> Off the picket guard forever.

Tuesday, 29th.—This morning the fallen soldier's comrades
bury him in a lonely place. Thus is this land being dotted all
over with the Union's noble defenders. As we stand by this soldier's last resting place we are tempted to pray to heaven that
some blighting and dread malaria would settle on the godless
traitors—that their widows might weep until their eyes are

weary, waiting for the return of their husbands—murderers from the field of strife. The command soon moves. We are now following winding paths through the woods and swamps, hunting for the marauding bands that are infesting West Tennessee. The regiment is now divided, moving in different directions. About noon we enter Jack Creek and capture three guerrillas. We remain here waiting for the different companies and detachments to come in. The junction formed, we move in the direction of Saultilla Landing, Tennessee river. All day we have been on the trail of Colonel Newsom; at one time the scouts fired upon him fifteen or twenty shots, but they failed in their object. To-night we camp six miles from the Tennessee river.

Wednesday, 30th.—This morning the command is again divided into detachments and directed to operate on different roads. Colonel Rowett with one detachment of the command formed from the Seventh Illinois and Seventh Kansas, moves with full speed towards Swallows Bluff to intercept a battalion of rebels said to be crossing the Tennessee at that point. Coming up, the Colonel discovers that the guerrilla leader has already succeeded in crossing all his horses and men with the exception of about thirty who were now waiting for their raft to return. As soon as Rowett and his troopers were seen above them on the bluff, they saw at once their situation, and for the first time during our raids in West Tennessee the rebels offered us battle, being well protected by the bluff and readily aided by the more lucky portion of their command on the opposite shore, who were in easy musket range. A casual observer would not have considered their resistance altogether hopeless with these advantages in position. The Colonel discovered at once that to capture them could not be accomplished without a fierce assault. The assault is made, the enemy's resistance is determined. Showers of leaden hail come rattling on the bluff from beyond the river, but they do not check the two Sevenths. Led by the gallant and fearless Rowett they charge up the bluffs, raining a shower of bullets from their superior guns into the rebels on the other bank. Some Fall, and the remainder retreat back under cover. A portion of the command with their long range muskets succeed in keeping the enemy back; while the remaining portion pay their attention to the squad under the bluffs who are soon compelled to run up the white flag. Among the number captured was a Major. We soon discovered that this battalion belonged to the regular confederate army, which accounted for the stubborn resistance. In this encounter the Seventh Kansas lost one man killed and two wounded.

The entire command now forms a junction, and with our prisoners we move on about eight miles and go into camp for the night. It soon commences to rain, threatening to be a dark dreary night for the soldier, for of course we have no shelter.

Thursday, October 1st, 1863.—It is still raining this morning and in lieu of dust we have mud. We are now fifty miles from Corinth, whither the advance is headed. We arrive at Purdy at 2 P.M., where we find Captain Clark with Company "D" barricaded in the old court house, where they had been sent yesterday with an ambulance and some sick soldiers. Captain Clark informs us that he was attacked by the guerrillas, but by determined resistance stood the ground against twice his number. Being well protected no casualties occurred. We halt in the outskirts of the town and feed, after which we proceed on our way towards Corinth. Arrive in camp 10 P.M., very much worn by the hard day's ride.[128]

Friday, 2nd.—This morning the bugle fails to arouse the Seventh. The sun's rays have long been shining through the crevices in the barracks ere they awake, but by and by the stern orders come and the Seventh is brought forth. The prisoners (some forty in number) having been safely guarded in our oats house, are to-day reported and turned over to the Provost Marshal. The boys are busily engaged this evening cleaning up their guns preparatory to another scout.

Saturday, 3d.—Last night some guerrillas made a demonstration on the Memphis and Charleston Railroad, burning a bridge between Chewalla, Tenn., and Corinth. In the evening we receive marching orders with camp and garrison equipage, destination Chewalla, to relieve the Eighteenth Missouri, now stationed there guarding the railroad.[129]

Sunday, 4th.—This morning at seven A.M., we leave our old camp at Corinth, with all our camp and garrison equipage. The Seventh, as they move through Corinth with their knapsacks strapped to their mules, and with their long train of pack mules, look very much like an immense caravan starting on a pilgrimage. After about three hours ride we arrive at Chewalla, finding fine quarters and fine grounds, &c. The Eighteenth Missouri are now leaving, and as fast as they vacate we take possession. This evening the men are busy cleaning up and arranging their quarters

Friday, 9th.—The swamps and bottoms along the Tuscumbia and the Hatchie rivers are now being thoroughly scouted. The guerrillas are finding their favorite haunts hot quarters. Go in whatever direction we may, and scouting parties from the Seventh can be seen.

Saturday, 10th.—This morning Captain Ring proceeds with a detachment on a scout towards the Hatchie river, but nothing hostile being discovered, he returns in the evening.

Friday, 16th.—A brigade of infantry pass through Chewalla on their way from Vicksburg to Corinth. They look as though they had seen hard service down on the Yazoo. This evening the order comes for five companies to report back to Corinth.

Saturday, 17th.—This morning companies A, B, C, D and E, proceed on their way to Corinth, companies F, G, H, I and K, remaining at Chewalla. Troops from Vicksburg keep passing through Chewalla all day on their way to Corinth.

October 19th.—To-day the cheering news comes to the army that Ohio's arch traitor has been defeated by 100 000 majority. Well done Ohio! The Illinois boys send greeting to your soldiers who fought the battle at the ballot box, gaining as important a victory over treason as has been gained on any of the great battle fields. This news carries cheer to every soldier's heart in the tented field.[130]

Wednesday, October 21st.—Last night Captain Johnson with part of the command started on a scouting expedition— has not returned yet. This evening he returns, after giving the notorious guerrilla, Captain Smith, a chase, capturing six of his horses, but owing to the dense undergrowth of the woods, Smith and his band made good their escape.[131]

Saturday, 24th.—This morning our detachment leaves Chewalla with their camp and garrison equipage for Corinth. We again go into our old quarters, which we now denominate our "old homestead." The arrival and moving of troops seem to instil new life into Corinth. The indications are that some aggressive movement is contemplated.

Chapter XI.

[October 26, 1863–January 7, 1864]

General Sherman's command—Marching orders—Camp at Jacinto—Camp at
Iuka—Payment of the Regiment—On Picket—Foraging—Troops leaving
Iuka—Standing in the rain—March to Eastport—Crossing the Tennessee—
Camp on the hill side—The Regiment divided into detatchments—Baily
Springs—Sergeant Hackney whipped by a woman—Seventh on the left flank—
The wild rocky country—Arrival at Pulaski, Tennessee—The trip to Columbia,
Tenn.—Return to Pulaski—Trip to Corinth after the division, camp and
garrison equipage—Encountering Roddy and Johnson—Camp at Waterloo—
Camp at Hamburg Landing—Companies sent to Corinth—Returning to
Pulaski, Tenn.—Fray at Waynesboro with the Fifth Tennessee Union
Cavalry—Arrival at Pulaski—Lieutenant Robert's trip to Eastport, Tennessee
River—His narrow escape, and safe return to Pulaski—The expedition to
Lawrenceburg—The loyal ladies of the south—The Veteran propositions—The
pulse of the Seventh—Re-enlistment—The cry for the mustering officer—His
arrival—The Regiment mustered as Veterans.

Gen. Sherman's command for the last week has been
thronging Corinth, and moving on towards Iuka. Marching orders is now the cry in camp. Four o'clock P.M. we are in the saddle with three days' rations. General Dodge's entire command
is now in motion. Our regiment moves on the road leading
through Jacinto, Mississippi, to Iuka. Nine o'clock in the
evening we go into camp at Jacinto.

Monday, 26th.—This morning at two o'clock the bugle's
blast is heard and soon the regiment is moving towards Iuka.
At daylight we come to a halt one and a half miles from Iuka
where we tie up and feed, after which Colonel Rowett proceeds
with the regiment to Iuka, and reports to General Sherman.

Companies A, B, C, D, E, G and K, go into camp in the woods
west of Iuka. Companies H, I and F, under the command of
Captain Johnson, pass through Iuka and go into camp as an
out-post, on the road leading south.

Wednesday, 28th.—Rumor has it that the regiment will be
paid off to-day, and for once rumor proves correct. Captain

Johnson receives orders to report with his detachment to regimental headquarters. In the afternoon the regiment is paid.

Thursday, 29th.—To-day the sullen roar of artillery is heard in the front, towards the Tennessee river. The troops are soon in motion. Sherman and staff are now leaving Iuka for the advance; the conjectures are that a storm is brewing down by the Tennessee. Sherman is now moving with his army to form a junction with General Rosecrans, and the probabilities are that Bragg will attempt to check him.

Friday, October 30th.—This morning a portion of the Regiment is placed on picket duty. It is now raining. The winds blow coldly. The day is waning. A dismal night is approaching. Amid the falling elements, chilly and drear, the Seventh boys are now standing, but all seem in fine spirits. "Their hearts beat high," "And they heed not the wild wind's wailing cry." About midnight some of Colonel Spencer's First Alabama Union regiment arrive at our lines—a sergeant and four privates, who got cut off from their command during Spencer's late fight with the rebel General Furgeson, and have ever since been brushing it.[132] It is now

> "Past the midnight hour, and we long to hear
> The step to the Soldier's heart most dear—
> A sound that banishes all his grief—
> The welcome tread of the "next relief."
>
> Ah! here they come, and now we can keep
> Our next four hours in the land of sleep,
> And dream of home and the loved ones there,
> Who never may know a soldier's care."

Saturday, 31.—This morning, after being relieved we return to camp, dry our clothes, and seek some rest. All quiet to-day. Sherman is now making his base at Eastport, Tennessee, whither the transports are now moving.[133]

Sunday, November 1st, 1863.—This morning companies C, G and H, commanded by Major Estabrook, go out on a foraging expedition. We go about three miles—load our wagons with corn, fodder and sweet potatoes, and strap all we can to the mules, and then start for camp. Entering camp the detachment reminds us of what might be called a moving "fodder panorama."

Wednesday, 4th.—This morning companies H and A escort the Second Michigan Battery out to the camp of the Fifty-second Illinois Infantry. Rumor has it now that the troops will all leave Iuka in the morning for Eastport, Tennessee river. All are in confusion this evening. Considerable excitement amongst sutlers and "civilians," for the order has come for the command to move to-morrow, at 7 A.M.

Thursday, 5th.—The bugle blows at early dawn, all are soon up and prepared to move; it is now raining in torrents. All the infantry are now in motion. During the morning the Seventh stand in the rain, expecting to move every minute. We wait and wait; mid-day is now passed and the Seventh still at Iuka. After this standing in the rain all day waiting for an order to move forward, we receive orders to unsaddle and remain another night, and in consequence the Seventh are far from being in a good humor this evening.

Friday, 6th.—This morning, the troops being all gone, we leave Iuka for Eastport, where we arrive about noon. The troops are now busy crossing the river. We go into camp for the night with orders to be ready to cross early in the morning.

Saturday 7th.—This morning the Seventh is aroused early. Cross in twenty minutes is now the order. We feed and proceed to the river and halt to await our time. The twenty minutes have now grown to hours. We succeed in getting across the river by noon, where we go into camp, feed, and eat our dinners. The last of the army is now across the Tennessee, moving on towards the front, the Seventh bringing up the rear.[134] We move out about eight miles and go into camp on the side of a large hill (no other place being found where we could tie our mules.) After feeding, and eating our supper, we remove some of the larger rocks and make "our beds." We all lie down, but it is with difficulty that we maintain our position. We predict that by morning we shall be down at the foot of the hill. All is still now. Nothing is heard save the watchful sentry's quiet tramp.

Saturday, 8th.—We are aroused early this morning. We are made to conclude that the Seventh is indeed a tenacious regiment, to have held their position so well on this hill-side dur-

ing the night. None are found at the foot of the hill, as was pre-
dicted. The mules too have been good in holding their positions. The Seventh being ordered to take the advance, we soon
move forward, through north Alabama on the north side of the
Tennessee, halt and feed about twelve miles from Florence, after which we move on, and about three P.M. pass through the
suburbs of Florence; we march about six miles farther and go
into camp. Where the main army is to-night we do not know.
We are now away off on the flank, isolated and alone.

Monday, 9th.—The regiment is to-day divided into detachments and ordered to move on different roads on both flanks of
the army. About noon the detachment which we accompany arrives at Baily Springs, one of Chivalry's fashionable resorts.
But we find none of her devotees pacing the building's dim cor-
ridors. War's stern voice has called them away. The springs are
beautiful, sparkling with nature's purest liquid—dashing in
playful sprays from granite rock. The weary soldiers love so
well to linger here—love to kneel at the healing fountain. After
feeding we move on our way. Before entering the main road
three men from the detachment stop to do some foraging, but
the chickens are difficult to capture, making strenuous efforts
when pursued by a yankee. The lady of the house comes to the
door and smiling sweetly says: "Soldiers, there's my little dog,
he can catch them for you." "Thank you, madam, we don't want
your chickens," replied Sergeant Hackney, of Company H, and
the soldiers make their exit. How well did that woman know
where man was weak. The column is now moving on the old
"military road." The main body of the Seventh is now on the
left flank. Striking out through the woods and brush we come
up with the regiment about 4 P.M. We go into camp at 8 P.M.

Tuesday, 10th.—This morning the Seventh takes the left
flank, the Ninth Illinois the right. We pass through a wild
country to-day: hills and rocks seem to look frowningly upon
us. The flinty roads are hard on the mules; their feet are becoming sore. We go into camp to-night thirty miles from Pulaski, Tennessee. Our supplies run out to-day, and this evening
we draw largely from the surrounding country.

Wednesday, 11th.—This morning a wagon with rations arrives from the column—quite a welcome arrival. We discover

that we are now some distance from the main command. The regiment is soon moving; we continue to pass through a hilly and rocky country, interspersed with springs and running brooks. We arrive at Pulaski, Tennessee, by dark; find the division already up and in camp. Pulaski is a beautiful town on the Tennessee and Alabama Railroad, running from Nashville to Stevenson.[135]

Thursday, 12th.—It appears that our Division has come to a stand; that Sherman and his corps have gone on unchecked to join Rosecrans. In the afternoon we move across Richland Creek; pass through Pulaski, and go into camp. All quiet this evening.

Friday, November 13th.—This morning a large detail from the regiment, under the command of Major Estabrook, reports to Colonel Weaver, Second Iowa, to accompany the Division train, now headed for Columbia, Tennessee, to draw supplies.[136] We are ordered to take the advance on the pike running through Columbia to Nashville. Traveling briskly all day, we go into camp for the night six miles from Columbia.

Saturday, 14th.—Early this morning we move on and arrive in Columbia about nine o'clock. Columbia is a beautiful and wealthy town, situated on Duck River. Captain Carpenter, Commissary of Subsistence, receives a dispatch informing him of no supplies now on hand at Davis' Station, the point beyond Duck River as far as the trains from Nashville run on this railroad. We immediately cross the river and proceed about five miles from Columbia on the Nashville pike, and go into camp, with orders to remain there until supplies arrive from Nashville.

Monday, 16th.—This morning the train arrives at Davis' Station, from Nashville, with supplies. The wagons are now being loaded up; this evening all being loaded, we receive orders to be ready in the morning to return to Pulaski, Tennessee.

Tuesday, 17th.—We move early this morning; it takes some time to cross Duck River, the river having risen considerably. We go into camp for the night, half way between Columbia and Pulaski.

Wednesday, 18th.—By day-light the train is moving; we arrive in camp at Pulaski by sun-down, and find it deserted, the regiment having gone on a scout.

Thursday, November 19th.—It is raining this morning, but soon ceases and clears off; the sun now shines refreshingly. This evening the regiment arrives back from their scout, with thirty rebels captured at Lawrenceburg, Tennessee. All seem in fine spirits; much elated over the success of their expedition, and none more so than Colonel Rowett, who never seems more in his element than when on Charley at the head of his regiment, thundering over the hills and through the ravines of Tennessee. There is always power felt where he moves.

Friday, 20th.—The companies are busy to-day getting their foot-sore mules shod, preparatory to another expedition, for rumor already has it that the regiment will leave Pulaski to-morrow morning on some mission.

Saturday, 21st.—Again rumors are verified. Pursuant to order, the regiment moves from Pulaski this morning with three days' rations. It is said we are bound for Corinth, Mississippi, to look after the camp and garrison equipage belonging to the Second Division. After travelling thirty miles, we go into camp at Lexington, Alabama. As usual the regiment forages, and chickens still continue to fall victims to the Seventh. We have a good supper to-night; such as soldiers enjoy.

Sunday, 22d.—Ere it is light the bugle is sounded, and after hastily dispatching our breakfast, we move on our way. All along the road to-day we encounter squads of rebels, scouting parties from Johnson's and Roddy's commands, all of which goes to prove that the raiders Johnson or Roddy, or both, are on the north side of the Tennessee, and in consequence we anticipate considerable opposition before we reach our destination.[137] Sure enough, at four o'clock P.M., our advance is checked. Colonel Rowett soon dismounts the regiments and forms a battle line. Our skirmishers are advanced and firing soon commences in every direction, sounding as though we were surrounded. A scout is now seen dashing from the brush to where the Colonel stands. He informs him of our danger and the fearful odds against us; that the rebels would soon be upon us if we remained there any longer. The bugle is sounded; the men spring into their saddles. Charley is champing and neighing. The Colonel's eye seems to be everywhere. He is now dashing down the road, with the regiment closely following. On we go towards Waterloo. The rebels hover on our flanks, front and rear. There is promiscuous firing all evening. They seem loth to throw any considerable force against us; feel loth to try our steel. By nine P.M., we arrive at Waterloo, four miles from East-port, Tennessee River. The rebels soon abandon their expected game. At Waterloo we go into camp, having traveled sixty-five miles since morning, capturing twelve rebels during the day and evening.

Monday, 23d.—This morning we proceed to the river, find some transports and two gun-boats up. We go into camp here for the night.

Tuesday, 24th.—The regiment will not go to Corinth as in-tended; only two companies will be sent. This evening they are taken across on a steamer. All quiet this evening. It rains all night.

Wednesday, 25th.—This morning a foraging expedition is sent out under the command of Captain Yeager, of Company G. Nothing discovered, nothing obtained—a fruitless expedi-tion.[138]

Thursday, 26th.—This morning the regiment moves down the river to a point opposite Hamburg Landing, where the three companies are ordered to report with the Second Divi-sion's equipage. Our way is a winding one over the hills and bluffs of the Tennessee. By night we arrive opposite the Land-ing, having captured four prisoners during the day. Here we find a transport anchored in the river, and a force stationed at Hamburg. We go into camp for the night. The Colonel obtains a skiff from the steamboat and sends a detail across the river to Hamburg to draw some rations. In the meantime the regiment kills a number of hogs. The detail sent across the river have now returned with plenty of rations. We do not hunger to-night. The three companies sent to Corinth have returned with the camp and garrison equipage. It is now raining, a cold driz-zly rain. Our camp is in a low swamp by the Tennessee. We an-ticipate that we shall lie or stand in water ere it is morning.

Friday, 27th.—To-day the Second Division's camp and garri-son equipage is loaded on board the steamer Nashville, to be sent around to Nashville. Still it rains. The camp seems to be floating in mud and water. Clothes wet, blankets drenched, and a cold piercing north wind blowing. Night comes on cold and gloomy. The men are now shivering around the camp fires, with no place to lay their weary heads. Gloomy picture!

"Out alone to-night we're sitting,
Watching shadows that are passing
To and fro upon the canvas,
In our spirit's penetralia.
Go, ye idle, cursed complainers,
Who complain at home of trouble;
Think upon the soldiers' sorrow,
Weary, weak and wakeful soldiers;
Guarding you from foul oppression,
Keeping you a home of pleasure.
If your coward heart will let you,
Then refuse him aid and shelter."

Saturday, 28th.—This morning three companies are detailed to escort back to Corinth the teams that hauled the Division's camp and garrison equipage to the river. All quiet this evening, and it is still muddy and wet.[139]

Sunday, 29th.—The three companies sent with the teams to Corinth return to-day. The order this evening is to be ready to move in the morning.

Monday, 30th.—This morning the regiment starts over the hills towards Pulaski, Tennessee; and moves on the Waynesboro road. Night coming on we go into camp at Pin Hook.

Tuesday, December 1st, 1863.—We are now on the road leading to Waynesboro. When within two miles of the town we halt and feed. After dinner we mount, put spurs to our steeds and charge into the town, from which place we start a citizen who mistook us for guerrillas, running him from town. He meets the Fifth Tennessee Union Cavalry approaching in an opposite direction; halting, they inquire if there are any guerrillas in Waynesboro? "Yes; down the road they are now camping," (pointing towards the Seventh's advance guard). The Seventh boys and the Fifth Tennessee meet and commence firing. The Colonel soon discovers the mistake, but is unable to stop the fray until three are wounded; two belonging to the Seventh and one to the Fifth Tennessee. The Fifth Tennessee having been deceived so often by guerrillas dressed in federal uniforms, they have in consequence become very vigilant. After the excitement, we move on five miles and go into camp at the iron foundry.

Wednesday, 2d.—Early this morning we are on the road leading towards Pulaski, Tennessee. When within twelve miles of Pulaski we go into camp; we have honey, chickens and hams in abundance to-night. The boys are cheerful.

Thursday, 3d.—We arrive in Pulaski by noon to-day, and find all quiet in camp; receive a large mail, which the boys are now reading.

Friday, 4th.—All still to-day; a dull monotony in camp. The Seventh are now making shelter out of rails and their oil cloths, and what few boards they can gather up; no tents; on duty every day, scouting and running everywhere. This evening a call is made upon the different companies for twenty volunteers to carry dispatches one hundred miles across the country to Eastport, Tennessee River. To be relieved from the camp's dull life, we conclude to be one of the number. The remaining nineteen soon report. About nine o'clock P.M., we leave Pulaski under the command of Lieutenant Roberts, of Company C. We travel until four o'clock in the morning, when we halt at a plantation, feed and get our breakfast, prepared by the negroes. At daylight we move on, pass through Waynesboro, and go as far as Pin Hook, where we go into camp for the night.

Sunday, 6th.This morning we move early; we are now in the enemy's country, far from support; all keep closely together, moving briskly, for to-day we are ordered to be at Eastport. At Pin Hook some of the loyal citizens informed us that the noted guerilla Moore was now at home, and as we were to pass his house, they urged us to capture him, as he was a terror to that whole country. When within a short distance of the house, the Lieutenant divides the command, directing one portion to file off and come up in the rear of the house. Arriving in sight we make the charge, but his little boy who was standing picket, soon gives the alarm, and Captain Moore seizes his gun and is soon in the brush. We jump the fence in front of the house, and on the charge we are met by the Captain's wife and daughter, who endeavor to scare our horses, but no scare; on we go in close pursuit of the Captain, with whom we exchange several shots—but no capture. He succeeded in evading us in the brush, and as it was taking us too far from our route, we abandoned the pursuit. Taking his horse we move on.[140] Near Waterloo we capture two conscripting officers from Bragg's army. Soon after we arrive at the landing opposite Eastport; we find the river swarming with transports loaded with troops; we feel more safe now. Lieutenant Roberts giving the signal, a skiff is brought over. The Lieutenant and two of the men take the prisoners over, deliver the dispatches, draw some rations and return, after which we go into camp for the night.

Monday, 7th.—This morning the transports and gun-boats all move down the river, leaving us isolated and alone, and in consequence we are soon on our way back towards Pulaski. Thinking it policy, we move on a different road. We travel briskly; capture three guerrillas during the morning; run one about three miles and capture him in a brush pile. When about thirty miles from Eastport, inland from the river, and while moving on a quick pace, we suddenly come upon a battallion of rebels numbering about two hundred. "Lieutenant, no time to be lost now! back we must get or be captured!" says Lowery, the scout.[141] So from the road over the hills and through the woods we plunge, and getting on the Waynesboro road, we make good our escape. We travel until about eleven o'clock and go into camp on a plantation seven miles from Waynesboro, making a distance since morning of eighty miles. It is now raining; the winds howl fiercely; the boys seek shelter in stables and sheds. We now think of those who are on picket tonight, after riding so hard all day. Stern necessity demands it, and no one complains. What noble types of untiring fortitude!

Tuesday, 8th.—This morning it still rains; we move on and arrive at Waynesboro at nine A.M., and find the Fifth Loyal Tennessee Cavalry garrisoning the town, and we conclude to remain here until the following day to rest ourselves and horses.

Wednesday, 9th.—This morning we start on our way for Pulaski, with a squad of guerrillas given into our charge before leaving Waynesboro, to take through to the Provost Marshal at Pulaski. A detail of the Fifth Tennessee accompany us. We go into camp for the night near Lawrenceburg. This evening a plot for the prisoners to break guard to-night is overheard by one of our men, and in consequence we are all compelled to be on guard, but no such attempt was made.

Thursday, 10th.—We arrive in Pulaski at noon to-day, and turn over our prisoners to the Provost Marshal and report to camp, having performed the journey without the loss of a man. All express themselves surprised to see us in Pulaski this evening, having given Lieutenant Roberts and squad up as captured, and candidates for some southern prison hell.

Friday, 11th.—This morning the regiment leaves Pulaski with three days' rations; Lieutenant Roberts and squad are ordered to remain in camp. Oh! how lonely here since the regiment has been out on the war line making inroads in West Tennessee and North Alabama.[142]

Wednesday, 16th.—A cold north wind is blowing all day. This evening the regiment comes in from its expedition—cold and hungry, but we see success beaming from every face, and soon we are told that the regiment met and routed the famous guerrilla Moorland and his band.[143] Killed ten and left them on the field, wounded about thirty, and captured forty prisoners, and strange to say without the loss of a man from the regiment. This can be accounted for from he fact of the superiority of our guns over those of the guerrillas at a long range. The boys are all in a glee over their scout, relating many incidents worthy of record. But we will only record one. Close by where our regiment encountered Moorland, two rebels entered a house to obtain their dinners, and in this house dwelt a young lady whose love for the old Union no one ever questioned. Though against her will, their dinners were prepared, and while eating, the young lady walks to the door and down the road she beholds the old Union's flag come flying. She immediately turns, seizes both guns and with one kills one of the rebels and with the other gun takes the other rebel prisoner, turning him over to our men when they advanced. Tell me not that woman is not performing her part in this war. Reader, will you believe me when I tell you that the world in all its knightly history, never produced brighter examples of heroism than have been produced in this southland during these years of terrible strife. The daughters of the south who love the bonny stars and stripes, deal with weapons of death; stemming war's wild current, braving what men have ever dared to brave, lending a helping hand to those who would perpetuate this union and save liberty from its final grave. We see her walking the battle field at the midnight hour where the messengers from the cannon's mouth have done their fearful work; we see her at the hospital where the angel of death lingers at the threshold waiting for life's brittle thread to break, when it could upon its wings bear the hero-spirits home to an approving God. We see her at the warrior's tomb, see her tears sparkle and her flowers fall on their silent mission of love and peace. Flowers of many hues from many hands, and tears from many heart fountains may fall there, but no brighter treasure, no holier tribute will ever be offered, than noble woman has already offered on the fallen soldier's hallowed tomb.[144]

Sunday, December, 20th.—To-day we receive the government's veteran propositions, which are now being discussed by the Seventh; whether the boys will catch the fever, remains to be seen.

Monday, 21st.—To-day a meeting of the regiment is called for the purpose of feeling its pulse, and it is found to beat to the veteran time. The ball is now rolling, old soldiers who have stood unblanched on many a battle field, seeing that war's storm king is still moving with fearful power, that the flag is still assailed and their second term of enlistment is drawing towards its end, are now re-enlisting and contracting for a third term of service.

Tuesday, 22d.—To-day the veteran spirit rages high. The chill winter winds are now blowing. We move through the Seventh's camp. There they stand shivering around the camp fires with no tents and scarcely any covering to shelter them from the winter frosts. Can it be possible that the men will contract to prolong this life of privations and arduous duties. But it is nevertheless a fact, the regiment is going almost to a man, showing the world examples that should move the mighty north as it has never before been moved, move it in such a way, that the southern army that to-day claims to be legion would be crushed into atoms.

Wednesday, 23d.—This morning Captain Ahern with two men from each company leave for Illinois to recruit for the regiment.[145] The entire regiment is now making preparations to go home on furlough, which is one of the conditions in the veteran contract. All are now busy preparing for muster, making out rolls, filling up enlistment papers, &c.[146]

Thursday, 31st.—The last week of 1863, the Seventh will never forget in mid-winter—standing in the rain, snow and storm anxiously waiting for the finishing of the rolls. This evening they are done; the cry is now for the mustering officers; all are anxious to start northward.

January 1st, 1864.—Sixty-four is ushered in bleak and rough. The year has died, but its blood-wrought history will live co-equal with time. The war clouds have hung long over a stricken people bringing sadness and tears to many a hearthstone; but the voice of the boys in blue now rolling from the tented field is positive. Shivering around the camp fires they say we will give the lie to modern democracy; we will show them that we are not tired of this "abolition war," that we will not leave the field while one hostile foe assails the flag.

"The mustering officer!"—"The mustering officer!" is now the universal cry. Colonel, can you not toll him out here? some one asks; "you know, Colonel, that he always goes where they have the best and the most for the 'neck'" utters one. But we will be compelled to wait his pleasure, for the colonel, as it happens, don't work with men in that style.

January 7th.—The weather still the same—cold and windy. The camp of the Seventh is indeed a place of suffering, but men of steel stand here, and despite the warring elements they manage to keep cheerful. Another long week of anxious waiting for the mustering officers has passed away. At last he comes. How welcome is his presence. This evening though they have long been veterans in practice, the Seventh is denominated by name the Seventh Illinois Veteran Volunteer Infantry. Thus ends our second enlistment, and commences our veteran organization.[147]

PART II.

VETERAN SERVICE.

Chapter XII.

Leaving Pulaski on Veteran furlough—Arrival at Springfield—The Reception—
The Regiment in the Representatives Chamber—Welcome speech of Governor
Yates—General Cook and the Seventh's old flag—General Cook's speech—The
hospitality of the people—The Seventh at home.

Corraling our horses and mules and leaving them in charge
of the non-veterans, the regiment on the 8th of January, with
drums beating, colors flying, and hopes beating high, march
from Pulaski, Tennessee. Arriving at Columbia we take the
cars for Nashville, where we remain in the Soldier's Home until transportation is furnished. Transportation being furnished
we proceed by rail to Louisville, Kentucky, where we remain
until we receive our pay and bounty—after which we cross the
Ohio and take the cars for Springfield, Illinois.

January 15th.—The train carrying the Seventh is now near
Springfield; soon we expect to meet a grateful people, who have
already been informed of the hour of our arrival. The train
moves slowly across Sangamon river, and as it emerges from
the timber and approaches the city we hear the cannon's roar.
The echoes roll across the prairie, telling to us that the great
loyal heart of Illinois still beats true for liberty and its defenders. The train moves into the Great Western depot, and a vast
crowd is now moving towards us. The patriot fathers are here;
mothers, sisters and lovers, with anxious throbbing hearts
whose pulses have ever beaten true for Union and liberty,
come like a beautiful sun-tinted wave against the Seventh.
Tears fall like dew drops for the loved and lost, who come not
back, but when the returning comrade says to that sister or
that maiden, "your Willie fought bravely on Shiloh's field, until
liberty in her trying hours claimed him upon her hallowed altar," their faces sparkle with holy light and they reply: "How
proud I am to know that they were thus brave soldiers in the
war for republican nationality." Oh! how noble these loyal

hearts that open so wide for the boys in blue. The regiment sways back the crowd and forms in line. Wheeling into company column, Colonel Rowett commences to move through the city; a grateful people continues to follow the regiment wherever they march; the men move firmly—their steps are even. Some one says "they are proud," and another replies, "and well may they be; for the record they have made in this crusade for freedom is enough to create within them a feeling of pride." After marching through some of the principal streets of the city, the colonel leads the regiment into the State House yard, where he forms the regiment in divisions and closes in mass. Our old Colonel, now Brigadier General, John Cook, commanding the military at Springfield, appears at one of the windows, and with his loud and familiar voice says: "Colonel Rowett, by the direction of Governor Yates, you will proceed with your regiment into the Representatives Chamber."[148] The hall is now densely crowded with the Illinois Seventh and her loyal men and women. Governor Yates now comes forward and in behalf of the loyal people of Illinois he says: "Welcome! Welcome, Seventh! to your homes and friends. The heart of this great commonwealth goes out in love for you, starting tears to the memory of those of your number whom you have left in the sunny south. Again I say in behalf of the loyal people, welcome, welcome Seventh." His big heart being so full he could say no more, and was compelled to sit down. Brigadier General Cook now comes forward, carrying on his arm the Seventh's old Donelson and Shiloh banner, and as he unfurled it in that chamber, those men who stood around it amid tempest and smoke, like a pillar of steel and fire, seemed to move towards it with all their hearts, for men never appeared to love a flag more; they loved it because of its associations, for when they gazed upon its shot-torn folds they remembered the eventful past, remembered the terrible battle flames through which it had been carried, remembered the loyal soldiers whose hearts ceased their pulsations beneath its shadow. General Cook commences to speak, and for one hour holds the vast audience spell-bound by his eloquence. He pays a touching tribute to the regiment's fallen, and we dare say a more beautiful tribute was never uttered in this chamber than this tribute delivered by General Cook. He spoke to the loyal heart, and it seemed that every word as fast as uttered entered there, for when he closed few eyes were dry in that vast audience. After a few apt and appropriate remarks by Colonel Rowett and Major Estabrook the audience disperses. The hotels are thrown open and the loyal people invite the regiment to throw themselves upon their hospitality during their stay in the city. Having free access, a portion of the regiment remains during the night in Representatives Hall.

Remaining in Springfield until the furloughs are issued the different companies on the 19th day of January, leave for their homes. We will now for a while leave the Seventh Illinois Veteran Volunteer Infantry with their friends, trusting that the loyal people will lavish upon them their hospitality and love in consideration of the noble part they have played thus far in the war for human freedom.[149]

Chapter XIII.

[February 18, 1864–June 1, 1864]

Rendezvousing at Camp Butler—Southward bound—Arrival at Louisville—
Arrival at Nashville—The Zollicoffer House—Arrival at Pulaski, Tennessee—
Marching orders—March to Florence, Alabama—Return to Pulaski,
Tennessee—Marching orders—March to Waynesboro—March to Raw Hide—
March to Florence—March to Baily Springs—March to Blue Water—Companies
H and K at Raw Hide—Company F at Cheatam's Landing—Headquarters at
Baily Springs—Companies H and K at Jackson's plantation—Arrival of
Company F at Jackson's plantation—Colonel Rowett's return to the regiment—
Captain Ring's detachment ordered to Center Star—Camp at Douglass'—Camp
at Taylor's—Camp at Williams'—The arrival of the supply train—The attack at
Shoal Creek—The crossing of Roddy—The fight at Florence—Rowett driven—
Captain Ring falling back across Elk River—Forming Junction at Florence,
Tennessee—The return to Florence—The march to Athens—Lieutenants
Sullivan and Rowett sent to Florence under flag of truce to negotiate an
exchange—The bad faith of the rebel Colonel Johnson—The regiment
dismounted.

"Southward, ho! How the grand old war-cry
Thunders over the land to-day,
Rolling down from the eastern mountains,
Dying in the west away.

Southward, ho! Bear on the watchword,
Onward march as in other days,
Till over the traitors' fallen fortress
The stripes shall stream and the stars shall blaze,
And the darkness fly from their radiant van,
And a mightier empire rise in grandeur
For freedom, truth, and the rights of man."

After mingling for a while so pleasantly with the good people of Illinois, enjoying their hospitality and receiving from
them many words of cheer, we rendezvous at Camp Butler,

February 18th.[150] While here we add to our rolls a large number of recruits. Noble men they are who have been waiting patiently to arrive at the necessary age for a soldier. That period having arrived, they now seem to feel proud in their uniforms of blue. Colonel Rowett having been by special order, (contrary to his wishes,) assigned to the command of Camp Butler, on the twenty-second of February the regiment, under the command of Major Estabrook, takes the cars for Dixie. Arriving at Louisville, Kentucky, we receive transportation for Nashville. On arriving there, we are furnished lodgings in the Zollicoffer House. The regiment will long remember the accommodations received there at the hands of the government contractors. How the bristling bayonets clashed together at the entrance, and how they practiced their expert chicanery to work their egress therefrom.

Remaining here until transportation is furnished, on the twenty-eighth we proceed on our way to Pulaski, Tennessee. The trains running all the way through, we arrive in our old camp at five P.M.; all seem glad to get back; the non-veterans are glad to see us, and hear from their friends at home; and even the mules send forth their welcome.

Monday, 29th.—All quiet to-day; the officers all busy equipping their companies. Soon we will be in the saddle in obedience to the call of the bugle.

March 6th.—Since our return to this land of cotton, sallow humanity and scotch snuff, the boys have been looking blue. The fond caresses and the beautiful smiles they received while among the loyal people, have well nigh spoiled the Seventh, but the bugle's blast, the whoop, the charge and the fray will soon give new vigor and point to the soldier's life; will soon draw their minds in from their wanderings and concentrate them on naught but the war line. Though they will not banish those images, they will think of them only secondary to war and victory. This evening we receive orders to be ready to move in the morning with six days' rations.

March 7th.—This morning we move early, heading as usual for North Alabama or West Tennessee; travel hard all day; pass through Rodgersville and go into camp for the night. The sky is cloudy; threatening rain.

March 8th.—This morning everything is wet, for it rained hard all night. A fine introduction to the new recruits, though all seem cheerful. We soon move from camp; marching on the military road leading to Florence, Alabama. We arrive at Florence in the afternoon, capture one rebel, and one seeking to make his escape gets killed. We go into camp close to Florence to await for transports that are expected up the Tennessee.

March 14th.—We are still in camp at Florence; no steamers have yet come up; don't look for any now; the river is low. Our rations have run out, and we are compelled to forage from the citizens, who are almost destitute themselves. Our pickets at the river keep up a continual firing with the rebel pickets on the opposite shore.

March 15th.—This evening we leave Florence; travel nearly all night; go into camp early in the morning, tired and sleepy.

March 16th.—This morning we proceed on our way to Pulaski; arrive in camp in the evening, very much worn by hard riding.

March 20th.—Since our return from the Northland, a dull monotony reigns in camp; nothing greets our ears but an occasional braying of some hungry mule and the rumbling of the waters over the mill-dam in Richland creek. All seems quiet with the military. We wonder if there will be any more blood made to flow in the South-land. There may be and there may not; God only knows. We would love to believe that ere long there shall be consummated an uncompromising peace, with the Union triumphant and traitors in the dust. Though things in and around camp are dull, the boys are cheerful and happy.

March 21st.—We again receive marching orders; Forest said to be crossing the Tennessee at Eastport. We are ordered to reconnoiter.[151] Oh! how sleepy the soldiers become; some fall off of their mules while riding along the road. About two o'clock, A.M., we come to a halt at Lawrenceburg, and feed and lay down to sleep, but very little do we obtain, for at day-light the bugle blows. The command is divided. Companies H and F, commanded by Captain Ring, proceed to Waynesboro; we find nothing hostile here. The report that Forrest was crossing the Tennessee has proved to have been only an idle rumor. We go into camp for the night. We feast to-night upon chickens, ham and honey. A scout is sent to Clifton, Tennessee river, this evening, to see and learn what he can about the movements of Forrest.

March 23d.—Still in camp in the woods near Waynesboro; we will remain here until the scout sent to Clifton, Tennessee river, returns. About nine o'clock the scout returns and reports all quiet on the river; we immediately leave Waynesboro, and after traveling briskly all day, go into camp five miles from Raw Hide.[152]

March 24th.—This morning we move on to Raw Hide; nothing to be found; we learn here that scouts from the regiment were here this morning in quest of Captain Ring's detachment. The regiment is reported to be at Florence, Alabama; we now lead out on the Florence road. In the evening we arrive at Florence, but find no regiment; we immediately move on to Baily Springs, nine miles from Florence and go into camp for the night. We learn here that the headquarters of the regiment is to-night on Blue Water.[153]

March 25th.—This morning it is raining; we are now out of rations; report to the regiment on Blue Water, where we go into camp and draw from the teams three days' rations, and after feeding and enjoying each a quart of fine coffee, as good (so we thought then) as any woman ever made, we again receive orders to saddle up and be off. We proceed back to Raw Hide, where we join Company K, who came before us in the morning. Our orders are to remain here and patrol the river between this point and Eastport.

March 26th.—This morning a squad of twenty men, under the command of Lieutenant Fergus, is sent out on a scout to Eastport, Tennessee river, and another squad, under the command of a non-commissioned officer, is sent to Cheatam's Landing, seventeen miles from Raw Hide. We make the point by noon; find Company F, Captain Knowlton, in camp here. Returning, we bring through a prisoner captured by Company F, who reports Forrest in Memphis and Longstreet in Knoxville.[154]

March 27th.—Our scouts and patrols are now continually picking up stray guerrillas. This morning Captain Ring sends to headquarters at Baily Springs, seven prisoners captured since our arrival here. Patrols are again sent to the Tennessee river, which now is a daily duty. Nothing new to-day, save some fine horses brought in this evening by the foraging parties. The Seventh is feasting high to-night.

Monday, 28th.—The details are now very heavy—patroling, foraging, scouting, &c.—but we live sumptuously upon what little fat of the land yet remains.

Tuesday, 29th.—The boys are scouring the country in every direction for horses and mules. All quiet this evening.

Wednesday, 30th.—To-day we move camp to the widow Jackson's plantation. This evening Captain Knowlton, with Company F, arrives from Cheatam's Landing and reports to Captain Ring. The detachment now consists of Companies F, H and K. We are now eight miles from the headquarters at Baily Springs, and eight miles from the Tennessee river. Orders are issued this evening to move at two o'clock in the morning.

Thursday, 31st.—Three o'clock, A.M., we move out on the Florence road; rebels reported crossing the river. At day-light we charge into Florence and intercept two rebels in the act of crossing the river to their command. Remaining in Florence a short time, we move out on the military road; proceeding a short distance a squad is sent to the residence of Dr. Riles, a rebel aider and abetter, whom they arrest, and with him and the two rebels captured at Florence, the squad is sent to regimental headquarters. In the evening the detachment returns to camp on the Jackson plantation.

April 1st.—Still we look out upon the fields of the South and behold the effects of desolating war. The plow is standing still; starvation and suffering are inevitable if the angel of peace comes not soon upon its mission to this stricken people.

April 7th.—Still at Jackson's plantation; duty heavy; daily patroling and scouting continued along the river. This evening a detachment is sent to Pulaski with dispatches; return to the detachment with a large mail, which seems to instil new life into the men. The little "billets" bring sunshine to the soldiers.

April 8th.—Negroes by the hundreds are flocking to our camp; all sizes and ages, ranging from one year to one hundred years old. Poor deluded beings, how extravagant have been their conceptions relative to the Yankees. An order from headquarters at Baily Springs this evening informs us that Colonel Rowett has fought himself away from Camp Butler and returned to the command of the regiment. Remaining in camp at Jackson's until the fifteenth, we leave and report to regimental headquarters. Immediately Captain Ring receives orders to proceed with the detachment to Center Star, where we arrive in the evening and go into camp, after which patrols are sent out to Bainbridge and Lamb's Ferry. This detachment will long remember their camp and stay at the Jackson plantation; how Captain R, Sergeants N. and A. made journeys across the Blue Water, and how the Captain when coming in contact with one of the South's fair literary stars, discoursed so freely upon the American and English poets—especially upon the merits of the Bard of Avon.[155]

April 16th.—Forage being scarce at Center Star, the detachment is to-day marched to Douglass' plantation. The patrols report all quiet on the river this evening.

Sunday, 17th.—For some unknown reason the detachment is to-day moved on to Taylor's plantation; a fine place, and we all agree that it is a happy change, for the command gains shelter here.[156]

Monday, 18th.—The detachment seems to be making itself at home at Taylor's. Our headquarters are in the parlor. Our host's heart is warm for "the glorious cause of the South." Has two sons, officers in the rebel army, and in consequence we conclude that we will live here for some days.

Tuesday, 19th.—Everything seems monotonous in camp this morning; nothing but the regular routine of camp and patrol duty greet us. All quiet this evening. Nature smiling, a warm sun, a soft south wind, makes us almost feel that we are not engaged in the puny strifes of war. Oh! for something to dispel the dull care; if it be rebels with bristling bayonets. Hark! we hear a voice tuned by a musical soul. Miss P—— seems defiant, singing her Southern collections, "God save the South," "Southern Red, White and Blue." We are inclined to admire her bold spirit, though the heart is with a desperate cause. Hearing this voice, we wonder if she, from whom it comes, would play for the "vandals." We will try her to-morrow.

Wednesday 20th.—Nothing new this morning; reported all quiet all along the Tennessee. "Now Lieutenant A——, we will have some music this morning," says Captain Ring as he moves from the room.[157] Will she refuse a Yankee officer, wonder the remaining occupants of the parlor. Hark! we hear footsteps; she is coming. She is now seated at the piano; she plays sweetly, but oh! the language, the sentiment; rebellion deep, defiant, loud, echoes from her soul. Her heart dwells fondly upon the "Bonnie South," but the gallant Union soldiers blame her not. Though her heart is with a cause which aims at the foundation of human freedom, she has had encouragement has been made to believe that the land of her birth is engaged in a righteous cause. The democracy of the North have given that encouragement. We will look among the old files of papers that lie here. What do we find? A number of Cincinnati Enquirers of old and new dates containing the speeches of Ohio's exiled traitor, These speeches have been eagerly read by the southern people, and upon their factious and treasonable sentiments they predict their hopes of Southern independence. Oh! modern democracy, what have you done, and what are you doing? You have strengthened the South in their wicked aims to subvert liberty and thereby shut the gates of mercy upon mankind.

April 25th.—Up to this date nothing of interest occurs; nothing but a dull monotony seems to reign in camp. The weather is warm; nature clothed in its heavenly beauty; the feathery tribe chattering songs of praise to their creator. We look out upon these fields and are made to ask ourselves the question: "Why the tramp of warriors here?" Something seems to answer, "Because wicked men were lured by an ambition to ride to power upon the crimson tide of blood.

April 26th.—We move camp to-day to Williams' plantation. Says our commander: "We will exhibit a sociableness and divide our visits while sojourning in the neighborhood.

May 5th.—Up to this time there has been quiet along the Tennessee; no hostile demonstrations apparent.[158]

May 6th.—Flat-boats have been seen floating down the Tennessee, which seems indicative of some hostile movements. The enemy may attempt to cross ere long; they may succeed despite our vigilance. This evening the supply train from Athens, Alabama, arrives at our camp on its way to regimental headquarters, now removed to Florence, Alabama; it will remain in our camp all night.

May 7th.—This morning the train proceeds on its way to Florence; gone but one hour when a courier comes dashing back to the detachment headquarters with the word "Attacked at Shoal Creek bridge! The train is in danger! Captain Ring, you are requested to send one company immediately to Captain Yeager's aid" (who was commanding the train and escort). Company F, Captain Ahern, is sent. The train is turned back towards our camp, where it soon after arrives. Company F reports back to Captain Ring with the intelligence that General Roddy and Colonel Johnson, with about fifteen hundred rebels, were now crossing the Tennessee; that their advance had crossed early in the morning and captured Sergeant Josiah Lee and squad, standing as a picket guard at Bainbridge Ferry; that they now occupied the road leading towards Florence.[159] The situation is critical. Rowett, with a part of the regiment at Florence, Estabrook with a part camped on Sweet Water, three miles northwest from Florence, Ring with three companies one mile beyond Shoal Creek and nine miles from Florence. We attempt to communicate with Rowett and Estabrook, but the courier returns with no news from them. We only know that they have been attacked by an overwhelming force.[160] Captain Ring, with his detachment and the regimental teams, remains on the opposite side of Shoal Creek from Florence, anxiously waiting to hear from Rowett. We are now convinced that he has been driven; we expect every moment that the rebels will be upon us. Lieutenant Fergus is now sent out with twelve men on a reconnoisance towards Shoal Creek. He soon comes up with a squad of rebels, when he boldly gives the command "forward." Driving the rebels a short distance, a company lying in ambush spring into the road and succeed in capturing the Lieutenant and private Joseph Burkhardt of Company F, who happened to be on horses in advance of the rest who were mounted on mules, and being in consequence unable to afford any relief, are compelled to beat a retreat to Center Star. Scouts now report to Captain Ring that a part of the rebel force is advancing towards us. It is now night; we know that Rowett has been driven from Florence; that to night he is some forty miles from us; we know that if we remain here until morning we will be compelled to confront two rebel battalions and a battery of artillery. Nine o'clock.—We are still lingering around Center Star as if loath to leave. The train is now headed towards Athens, Alabama. Ten o'clock. Captain Ring concludes for the safety of the command and the train to move on and cross Elk River. We travel all night, and early on the morning of the eighth find Elk River between us and Florence. We are now fifteen miles from Athens. Soon after crossing we go into camp to await orders. We are now distinguished as the army of the Elk. We receive a dispatch this evening informing us that Colonel Rowett has made his appearance at Pulaski, Tennessee, having lost from his command Captain McGuire of Company A, and Lieutenant Roberts of Company C, and thirty men, all taken prisoner.[161] The particulars of Rowett's engagement with Roddy we have not yet learned. We receive orders to-day to report to the commanding officer at Athens, where we arrive and go into camp late in the evening.[162]

Tuesday, 10th.—This morning Captain Ring receives a telegraphic dispatch from Colonel Rowett to proceed back to Elk River. The order obeyed, we go into camp in the evening on Dr. Blair's plantation.

Wednesday, 11th.—To-day parties are sent out to patrol along the Elk, and guard the crossings. This evening we receive a dispatch informing us that Rowett has moved from Pulaski on the road leading towards Lexington, Alabama.

Thursday, 12th.—This morning another dispatch informs us of the arrival of Colonel Rowett with his part of the regiment at Prospect, Tennessee, on the railroad, ten miles from Athens, Alabama. During the day, squads of rebels make their appearance on the opposite bank of Elk River, who fire a few random shots into our pickets. No damage done.

Friday 13th.—This morning Captain Ring receives orders from Colonel Rowett to report with his detachment to the regiment, now at Prospect, Tennessee, where we arrive by dark and join the regiment from which we have been for the last two months. Soon after going into camp we learn that there is another expedition to be started towards Florence, Alabama, commanded by our gallant Dick Rowett, to be composed of the Ninth Ohio Cavalry and the Seventh Illinois Mounted Infantry.

We will now go back and follow Rowett from Florence to Pulaski, thence to Prospect, Tennessee. As we stated, when Roddy crossed at Bainbridge Ferry, Rowett, with a portion of the regiment was in Florence, Estabrook in camp at Sweet Water, and Ring at Center Star.[163] Early on the morning of the seventh the rattle of musketry was borne to Rowett's ears from the direction of Bainbridge Ferry. In a moment he was on Charley and away towards Sweet Water, five miles from Florence, and two miles from the river. Arriving at Sweet Water he learns that a superior force, with two pieces of artillery, was on the north side of the Tennessee. Immediately Colonel Rowett dashes forward with Estabrook's detachment, consisting of companies E, B and C, to develop the strength of the enemy; finding it to be strong, Major Estabrook is ordered by Colonel Rowett to hasten back to Florence and bring out the remaining companies. In the meantime the companies on Sweet Water are routed, with the loss of Captain McGuire, Lieutenant Roberts and thirty men, all taken prisoner. The woods are now swarming with rebels. Rowett's attention is now directed to the train corraled at Florence, whither a retreat is ordered. Captain Hector Perrin being left to conduct the retreat, Rowett hastens on to Florence to make preparations for the worst. Fifteen hundred rebels, led by Roddy and Johnson, are now driving Captains Perrin and Smith towards Florence, yelling like so many infuriated demons. The train is soon put on the road and started towards Lawrenceburg. Eager for Rowett's capture, the rebels press hard. East of Florence, on a slight elevation, Captain Smith, with the invincible E, takes his position and gallantly holds in check for one-half hour the entire rebel command, thereby giving Rowett time to get the wagon train well on its way. Smith then brings up the rear on the Lawrenceburg road. The rebels continue to press hard; the crash of artillery makes the earth tremble on the road leading down to Lawrenceburg. About every half mile Rowett is compelled to halt and give battle to the rebels, who seem loath to let him escape. About eleven o'clock, the rebels having given up the pursuit, Rowett goes into camp between Raw Hide and Lawrenceburg. Some considerable time after going into camp, Captain Johnson, with his company, joins the Colonel, having been cut off at Florence from the main command. Passing by the way of Lawrenceburg, Rowett arrived in Pulaski, Tennessee, on the eighth. On the ninth he gets part of his stock shod. On the tenth he leaves Pulaski, Tennessee, for Prospect *via* Lexington, Alabama leaving Estabrook with the unshod mules and the teams at Pulaski. The Colonel, with his command, swims Elk River in the evening in the midst of a terrible storm; a hazardous undertaking, but information had reached the Colonel that the rebels were aiming to head him off and to burn the large railroad bridge spanning the Elk at Prospect. Early on the morning of the eleventh he reached Prospect in time to save the weakly guarded bridge from rebel wrath. Though we were not with the Colonel, we judge from the appearance of the men accompanying him, that he passed through some fierce hours. A colonel with less bravery than Colonel Rowett would have faltered had he stood like he did in that raging storm on the banks of the Elk River, and beheld its frightful current. But duty demanded it; the safety of the bridge at Prospect required it. Thus urged on, Rowett led and his men followed, and the daring deed was accomplished. It now seems that all the rebel force in North Alabama lent their aid for the sole purpose of capturing Dick Rowett and his regiment, who have in the last twelve months been a terror to them in that region. All are in fine spirits to-night. Edwin M. Stanton's war bulletin—how cheering to the soldiers.[164]

May 14th.—This morning Colonel Rowett, with the Ninth Ohio Cavalry and the Seventh Illinois Mounted Infantry, leave Prospect on the road leading towards Lexington, Alabama.

May 15th.—This morning we move early, the Ninth Ohio taking the advance. We strike the Huntsville road south of Center Star, and soon learn that Major Williams, with his battalion, is in camp on the Douglass plantation.[165] Colonel Rowett, with the advance of the Ninth Ohio, soon comes upon their pickets. The rebel battalion being saddled ready to start to church, upon seeing Colonel Rowett advancing, are soon in their saddles and away towards the Tennessee where they plunge in and succeed in making their way on to Cedar Island, and thence to the opposite shore. Charging upon their rear at the river the Ninth Ohio capture twelve prisoners, with the loss of one man killed.

Monday 16th.—This morning Colonel Rowett moves with the command towards Florence, leaving Company H, Captain Ring, near Cedar and Cox's Island to guard the crossings. This morning Company H buries the Ninth Ohio Cavalry's fallen soldier, who was killed yesterday evening. We lay him in a lonely place beneath the drooping branches of a large tree on the bank of the Tennessee. Though he is an Ohio soldier, we care for him with the same interest as we would were he one of our own company, and why should we not, since he has been a brave warrior, fighting in the same common cause beneath the same starry banner. A dispatch from Rowett this evening informs us that Roddy crossed the Tennessee last night at twelve o'clock; that he would not fight Rowett on an equal footing.[166] This evening Colonel Rowett arrested Buckee and Judge Foster as hostages for the delivery of Dr. McVay, now held by the rebels because of his devotion to the old Union.[167]

Tuesday, 17th.—To-day one company of the Ninth Ohio Cavalry reports to Captain Ring. The remainder of Rowett's command is now deployed along the Tennessee River to intercept squads of rebels on the north side of the river, seeking to cross to their commands. Late in the evening Rowett arrives with his force at Center Star. Our rations are now out and in consequence the soldiers are making heavy requisitions upon the citizens, who no doubt before morning will come to the conclusion that they have not gained much by inviting Roddy and Johnson across the Tennessee to drive Dick Rowett and his troopers from North Alabama. How true it is "that every dog has his day." At ten o'clock P.M., we receive orders to report immediately to Athens, Alabama.[168] We are soon in the saddle and on the road. We travel all night and cross Elk River early in the morning, and arrive and go into camp at Athens nine o'clock A.M.[169]

May 22d.—To-day Lieutenants Sullivan and Rowett are sent with a flag of truce into North Alabama, to negotiate an exchange for our men who were captured on the seventh. Upon promise that our men would be sent to Decatur the following day, Lieutenant Sullivan surrenders up to Colonel Johnson the rebel prisoners captured by us in North Alabama, and returns to Athens.[170]

May 23d.—Instead of sending our men as per promise, Colonel Johnson, C. S. A., sends a squad of Federal soldiers belonging to other regiments whose term of service would soon expire, thus breaking his pledge of faith. Most honorable man; a true type of chivalry. Thou art worthy a medal.

June 1st.—We receive orders to turn over to the Division A. Q. M., our long eared friends, which causes us all to give a sigh, for they have been faithful in many things.[171] Troops are now daily passing through Athens on their way South. From day to day we look for orders that will tell us to move. On the fourteenth they come. Our faces will soon be turned towards the far sunny South, where the angry passions of men run high, and ere long we anticipate days of fiery strife—days that will be marked with fearful sacrifice. May God be with us.

Chapter XIV.

[June 15, 1864–September 8, 1864]

Leave Athens for Chattanooga—Arrival at Chattanooga—Lookout Mountain—
Seventh boys on its Summit—Leaving Chattanooga—Camp on Chicamauga—
Moving down the Railroad—Camp at Tunnel Hill— Camp at Tilton—Leaving
Tilton for Rome—Camp on the Elwood river—Building barracks—The attack
by the guerrillas on foragers—Scout of the Seventh and Fiftieth Illinois in the
direction of Kingston.

On the evening of the 15th we take the cars for Chattanooga. All are in fine spirits, and as we move from Athens we
are wont to say, farewell mules! farewell North Alabama! Arriving at Stephenson the train stops until morning, when it
again moves on its way southward. We are now approaching
Chattanooga. Lookout Mountain is seen looming up in the dim
distance—it presents to the eye of the soldier an impressive
grandeur, impressive because on its highest pinnacle, a flag
honored and loved by earth's struggling people is flying as it
were in the atmosphere of heaven. Arriving at Chattanooga we
leave the train and march outside the city limits and go into
camp for the night.[172]

June 17th.—It is said we will remain here for a few days.
All is quiet this morning. Our camp is at the foot of Lookout
Mountain, in the Chattanooga valley. As we look around we
are reminded that blood has flowed and noble men died here.
Uncoffined graves dot the valley and the mountain side, and
here these hallowed mounds will ever appear as landmarks to
guide those who have for long weary years sighed for human
freedom.

To-day the Seventh boys wend their way up Lookout Mountain; it is a wearisome task; up and up we climb. Soon we are
above the clouds where Hooker's bayonets clashed in midnight
darkness, when the mountain was wrapped in one grand sheet
of battle flame. We are now on Point Lookout looking down in
the valley. Lowering clouds hide from our view the landscape;

presently the clouds vanish and we now behold Chattanooga and her fortifications beneath our feet; the winding Tennessee, the current of which is moving on towards the father of waters to tell its silent story of blood, and Mission Ridge where warriors moved in the grand pageantry of battle, flinging to the wind a hundred union battle flags. We now turn our eyes towards the Chicamauga, the river of death. As our eyes fall there we remember how General George H. Thomas mastered Longstreet and saved the army of the Cumberland from defeat. As we stand here looking down to where he stood that fearful day, we imagine we see him or them watching the dust as it rose from the feet of Gordon Granger's command. That was a moment of suspense, and we know that General Thomas's heart leaped with joy when Captain Thomas dashed from that cloud of dust to his side with the compliments of General Gordon Granger.

We now descend the mountain side over the rugged cliffs and rocks that have been stained with human gore. Brave men sleep beneath these rocks, but Lookout Mountain will ever stand as monument to their memory, and through the eventful years to come will guard this fearful silence from tempest and storm.[173]

Monday, 20th.—We receive orders this morning to move, which are hailed with cheers from the Seventh. We proceed to the Chattanooga depot where we take the cars and are soon moving towards Atlanta. We are all expecting that ere it is night we will be away down in Georgia, but alas we are disappointed. The train stops at Griggsville and the regiment is ordered off. Many rumors are now flying about the railroad being cut. About Wheeler's demonstration, all seems dark and mysterious to the soldier.[174]

Tuesday, 21st.—We are now camped upon the banks of Chicamauga, a name that has gone to history inscribed with deeds of blood. This evening companies D, H and I receive marching orders, and under the command of Lieutenant Sullivan of company I, (the captains of companies having been left back at Athens to settle their mule accounts with the A. Q. M.) we now move down the railroad. We stop and draw rations at Ringgold, after which we move on about two miles and go into camp for the night. The country every where along the railroad is all desolated. Trains pass up this evening from Atlanta loaded with wounded soldiers from Sherman's army, which tell us that there has been a fearful work of blood down there.

Wednesday, 22d.—This morning Co. H move on to Tunnel Hill and go into camp in a brick church. It seems that the regiment is being deployed along the railroad to do guard duty, and in consequence the boys are not in a very good humor.

Thursday, 23d.—This morning the regiment with the exception of Companies D, H and I, pass down on the train to Tilton, leaving orders for these three remaining companies to follow.

Friday, 24th.—To-day companies D, H and I, leave Tunnel Hill on the cars for Tilton, where we arrive late in the night. We remain here guarding the railroad, scouting and running after guerrillas until July 8th, when we take the cars for Rome, Georgia, to join our division and brigade stationed there. Arriving at Kingston we change cars for Rome, where we arrive on the evening of the 9th. We immediately cross the Etawah river and go into camp one-half mile from the city.[175]

Sunday, 10th.—All quiet this morning, weather intensely hot. Rome is a beautiful town situated on the Etawah river, and is now converted into one vast hospital for the wounded and sick soldiers of the army of the Cumberland.[176]

Monday, 11th.—This morning the regiment receives orders to build barracks, and we are told that we will remain here during the summer. On the 14th our barracks are finished and the regiment cosily quartered therein. The picket line is now affording considerable attraction. The citizens are making daily pilgrimages thither with produce of every kind to trade to the soldiers, and now and then some one becomes victimized by some shrewd trader.

On the 1st day of August Major Estabrook with Lieut. Pool of Company B, Captain Lawyer of Company C, Captain McGuire of Company A, Captain Clark of Company D, Lieutenant McEvoy of Company D, Captain Knowlton of Company F, Captain Yeager of Company G, Lieutenant Sayles of Company G, Captain Ring of Company H, Lieutenant Pegram of Company H, Lieutenant Fisher of Company I, Lieutenant Judy of Company E, and the non-veterans of the different companies, leave for the north for muster-out and final discharge from the service; their term of service having expired on the 25th of July, 1864.[177] We all regret to see these officers and men leave the regiment; for we remember that in dark days they stood with us: that when the flag trembled and brave men were dying, they were never found wanting. They have now finished their contract—have performed their part, and performed it well. Some bear upon their persons honorable scars, which tell a silent story. Farewell, gallant men.

August 15th.—To-day Colonel Rowett assumes command of the Third Brigade, consisting of the Seventh, Fiftieth and Fifty-seventh Illinois Infantry, and the Thirty-ninth Iowa Infantry, with head-quarters in Rome.[178]

August 19th.—Up to this morning nothing has transpired to disturb the quiet of our camp near Rome; but this afternoon a little excitement is created in camp by the attacking of a foraging party sent out in the morning under the command of acting-Lieutenant Billington of Company C, which resulted in the killing by the guerrillas of acting-Lieutenant Billington of Company C, and the wounding of privates William Ross and Frits of company D, and Dr. Felty of the hospital department, and the loss of all the mules belonging to the teams. Companies H and K are despatched at once to the scene of death and robbery, but no guerrillas are to be found, all having fled in great haste. The fray happened at a noted rebel's house, to which we apply the torch, and return to camp.[179]

Sunday Afternoon, August, 21st.—Six companies of the Seventh, and six companies of the Fiftieth Illinois Infantry, under the command of Colonel Rowett, leave Rome on a scout. We march about nine miles out on the Kingston road and go into camp for the night. Hogs, chickens, roasting-ears and fruit abound in abundance. We live high to-night. After all is quiet in camp, scouts are sent out to see if they cannot discover something hostile said to be threatening these parts.

Monday morning the scouts return to camp reporting nothing threatening in the country, whereupon we return to camp, thus ending another "wild goose chase."

On the 8th of September the regiment moves camp across the Etawah, north of Rome, where they are again ordered to build barracks. The boys are fast becoming apt workmen in architecture. After building quarters and remaining in them a few days we are again ordered back across the Etawah and the third time we build barracks since our arrival at Rome; but in these we remained quietly until Hood commenced his movement northward. For awhile we will leave Rome, and invite the reader to go with us to the Allatoona Pass.[180]

The regiment is now armed with the Henry repeating rifle (sixteen shooter,) which were obtained by the men at their own expense. These examples of self-sacrifice are worthy of loyal commendation.

Chapter XV.

[October 1864]

The situation—Hood's retrograde movement—Gen. Corse ordered from Rome to the Allatoona Pass—Arrival in the evening—Finding the garrison surrounded—Preparations for battle—Battle of the Allatoona Pass—Companies E and H deployed on Skirmish line—The demand for surrender—The skirmish line ordered back—Rowett's command in the outer works—Captain Smith holding at bay one rebel regiment—The desperation of the rebels—The retreat to the fort—The fearful sacrifice—The first charge—General Corse wounded—Colonel Rowett assumes command—The first rebel charge repulsed—Rowett's first order—The attempt by the rebels to burn the two million rations—The second charge—The second repulse—The third charge—Sherman on Kenesaw Mountain—Sherman's dispatch to General Corse—The third repulse—The fourth charge—Colonel Rowett's fort at Slaughter-pen—The rebels compelled to give way in despair—Colonel Rowett wounded—Captain Rattrey assumes command—The Seventh with their sixteen-shooters—The close of the battle— The dead and wounded in Rowett's fort—Companies E, H and K on picket—The rain—The list of casualties—Honorable mention—Burying the dead—Caring for the wounded—Return to Rome—Death of the Seventh's drummer boy— Hood contriving to move northward—General Sherman—Indications of some gigantic movement.

On Monday, the third of October, it was known to General Sherman that General Hood, with thirty thousand foot and ten thousand horse, supplied with the necessary munitions of war to give battle, was on the north side of the Chattahoochee River, moving northward. Never before in the annals of American history had there been such a succession of startling events. The bridge over the Chattahoochee and been washed away in a storm, Forrest had severed communications between Chattanooga and Nashville, drift-wood had leveled the bridge spanning the Austanula River at Resaca, and a large body of rebel cavalry held Big Shanty. Such was the situation when the stars peeped out from their ether bed in the clear blue sky

Monday morning. It was apparent to Sherman that Hood would throw a considerable force against the weak garrison at Allatoona Pass, where were stored over two million of rations. Sherman knew if these were taken his men would be in a perilous condition. A commander with less resources than General Sherman would have contemplated the situation with horror; but not so with the hero of Rocky Face, Kenesaw and Atlanta. Signaling from the summit of Kenesaw, thirty miles across the country, to General Corse, commanding at Rome, he directs him to take all his available force to the Allatoona Pass, and hold it against all opposition until he (Sherman) himself could arrive with help.[181] In compliance with these orders General Corse, with the Twelfth Illinois Infantry and Colonel Rowett's brigade, consisting of the Seventh, Fifteenth and Fifty-seventh Illinois Infantry, and the Thirty-ninth Iowa Infantry, in all about fifteen hundred, proceeds by rail towards the Allatoona hills, where we arrive late in the night and find that one division from Hood's army, commanded by General French, was already surrounding the place.[182] The train that carried Corse and his fifteen hundred might have been checked. The enemy saw the train approaching and permitted it to pass in unmolested, thinking it was a train from Chattanooga loaded with supplies for Sherman's army, and therefore would make a fine addition to their game, which with their overwhelming force they were considering as good as captured. Sad, sad mistake was this, as the sequel will show. As soon as the train moves through the pass the regiment leaps from the train; General Corse and Colonel Rowett soon form their battle lines, making all necessary dispositions for the threatening battle, after which the men are ordered to lie down upon the ground to rest; but it is a night before the battle and the soldiers cannot rest. Men are hurrying to and fro; their voices are hushed, for thought is busy with them all; they are thinking of the coming strife, thinking whether they will live to see the old Union's battle flag float over these hills triumphant; thinking of the sables of grief that will be unfolded in memory of those who will lie down to sleep death's silent sleep ere the sun sinks again beneath the ocean's wave.

"Day is dawning dimly, grayly;
In the border of the sky;
And soon the drum will banish
Sleep from every soldier's eye."

The sun is now rising from behind the eastern hills. The rebels have been at work all night preparing for the assault. Companies E and H, commanded by Captain Smith, are now deployed forward on a skirmish line down the railroad south of the depot. A demand for General Corse to surrender is now made by General French. Says he to Corse: "I have Allatoona surrounded by a superior force, and to stay the needless effusion of blood I demand your surrender." General Corse replies: "I am prepared for the 'needless effusion of blood.'" Firing soon commences upon the skirmish line from the south, and directly a rebel battery opens with grape and canister upon our line, killing one man belonging to Company H—private John Etterline, the first to fall in Allatoona's great battle.[183] About ten o'clock we discover the enemy massing their forces on the Cartersville road west of the railroad. Colonel Rowett perceiving that the main battle would be on his front, sent Captain Rattray, of his staff to order the companies forming the skirmish line south, to report to the regiment immediately.[184] The skirmish line falls back in order, contesting manfully every foot of ground.

"Hark! A roaring like the tempest!
'Tis a thundering of the war steeds!
Like a whirlwind on they're rushing;
Let them come, but come to die;
Finding foemen ever ready
For the fry, but not to fly."

We cast our eyes to the south-east and behold a heavy force moving towards the depot. This force soon strikes our left and forces it back. The whole rebel force, six thousand strong, is now sweeping on to the Allatoona hills. The Seventh Illinois and the Thirty-ninth Iowa are standing like a wall of fire in the outer works to the right and left of the Cartersville road.

The storm breaks upon them in all its mad fury; the Seventh is now struggling against the reckless rush of the infuriated rebels that are swarming towards their front. The sixteen-shooters are doing their work; the very air seems to grow faint as it breathes their lurid flame. Colonel Rowett soon after the first onset discovers a rebel regiment charge on to the right flank from the northwest threatening to sweep it back like so much chaff. Captain Smith, with noble Company E, is ordered to stem the wild tide in that direction. In a moment he doubles into confusion this rebel regiment. It is soon discovered that it will be madness to attempt to hold the weakly constructed outer works. A retreat is ordered; the Seventh and Thirty-ninth Iowa fall back slowly; rebel shot are plowing great furrows in the earth; rebel shot fill the air; they fly everywhere; men are falling; the ground is being covered with the dead and dying. Colonel Rowett is taken to the fort wounded, from which he soon recovers and vigorously enters into the fight. The forts were gained by a fearful sacrifice. Colonel Rowett, with the Seventh and a few companies of the Fifty-seventh and Twelfth Illinois and the Thirty-ninth Iowa, is now in the fort, west of the railroad. Colonel Toutellotte, with the Ninety-third Illinois, Fiftieth Illinois (Colonel Hanna's old half hundred), takes possession of the fort east of the railroad.[185] General Corse takes his position in the fort with Colonel Rowett's brigade, where seems to be the main drift of battle. The retreat into the forts and the necessary dispositions were all performed in a moment—performed amid fire and smoke, while noble men were dying. The hurried retreat into the fort seemed to encourage the demons.

> "At once they raised so wild a yell,
> As if all the fiends from heaven that fell
> Had pealed the banner cry of hell."

On, on, with fiendish yells they come rushing to the breach. Over the hills and up the ravines they charge; it is now hand to hand, man to man; Colonel Rowett and his men fight desperately. General Corse is now wounded; he has been fighting manfully; man never before stood as he stood in this scene of death; never before contended as he contended against these fearful odds. Fainting from loss of blood, he has fallen back upon the blood stained ground. It is now half-past ten o'clock. Colonel Rowett assumes command; his first order is to send for Colonel Hanna and his "half hundred." He knows they are the true steel. By the severe fire from the fort west of the railroad the enemy's lines are broken. Colonel Hanna is now cutting his way to Rowett's fort. Crossing the railroad near the depot, he strikes the enemy attempting to burn the warehouse containing the two millions of rations and in a gallant manner drives them back; he rushes into Rowett's fort with a heavy loss. The rebels are now preparing for another desperate charge; reformed, they rush up like mad men threatening to crush into dust the gallant fifteen hundred.

> "I heard the bayonets' deadly clang,
> As if a hundred anvils rang."

The hills tremble; the fort is wrapped with fearful flame. Amid dying groans the cannon crashes, to sweep down the angry rebels to a suicidal death. The grand one-half hundred, the reckless Seventh, the undaunted Fifty-seventh Illinois, and the fiery Thirty-ninth Iowa, barricade the Allatoona walls with their frightful steel. Men are falling; their life blood is streaming. The rebels driven to desperation, attempt to cross the defences, but they are thrown back in wild confusion. But lo! they are rallying again, preparing for a third charge. Again they rush on to engage in the awful work of carnage. The smoke from our cannons makes wrathful heaves. Terrible red hot flames of battle shoot from the hill. During the last three hours an interested spectator has been standing upon Kenesaw, watching the progress of the battle. Soon a dispatch is read in the fort:

> "Hold Allatoona! hold Allatoona, and I will assist you.
> (Signed)   W. T. SHERMAN."

Closer and closer the determined rebels come; Many have already fallen. Weaker and weaker the command is becoming. The Seventh, with their sixteen-shooters, which has been the

main dependence, is now running short of ammunition, and
Colonel Rowett orders them to hold their fire, and let the Fiftieth Illinois and the Thirty-ninth Iowa bayonet the rebels in
case they attempt again to scale the defences. General Corse,
as brave a spirit as ever battled in the cause of human freedom,
raises from his matress and cries "Hold Allatoona! hold Allatoona." The third time the rebels are driven back from the fort;
they are now preparing for the fourth charge; Colonel Rowett's
fort has become one vast slaughter-pen. But look! the frenzied
rebels come swarming on to the breach again. This is the hour
that will try our steel. They are now passing over their already
beaten road, stained with blood. Again they are charging up to
crush the Spartan band. It is now one o'clock; for three long
hours clouds of darkness have mantled these hills; they now
seem to be growing darker. The command is every moment
growing weaker and weaker; a large portion of the fifteen hundred have been killed and wounded, and still the battle rages
in its mad fury; still the besieged are pressed hard. Colonel
Rowett now succeeds in getting the artillery loaded and
manned, which for some time has been silent. It is shotted to
the muzzle; all ready, the men are commanded to raise the yell,
and into the very faces of the rebels the death messengers are
hurled, which is repeated several times until the rebels commence to give way in despair. Just at this moment, half-past
one o'clock, Colonel Rowett is badly wounded in the head. Captain Rattray, a member of his staff, being the ranking officer
left, now assumes command and heroically carries on the battle. The awful work of death is drawing to a close; the rebels are
now flying. The Seventh, with their sixteen-shooters, are performing a terrible work of death; the enemy is driven from the
Allatoona hills like chaff before the winds of heaven.

> "None linger now upon the plains,
> Save those who ne'er shall fight again."

The great battle of Allatoona is now over; the six thousand
rebels, save those who are dead and wounded, are now retreating in commotion from the Allatoona hills. Corse, Rowett and
Tourtellotte, with the survivors of the gallant fifteen hundred,

fling their tattered and blood washed banners triumphantly over this field of death. As victors of the Pass they stand with about half of their number lying dead and wounded at their feet. We now look around us and behold the forts dripping with blood. Who do we see lying here, cold and stiff? It is our comrade, Samuel Walker. We cast our eyes to another spot; who is that who lies there in such agony, so fearfully wounded? It is the brave Sergeant Edward C. Nichols. Gallant spirit, we fear it will soon take its flight from its tenement of clay. Noble soldier, thy work is done; no more will you be permitted to stand in war's tempest of fire; no more will you battle in this struggle for man's equality. We attempt to move through the fort defended by Colonel Rowett's brigade, and we find it almost impossible without trespassing upon the dead. Oh! what an awful work of death! Has the blood-wrought history of the nineteenth century equaled it! We think not, and we dare say that this generation will pass away ere another Allatoona shall be given to the history of the western world. We succeed in changing our position. Who do we see here, wounded and bleeding? we look again. Our heart beats quick. 'Tis the Hackney brothers, lying side by side. We are wont to say, here we see the embodiment of manhood. They looked like boys before the battle, but they look like men now. Look at that cheek, behold that frightful gash. 'Tis a mark of royalty. When future years shall have rolled down the stream of time, and when the country is at peace, on that cheek will be a scar that will lead the mind back to the eventful years that saw this nation leap like a giant from her thralldom of tyranny. Night now comes on, and soon it commences to rain. The larger companies, E, H and K, with what men they have left, are placed on picket. This is the most doleful night that ever dawned upon the Seventh. While we stand here on these hills, amid storm and rain, our hearts are sad when we look around and see so many of our number still and cold in death, and so many wounded and dying.

> "Ah! this morning how lightly throbbed
> Full many a heart that death has robbed
> Of its pulses warm, and the caskets lie
> As cold as the winter's starless sky."

But we all feel glad to-night to know that we hurled back from the pass Hood's angry hosts; that we sustained the flag, saved the two millions of rations, saved Sherman's army, and helped to save the Union. While out here in these dark woods, while the cold winds are blowing, we are thinking of our noble comrades who were wounded to-day. We know that they are suffering to-night. We are all anxious about the gallant Rowett, for the Surgeon tells us that he is dangerously wounded. The prayer of the Seventh to-night is that he may recover; that he may yet live to lead forth, if need be, the gallant old Third Brigade in other battles in the war for the Union.

The morning of the sixth dawns beautifully, but upon a field of death—a field of blood; but thanks be to God, it dawns with the old flag triumphant. We will again walk among the dead and wounded. The loss of the Seventh has been fearful. At Fort Donelson, Shiloh and Corinth our loss was heavy, but our loss in this battle exceeds our whole loss in those three great battles. The following list of the Seventh's casualties in this battle will speak for itself; will alone tell how fierce was the storm of battle that raged on these hills.

STAFF.—*Wounded:* Colonel R. Rowett, in the head, severely; Adjutant J. S. Robinson, severely.

COMPANY A.—*Killed:* Corporal Henry C. Hasson. *Wounded:* Sergeant James O'Donnell.

COMPANY B.—*Killed:* Privates Philip Saules, Jonathan Bishop; *Wounded:* private John Hunter.

COMPANY C.—*Killed:* Privates Andrew Hellgoth, John McAlpine; Corporal John B. Hubreht.

COMPANY D.—Company D was left at Rome on guard duty, therefore was not with the regiment at the Allatoona Pass.

COMPANY E.—*Killed:* Privates James F. Burk, George W. Eversole, Michael F. Galbraith, Marion R. Kampf, Francis Love, David Roberts, Lewis C. Stroud, Calvin A. Summers, John W. Watt, W. H. Burwell, Lewis J. Allman, Levi Allen, Ezra M. Miller, Elias Hainline, Leonidas Burkholder, Corporal William Smith. *Wounded:* Sergeant and Color Bearer Joseph Bordwell; Privates L. D. Barnes, George G. Brooks, Lewis A. Burk, Abner W. Burwell, Samuel H. Ewing, Angelo V. Faucett, Albert Gardner, Phillip J. Gossard, John F. Hainline, James A.

Hedges, George Sullivan, Edwin R. Jones, Thomas Gardner, A. N. Roelofson, James M. Allman, John L. Forbes, Joseph Lancaster, Eli Mushrush, Samuel M. Watt. Corporal Henry C. Montjoy; *Taken Prisoner:* N. A. Bovee, Samuel H. Jones, William E. Verry, William H. Miller.

COMPANY F.—*Killed:* Privates Philip Hale, John Phillips, Henry M. Robbins, Eldridge Walton, Nathan D. Atchison. *Wounded:* Privates James Kelley, Robert B. Kelley, George Brenton; Sergeant John McTurk.

COMPANY G.—No separate record given—consolidated with Company I.

COMPANY H.—*Killed:* Corporal Samuel Walker; Privates Henry Bigler, John Etterline, William T. Taylor, John White, Timothy Hoblitt, James L. Parish. *Wounded:* Sergeant William P. Hackney, severely; Edward C. Nicholas, severely; Privates Oscar J. Hackney, slightly; John E. J. Wood, severely; Richard P. Graham, severely; James M. Halbert, slightly; Aaron Watkins, slightly; Ferdinand Capps, severely. *Taken Prisoner:* Thomas Caylor, William R. Skiver, George W. Ballard.

COMPANY I.—*Killed:* First Lieutenant John E. Sullivan, Sergeant Charles Myres, Corporal William Ecker, Privates John W. Johnson, Ira Carey. *Wounded:* Privates Daniel O'Keefe, Alfred Scott, James Andrews, George Harris, William Massey.

COMPANY K.—*Killed:* Privates E. Thompson, Martin V. Kelton, Jesse C. Botkins. *Wounded:* Corporals John W. Bowman, Walter smith; Privates Grundy McClure, Thesbold Steinberg, Lewis P. Moore, Albert H. Duff, John P. Van Dyke, Julius Wolf. Total Killed, 42, total wounded, 53.[186]

Though the Union loss is heavy, though Illinois, Iowa and Minnesota, offered a fearful sacrifice; we behold in looking around us a great many more of the traitors weltering in their gore. Six hundred rebels poured out their life blood—poured it out upon these hills for naught—six hundred lie still in death, and as many more are wounded. Ah! what an ill-fated field Allatoona has been to them. "They came for bread; Corse gave them war and lead." Their wounded tell us they never fought such men. Says a rebel officer, "I believe those Illinois and Iowa boys who were in yonder fort (pointing to the fort General Corse, Colonel Rowett and his Third Brigade occupied,) would have all died before they would have surrendered." All day the 6th we are engaged caring for the wounded and burying the dead. On the hill the Seventh bury their fellow-heroes. The regiment is now small, the survivors look sorrowful; now and then we see tears steal down the bronzed cheeks to fall and perish upon the lonely graves. Praises for Colonel Rowett are on every tongue. Allatoona tells us that no braver warrior ever drew a sword in battle. In the thickest of the conflict he was ever found, cheering his men when disaster threatened, leading amid dire confusion. In Allatoona's great battle he stood by the flag, and around him and it his men rallied; rallied to fall and die; rallied to see it victorious. But how sad were his men when they saw him fall; when they saw him bleeding; when they saw him fainting from loss of blood. But remembering his words of cheer; remembering his command to die rather than let the flag be lowered; his men struggled on and proved themselves true to their Colonel and their flag, and the sun went down with the fifteen-hundred triumphant, and that evening the Union's proud banner looked more beautiful than it had ever before looked—more beautiful because it stood upon another victorious field.

Lieutenant John E. Sullivan, of Company I, fell fighting like a Spartan. Heroically he braved the frightful tempest and went down crowned all over with laurels of glory. He fell mortally wounded in the early part of the day, and died about ten o'clock the next morning. We were called to his side as his last moments of life were drawing nigh. Says he, "Give my sword to the gallant William Hackney of Company H," (which company he commanded until he fell.) "Brave men, I will soon leave you,—will soon pass the river of death." We stood by his side again, but his spirit had departed, and the noble warrior was free from the angry strife of men.

Lieutenant John S. Robinson, A. A. A. G. on Colonel Rowett's staff, was severely wounded during the last charge of the rebels, and no one performed his part more gallantly in this great battle than did this officer.[187] Where the battle raged fiercest there he was ever found. He was standing by the side of Colonel Rowett, struggling against the wild tide of battle as but few men have ever struggled in this terrible war, until the scales began to show signs favorable to the fifteen-hundred, when he was stricken down, (which was but a short time before the battle closed.) He is dangerously wounded and we fear his days will soon be numbered. Courageous soldier! we can only say of him he was true; that he did his duty, and did it well.

Colonel Hanna, the dashing commander of the Fifteenth Illinois, was among the most conspicuous in this battle. With his impetuous and irresistible regiment he stood as firm as a gigantic rock, and against his front of bristling steel French's hungry rebels hurled themselves, but in vain did they attempt to crush the gallant "half-hundred," for when the fearless Hanna threw himself into the most dangerous ordeal, making his clarion voice heard above the loud din of battle, the eyes of his brave men grew brighter and each heart was kindled with the fire that ever warms the patriot's heart. We remember when the very air was red with flame, when the earth was strewn with the mangled dead, when the sun seemed to be hid behind an awful sheet of fire; how anxiously we watched Colonel Hanna moving with his regiment from beyond the railroad to the support of Colonel Rowett. Oh! that was a trying hour; the leaden hail flew thick and fast; it was a march of death, for ere they reached Colonel Rowett's fort many of their number had fallen. But how glad were the men of the Seventh Illinois when that grand old regiment rushed into the fort and waved over the ramparts their shattered battle flag. It was a glorious hour, glorious because we felt encouraged and strengthened. We will never forget that period in the battle; will never forget Colonel Hanna and his noble men who made that memorable charge across the railroad and cut their way through to Colonel Rowett's fort, a work which for fierceness had, we believe, never been surpassed in this war.

Captain Rattrey of the Fifty-seventh, aid to Col. Rowett, excited the admiration of every one for his bravery, accompanied with so much coolness and judgment. He was found constantly by Colonel Rowett's side, executing his orders with promptness that was indeed remarkable. When the crushing tide of battle bore down Colonel Rowett, Captain Rattray could not find a field officer in the brigade to report to; every one down to his rank having fallen as victims—either dead or wounded. The gallant defenders of the Pass who had been struggling through long weary hours, were now making their last desperate struggle, and signs were appearing that seemed to tell of a turning point in the battle,—seemed to tell that the boys in blue were about to gain the mastery, were about to hurl back from the pass Hood's insane legions. There was no time to lose, and Captain Rattray fearing that the men who had fought so long, and so well, who had seen so many of their comrades fall and die, would soon become exhausted, leaped like a giant from where lay the bleeding and seemingly lifeless Rowett, and with the robust courage of an angel in his soul assumed command of the gallant old Third Brigade and conducted the battle to its glorious consummation. There seemed to be no post of danger that Captain Rattray did not wish to occupy.

In looking around us we miss many noble men who are now sleeping in death's cold embrace, Liberty in its great trial claimed them as sacrifices on its altar; but not for naught, as history will declare when this generation shall have long passed away. Private soldiers though they were, they performed their part, and hence are as worthy the country's gratitude as those in higher positions, who offered up their lives in this battle.

We cannot pass without alluding to the gallantry of Corporal Samuel Walker of Company H. He was standing with Colonel Rowett, and while fighting bravely in one of the desperate rebel charges the flag comes falling down over his head, and ere it reaches the blood stained earth, Corporal Walker is seen to grasp its shot-riven staff, and with its silken shreds falling around him, he mounted the works and there in one of the wildest battle storms that ever left blood in its wake, he waved it defiantly in the face of arch-treason,—waved it until a minie went crashing through his brain,—waved it until he fell, and there in blood under that grand old flag, the pride of his heart, the glory of his manhood, he died—died for the flag, died for his country, died for liberty. Glorious spirit! may his name ever shine bright in the book of perpetual remembrance as one of the boldest who helped to defend this second Thermopylae!

But all were brave, and like the legions of Bruce and the lovers of Sparta, they struggled against an adverse tide; for four fearful hours they held it in check; at last they turned it, and above streams of blood, the groans of the dying and the shouts of victors, light from the Union's proud banner seemed to flash against the sky. How proud were the Illinois and Iowa boys when the noble Corse, wounded and bleeding, said there was not a coward in the great battle of the Allatoona Pass; and prouder still were the men of the Seventh, when he said, "Colonel, your regiment sustained the heaviest loss; I will give it the post of honor."[188] Before leaving the battle-field, Sergeant Major S. F. Flint writes:

> Winds that sweep the southern mountain,
> And the leafy river shore,
> Bear ye not a prouder burden
> Than ye ever learned before?
> And the hot blood fills
> The heart till it thrills,
> At the story of the terror and the glory of the battle
> Of the Allatoona hills.
>
> Echo from the purple mountains,
> To the dull surrounding shore;
> 'Tis as sad and proud a burden,
> As ye ever learned before.
> How they fell like grass
> When the mowers pass,
> And the dying, when the foe was flying, swelled the cheering
> Of the heroes of the pass.
>
> Sweep it o'er the hills of Georgia
> To the mountains of the north;
> Teach the coward and the doubter,
> What the blood of man is worth.
> Toss the flag as you pass,
> Let their stained and tattered mass
> Tell the story of the terror and the glory of the battle
> Of the Allatoona Pass.

After burying the dead and caring for the wounded, which are placed on the cars to be sent to Rome, we return to our old camp on the Etawah. At no time during the war have we seen so much of sadness depicted upon the faces of the men as we have seen since our return to Rome. The men stand around in the camp lonely and silent, without a word to say to each other. There is indeed sorrow in the Seventh; sorrow for their brave comrades whom they left wrapped in death's pale sheet on the Allatoona hills. The Seventh felt sad when they stood on Shiloh's field and gazed upon their dead and wounded companions; their hearts were moved when they saw so many of their number who had perished on Corinth's plain, but the blood that flowed from the heroes of the Allatoona Pass has completely unnerved these strong men; and will our readers call it weakness when we tell them that after that work of blood at the Pass, while standing around the camp fires near the banks of the Etawah, we saw stalwart soldiers weep; saw tears sparkle in their eyes for those brave boys who had surrendered their lives in the great war for human liberty?

October 8th.—This morning we learn that Rome is in danger of an attack from Hood's northward bound column. We are early ordered into line, and soon we move out from our camp near the Etawah river. We do not march far until our advance is checked, when a brisk skirmish commences. All day we keep up a running fire with a considerable force of rebels with artillery, supposed to be a brigade sent out by Hood to reconnoiter. In the evening we return to camp with the loss of one man from Company F—private Hugh H. Porter, mortally wounded. And so another good soldier has fallen; another name to be added to the Union's roll of honor; a name with the prefix of private, but none the less worthy. As we look over the Seventh's mortality list, we see the name of none who was truer and more valiant than Hugh H. Porter, of gallant old Company F.[189]

Since our return from the Allatoona Pass, one of the Seventh's drummer boys has died; little Willie White, of Company H. His brother John fell a victim at Allatoona. Willie was left at Rome; he did not accompany the regiment, but when he heard of his brother's death, it weighed so heavily upon him as to prostrate him upon a bed of sickness, and soon he passed away—dies from grief, uttering as his last words: "Oh! what will mother do now?" We buried him in the soldiers' cemetery near the Etawah River, and a little white board marks the lonely spot where the Seventh's drummer boys sleeps.[190] General Hood, with his half starved army, has crossed the Coosa River, moving northward, making but a slight feint on Rome. Sherman's army is now swarming in and around Rome. Hood is far to the northward, and all is quiet on the Etawah and Coosa rivers. It is evident that Sherman is contemplating a movement that will shake the Confederacy and startle the world. The military are all active. Last night we chanced to be in Rome at the midnight hour. Who is that stately personage pacing to and fro in front of yonder tent? The guard tells us that it is Major General Sherman. He is in his night dress. Hood was then crossing the Tennessee. We know that some gigantic scheme is revolving in that master mind; a scheme the grandest and the boldest that ever flashed upon the world's greatest military minds, as the sequel will show when the future's sealed scroll shall have been unfolded a little way.

The wounded have all been sent northward. Noble company! May they soon recover and return to us again, for the regiment seems crippled without them. Ere we leave Rome we learn of the death of First Lieutenant and Adjutant J. S. Robinson and Sergeant Edward C. Nichols, of Company H—died from wounds received in the battle at Allatoona. Thus two more gallant soldiers have passed away. Long and patiently they endured their suffering, but at last the brittle thread of life broke, and these soldiers are now at rest. The indications as present are that we will soon leave Rome; how soon, we know not. The soldiers are conjecturing, but all is wrapped in mystery since Sherman has left Hood free to operate against Nashville. But for the present we are compelled to let the curtain hang; by and by it will be swung back; until that time we will wait.

Chapter XVI.

[November 11, 1864–December 22, 1864]

General Sherman—Army in the vicinity of Rome and Kingston—Hood moving northward—Leaving Rome—Camp on the Allatoona battle-field—Camp at the base of Kenesaw—Passing through Marietta—At Atlanta—The arrival of the last mail—The new commissions—The army launched forth upon the perilous march—Camp three miles from Atlanta—Burning of Atlanta—The army moving on four different roads—Camp near Cotton River—Crossing the Ocmulgee River—The orders to mount the Seventh—Passing through Clinton—Gordon—Irvington—The army subsisting on the country—The Third Brigade on the Savannah and Macon Railroad—Their work—General Corse lost in the pineries—The troops on half rations—The devastation—The obstructions—The Seventh on the Ogeechee—Standing picket—Skirmishing—Running on to a rebel fort—Before Savannah—Quarter rations—The fall of Fort McAllister—Captain E. R. Roberts escapes and returns to the regiment—His sufferings and trials—The troops subsisting upon corn and rice—Savannah evacuated—Entering the fallen city.

From October 3d to November 10th Sherman's army was continually marching, manoeuvering and skirmishing. The battle of Allatoona had been fought, the pass had been defended, the mad men who rushed up those rugged hills had been hurled back, the army of Georgia and Tennessee had been saved by the handful of men who stood there facing the grim monster as man never before had stood, and November 11th we find the armies commanded by General Sherman in the vicinity of Rome and Kingston. Hood was far to the northward. Sherman says: "He may push on his conquests; I will leave Thomas to confront him. I will enter the heart of the Confederacy. I will visit the South with war's stern realities."[191]

Orderlies and aids are dashing hither and thither. The order has been given. Hark! We hear the drum and the bugle, as if to say "Up boys and be ready, for Sherman is going to make a great stride in the South-land." The Seventh is now ready, shod and equipped, and in the evening, under the command of

Lieutenant Colonel Hector Perrin, we move from Rome about six miles and go into camp.

Rome is now burning, and to-night innocence, beautiful innocence is crying, all because its brothers rebelled; because they leaped from liberty's lap and struck the flag and swore this Union to divide, and her name and her glories to blacken.

November 11th.—The grand armies are now moving, headed towards Atlanta. To-night we go into camp upon the Allatoona battle field. The brave General John M. Corse, though his wound is scarcely well, is with us commanding the Fourth Division.[192] As we see him late to-night riding up to his headquarters (having refused to dismount until his division was all in camp), we thought to ourselves, "Brave Johnny, thou art a noble type of an American soldier." As we said, this is Allatoona's great battle field; here brave men sleep; here noble warriors fought their last fight; here sleep those who stood with us when Allatoona's hills were rocking amid the awful din and clash of steel; stood with us until they fell. We are now standing by their uncoffined graves. Boon companions lie here. How vividly the hour comes to us when they passed away under the shadow of the flag, the pride of their hearts. We cannot help but cast silent tears to their memory, and turning our faces towards the north star, we are wont to say: Oh! weep, heart of the North, for thy fallen dead who sleep here. The night is growing cold; we will now wend our way to where the weary Seventh lie sleeping.

November 13th.—This evening finds us at the base of Kenesaw. We are reminded that this name has gone to history, associated with deeds of valor; where Logan's battle flag flapped against the sky.[193] The heavens are all aglow to-night; to the southward red columns of smoke are curling upward. Signal lights are twinkling upon Kenesaw. Evidently Sherman is conversing with Howard and Slocum, his right and left bowers.[194]

November 14th.—At seven A.M., we move; pass through Marietta, which is now slumbering in ruins; we are now in the advance; pass the old rebel works, two P.M. In the evening we cross the Chattahoochee and go into camp for the night nine miles from Atlanta.

November 15th.—This morning the command moves by day-light. The Seventh is ordered to bring up the extreme rear from the Chattahoochee to where Companies H and K are now ordered to assist the pioneers in taking up the pontoons, after which we move on and join the division at Atlanta, where we find it halted for dinner. Here we receive our last mail, which brings the commissions for the new officers of the regiment. The promotions in the veteran organizations are as follows:

Captain Hector Perrin to be Lieutenant Colonel, vice Rowett, promoted.

Captain Edward S. Johnson to be Major, vice Estabrook, term expired.

Commissary Sergeant Frank Morse, to be First lieutenant and Adjutant, vice Robinson, killed in battle.

First Lieutenant Benjamin Sweeney to be Captain of Company A, vice McGuire, term expired.

Quartermaster Sergeant Henry L. Balcom to be First Lieutenant of Company A, vice Sweeney, promoted.

First Lieutenant Edward R. Roberts (now prisoner of war) to be Captain of Company C, vice Lawyer, term expired.

Second Lieutenant John Hubbard to be First Lieutenant of Company C, vice Roberts, promoted.

First Lieutenant Seth Raymond to be Captain of Company D, vice Clark, term expired.

Private Elias Lorey to be Second Lieutenant of Company E, vice Miller, term expired.

First Lieutenant Henry Ahern to be Captain of Company F, vice Knowlton, term expired.

Second Lieutenant Thomas B. Atchison to be First Lieutenant of Company F, vice Ahern, promoted.

First Sergeant William P. Hackeny to be Captain of Company H, vice Ring, term expired.

Sergeant D. Leib Ambrose to be First Lieutenant of Company H, vice Pegram, term expired.

Private William E. Norton to be Captain of Company I, vice Johnson, promoted.

Private James Crawley to be First Lieutenant of Company I, vice John E. Sullivan, killed in battle.

Second Lieutenant William C. Gillson to be Captain of Company K, vice Hunter, term expired.

First Sergeant Sanders to be First Lieutenant Company K, vice Partridge, resigned.

Commissions for the above promotions, with the exception of Lieutenant Colonel Hector Perrin's, Major Johnson's, and Captain Norton's, were received by to-day's mail, Lieutenant Colonel Hector Perrin's, Major Johnson's and Captain Norton's, having been received while in camp at Rome. The regiment is now newly officered by soldiers who have labored long and faithfully, and Allatoona tells us that the above list merit well their commissions. This evening at three o'clock we again move, our division being the last to pass through Atlanta; we go into camp three miles from the city. Up to this day communications have kept open. This evening the last train will leave for Nashville, by which Sherman will send his last dispatches to the Government, and ere the sun goes down we will have launched forth upon the perilous march. The destination we know not—everything seems to be clouded in mystery. The camp fires are now burning as it were upon a thousand hills, as if to rival the stars above. The boys are all in fine spirits. We to-night behold the conflagration of the great city. Atlanta is burning. "She sowed to the wind, she is now reaping the whirlwind."

November 16th.—This morning the army moves upon four different roads. The Seventeenth and Fifteenth A. C., comprising the right wing, commanded by Major General Howard, the Twentieth and Fourteenth A. C. the left wing, commanded by Major General Slocum.[195] All eyes are now turned towards General Sherman, as he sits upon his restless war steed, directing the perilous movements of a mighty army, which if successful, will add a new chapter to the arts of war. Will he succeed? Will he plant his banner upon the ocean strand? His countenance seems to say "I will, if these seventy thousand warriors keep thundering at my heels." To-night we camp upon the banks of Cotton River.

November 17th.—This morning our brigade takes the advance. At eleven o'clock we pass through McDonald, and in the evening go into camp four miles from Jackson.

November 18th.—We remain in camp to-day to let the Seventeenth A. C. pass. We live high to-day; plenty of fresh meat and yams. Five o'clock P.M., we move, go about eight miles and go into camp for the night. The soldiers are tired to-night; it is twelve o'clock before they lie down to rest. We are now far in the South-land, encompassed by foes in the front, the rear, and on both flanks, but the hearts of the seventy thousand warriors beat high, and this land is feeling their powerful tread.

November 19th.—We move early this morning and go as far as the Ocmulgee river, where we go into camp. Two pontoon bridges are now being spanned across the river, one for the teams and artillery, and the other for infantry. This evening Colonel Perrin receives orders from General Corse to mount his regiment as fast as stock can be captured. The order is received by the boys with great delight.

Sunday 20th.—Before daylight this morning we cross the Ocmulgee River, all the rest of the army having crossed last night. Our division is now in the rear guarding Kilpatrick's train; the roads are very muddy; only succeed in getting ten miles to-day, when we go into camp near Monticello. A cold rain is now falling; the chilling winds, how fierce they blow! The Seventh suffers to-night.[196]

Monday, 21st.—At seven o'clock we move. Oh! how terrible the mud; teams sticking all along the road, and in consequence we move slow. We go into camp about ten o'clock upon an open field. It is now raining. The regiment is upon half rations; the men are standing, shivering around the camp fires; it is a terrible night; the fierce, wild winds sweep through the Seventh's camp. Nothing to shelter the men from the howling storm, but this matters not. "Let the world wag as it will, we'll be gay and happy still," breaks forth from the soldiers as it were in harmony with the elements. There is manhood here; there is fidelity around these camp fires, and how sad the fact that there are men in America who would be loath to acknowledge it.

Tuesday, 22d.—We move at seven o'clock this morning; weather very cool. Mud, mud everywhere; this evening the trains all swamp; night comes on dark and dreary, and being unable to extricate the teams, we go into camp two miles from Clinton.

Wednesday, 23d.—We move at seven A.M.; the troops succeed in getting the train in motion; we go into camp in the evening five miles from Gordon.

Thursday, 24th.—We move slow to-day, reach Gordon, the junction of the Milledgeville Railroad, by noon. The work of destruction is now going on; the railroad is being destroyed; we cross the railroad and go into camp two miles from Gordon. The whole country is clouded with smoke. This mighty army is making a terrible sweep. The legitimate vengeance of this government is now falling upon this rebellious people.

Friday, 25th.—This morning we move early; pass through Irwinsville about noon. This was once a very beautiful town, but now lying in ashes. The roads are better to-day; we march twenty five miles and go into camp at five o'clock P.M. Our rations are now very short, and we are compelled to subsist chiefly upon the country.

Saturday, 26th.—Our regiment having received orders to take the advance, to-day we move at 5 o'clock A.M.; about noon we enter the swamps of the Oknee river. Here the enemy endeavored to check our advance, but from this great army's front they are hurled away like chaff. The pontoons having been laid we cross the river, 2 o'clock P.M., go about eight miles, and go into camp for the night.

Sunday, 27th.—This morning our brigade moves on three miles to the Macon and Savannah Railroad, and for our allotment destroy six miles of track. Night coming on we go into camp near the railroad.

Monday, 28th.—This morning Company H is detailed for foragers. The Fifteenth corps is thrown into confusion to-day. The Third and Fourth Division get all mixed up, General Corse with the Second Brigade takes the wrong road and gets lost in the Pineries, taking some time to extricate himself and get on the right road.

Tuesday, 29th.—We are still in the pine barrens of Georgia; darkness is now hovering around us. The troops are all on half rations, forage is scarce. We are late going into camp to-night, but the troops are all in fine spirits this evening. All seem confident that success with its glories will fall around this army.

Wednesday, 30th.—To-day finds us still in the Wilderness of Pines, not more than half way to the sea, which, it is now evident, is our destination. For two days we have not seen a habitation; has man ever penetrated these wilds before? It seems not. The roads are desperate; our supplies are becoming shorter and shorter; darkness seems to be falling on our path but the 70,000 warriors keep moving on with a silent but unceasing tread. Every step seems to say we will yet see the sunlight from the ocean flash on our serried lines—seems to say that we will yet see the ocean steamers from the great cities of the east, laden with supplies, deck the waters. This is our hope—our only hope. Late going into camp to-night; all tired and hungry marched 25 miles to-day.

December 1st.—Thursday morning we are soon on the way; we make a hard march and go into camp at 3 o'clock P.M.

Friday, 2d.—To-day we lay in camp while the work of destruction is going on along the Savannah Railroad.

Saturday, 3d.—The country is all wrapped in flame; how terrible the sweep of an unchecked army! We go into camp early this evening.

Sunday, 4th.—We are now marching parallel with the Ogeechee river. We go into camp early. Now and then occasional firing is heard on the flanks, front and rear, but nothing very threatening as yet has confronted us.

December 9th.—Companies I, E and F, are now mounted—are now moving upon the war path as of old.[197] The non-mounted portion of the regiment are in the advance of the Fifteenth Army Corps. To-day we find the roads all obstructed by the felling of trees, but not enough to check the army; the Pioneers keep the roads all free from impediments. Some skirmishing to-day but nothing serious. The weak rebel forces seem but idle toys for the moment.

December 10th.—We move early this morning. Meeting increased obstructions and encountering rebels in our front, we only succeed in getting about four miles, when we go into camp for the night. Soon after going into camp the Seventh is sent forward to the Little Ogeechee river to stand picket.

December 11th.—This morning we cross the Ogeechee, and do not advance far until skirmishing commences; Company K is deployed forward, and Company H barricades the road with rails. Soon the Thirty-ninth Iowa comes up and the entire Seventh is deployed forward; advancing a short distance we discover a rebel fort and camp swarming with rebels, who seeing our flag appear from the margin of the woods on to an open field, open their artillery upon us. Upon the field we find ourselves much exposed, and being unable to advance in consequence of the extensive rice swamps in front of us, we change position by the left flank under a heavy fire, cross the road and take our position behind an embankment thrown up from a ditch, where we remain until night comes on, and then return to the woods and go into camp.

December 12th—Finds us across the Ogeechee, finds us before Savannah, finds us twelve miles from the sea. A defiant foe is before us disputing our advance; this day we may fight a battle—may see what virtue there is in lead and steel. The army is now at a stand; some skirmishing and some fighting is continually going on. The troops are upon quarter rations. Will we fail? Our gallant Sherman says no, follow me, and I will lead you through. To-night we hear Slocum's guns echoing a death-knell to arch-treason. Tomorrow's sun may set upon a field wet with the heart's blood of warriors, for everything this evening looks warlike.

December 13th.—With but short intervals, Slocum's guns have been hard all day. About three o'clock in the evening we hear to our right a sullen roar, a desperate crash, a whoop, and all is over; and soon we are told that Fort McAllister has fallen; that the immortal Hazen, Ohio's ideal son, has planted his battle-flag upon the ramparts there, making free our passage to the sea, and now we hope to receive supplies, as we have access to the fleet anchored in Ossabaw Sound.[198] This evening Captain Ed. R. Roberts of Company C, makes his appearance in camp, after an imprisonment of seven months in the southern prison hells. The reader will remember that Captain Roberts, together with Captain McGuire, Lieutenant Fergus, and about thirty of the men, were captured on the seventh of May, 1864, in our encounter with Roddy and Johnson at Florence, Alabama. The captain has now a large crowd of the Seventh congregated around him, listening attentively to his heart-rending stories of rebel cruelty. We will now follow Captains Roberts and McGuire and Lieutenant Fergus during their wanderings in the land of their captivity. After their capture at Florence, Alabama, on the 7th of May 1864, they, in company with the men, were taken *via* Mobile and Montgomery, Alabama, to Macon, Georgia, where they arrived May 28th. As soon as they entered the stockade Roberts washed his shirt, and after wringing it out, approached the picket fence immediately inside of the stockade to hang it thereon to dry, and just as he was about to touch the fence he was pulled back by a comrade who saved his life—saved him from being cruelly murdered; for it was the dead line he was about to touch, a line upon which many a noble patriot Union soldier poured out his life blood. At one time while here they were compelled to be two and a half days without anything to eat. After remaining in the Macon stockade for some time the officers were separated from the men, and transferred to the city work-house and jail at Charleston, South Carolina, and while here they were continually under the fire of Gilmore's guns. On the 5th of October they were all moved to Columbia, South Carolina, with the exception of those who were sick, among which number was the gallant Lieutenant Fergus, who was suffering with the yellow fever. After long weary months of suffering known only to those who were the sufferers, Captain Roberts and a number of other officers made their escape from those wicked men who sought their lives. The story of the Captain's march from bondage to liberty would alone fill a good sized volume. Guided by the trusty negroes they traveled one hundred and eighty miles in ten nights, (lying in the swamps by day) and reached Sherman's army, seventy miles above Savannah, Georgia, December 5th.

The Captain remained with Kilpatrick's cavalry until the 12th of November, when he joined his regiment and company. Brave, self-sacrificing soldier, the story of your trials, the longings that were yours, the revolting scenes that met your eyes, and the feeling of joy that came to your heart when your eyes fell upon the old flag, will never be known to any save those who experienced like trials, who witnessed like scenes and felt like joys. We now think of those of our number who are yet suffering in southern prison pens, and we are informed that some of them have been freed from their suffering, have been starved, have been murdered. It cannot be that these brave men's sufferings and sorrows which they endured in this land of cruel wrongs will not be righted in the world beyond the stars. We could not believe in a heaven if we should lose the faith that these men's wrongs will be made right above.

December 20th.—After the fall of Fort McAllister, we obtain some supplies, but for the seventy thousand hungry soldiers they soon run out. For the last week the troops have been sub-sisting upon corn and rice, the rice being obtained from the shocks in the swamps, and hulled out by the soldiers. Every-thing in the country for fifty miles around has been foraged. The army is still investing Savannah—the siege still going on. It will be over soon however, as a great battle will be fought where Count Pulaski's Monument stands; for Sherman's army is now in a good condition to sweep Savannah from the earth. The next forty-eight hours will tell the tale.

December 21st.—This morning we walk through the Sev-enth's camp, and everywhere we see the men with their clubs hulling out rice; this is all they have, but they are in fine spir-its, all seem firm; seem confident and hopeful that this the most daring march in the military history of the nineteenth century, will be successful.

December 22d.—Last night Savannah was evacuated—her power yielded. The grand army is tramping now. Soon Sher-man's terrible battle-flag will be flying beneath the shades of Bonniventure, where the chivalric knights have so often re-hearsed their gallant deeds to the South's fair ones. With drums beating and colors flying we enter a fallen city. Our work in this campaign is done.[199] We behold rebellion dying. The tramp of armies; the burning of cities; the destruction of railroads, have ruined Georgia. Such destruction and desolation never before fol-lowed in the wake of armies. History has never recorded a paral-lel. Sherman was terrible, severe, unmerciful. But his severity and unmercifulness have stamped his name high upon the "Table Rock of immortality" as the boldest, most fearless and most consummate leader of the nineteenth century, and second to none in the world. In the language of a Soldier Poet,

> Proud was our army that morning,
> When Sherman said, "boys, you are weary,
> But to-day fair Savannah is ours."
> Then sang we a song to our chieftain,
> That echoed over river and lea;
> And the stars in our banner shown brighter,
> When Sherman marched down to Sea.

Chapter XVII.

[December 22, 1864–March 21, 1865]

Major Johnson on the flanks of the army—Stopping all night with an old planter—Lieutenant Flint's poem—Our camp at Savannah—Fort Brown—Bonniventure—The wounded men ordered to Pocotaligo—Leaving Savannah—Crossing the Savannah River—Entering South Carolina—Crossing the swamps—Joining the Fifteenth Corps at Midway—Crossing the Edisto—Crossing the Congaree—In front of Columbia— Crossing the Soluda River—The surrender of Columbia—The burning of the city—The march to Cheraw—Crossing the Pedee River—At Fayetteville, North Carolina—Crossing the Cape Fear River—The march to Bentonville—The battle of Bentonville—The march to Goldsboro—Camp at Goldsboro—Arrival of new companies—The consolidation.

During the siege of Savannah Major Johnson was off on the flanks of the army with the mounted portion of the regiment, scouting, foraging, doing outpost duty, and gathering up stragglers from their commands. After the fall of the city General Corse sends a dispatch ordering him to join his regiment. On the evening of the twenty-second he halts on a plantation near the Ogeechee River, and after camping his men, accompanied by Lieutenant S. F. Flint, he wends his way to the planter's mansion. It is now dark and raining. The Major knocks at the door, and after an assurance of friendship, they are received into the household. Their sabres' frightful clang grates harshly upon the ears of the inmates—an old man, woman and daughter—and for a while they seem frightened, but the gentlemanly demeanor of the Major and Lieutenant soon wins their confidence, causing them to come to the conclusion that the Yankees were not the wild creatures they had been represented to be. The midnight hour approximating, they all retire, leaving the Major and Lieutenant the occupants of the parlor. In the morning, while all is quiet, they make their exit, leaving the following beautiful lines (written by the Lieutenant,) in the clock:

Where the Savannas of the South
  Spread out their golden breadths to sea,
The fearful tide of war has rolled
  Around this lonely household tree.

I know the hearts that linger here,
  Their broken hopes, their wounded pride,
Have felt what I may never feel,
  Are tried as I have not been tried.

This aged man, this fair browed girl,
  What wonder if they learn to blend
His memory with hate—the foe
  Who might in peace have been their friend.

One common tongue, one blood, one God,
  The God whose ways are dark, are ours;
And He can make war's blackened path,
  Rustle with harvests—bloom with flowers.

And here before he seeks his rest,
  The hated North-man bends his knee,
And prays, restore this household band—
  As dear to them as mine to me;
Oh! let the fearful storm sweep by,
  And spare this roof that sheltered me.

After our entrance into the city, we go into camp in the suburbs, where we remain during the night and the following day. On the twenty-fourth we are ordered to Fort Brown, two miles from the city, where we go into a more permanent camp. During our first days at Savannah, the Seventh's boys are seen strolling everywhere, viewing the fortifications and the great guns; they are also seen pacing the streets of the beautiful city, looking with admiration upon her gorgeous buildings, and standing in awe in the shade of the peerless monument reared by a generous people to that noble Pole, Count Pulaski, who fought, bled and died in America's first revolution for independence. Can it be that traitors have walked around its base and sworn that the great Union for which this grand and liberal spirit sacrificed his life should be consigned to the wrecks of dead empires? As we stand and gaze upon this marble cenotaph, we are constrained to say, Oh! wicked men, why stood ye here above the dust of Poland's martyr, seeking to defame his name and tear down what he helped to rear! May God pity America's erring ones! In our wanderings we are made to stop, by an acre enclosed with a high but strong palisade, the work of Colonel G. F. Wiles, Seventy-eighth Ohio Veteran Volunteer Infantry, commanding Second Brigade, Third Division, Seventeenth Army Corps, and his gallant command. This is God's acre and liberty's, and emphatically can this be said, for here three hundred or more of our fallen comrades sleep death's silent sleep. Here in trenches, unknelled, uncoffined, but not alone, "life's fitful fever over," they sleep well. They fell not in the deadly breach, nor yet on the grassy plain. For them no choir of musketry rattled, no anthem of cannon rolled, but unclad and unfed, their lamps of life flickered out in that worse than Egyptian bondage—a Confederate prison. For long weary months they suffered and waited for the time to come when they would inhale freedom's pure air; for long weary nights they watched the signal lights as they flashed upwards from the monitors to guide Sherman through the wilderness of pines, down to the sea; long did they wait to see the sunlight from the waters flash on his serried lines, but he came not. They suffered on, and died—died martyrs upon the altar of human freedom; died that not one single star, however wayward, should be erased from the Union's great banner of freedom. Has the world, in all its history of blood, from the creation to the christian era, from the reformation to the revolution, ever produced examples of such heroic endurance as this second revolution has given to the world? Echoes coming from the soft south winds that sweep along the Atlantic shore, answer no. These men were murdered! Yes, murdered because they wore the blue, and fought for the flag and freedom. The poet alludes most touchingly to an incident that caused the murder of one of these lonely sleepers, who plead for his wife's letters.

"First pay the postage, whining wretch."
Despair had made the prisoner brave—
"I'm a captive, not a slave;
You took my money and my clothes,
Take my life too, but for the love of God
Let me know how Mary and the children are,
And I will bless you ere I go."

This plea proved fruitless, and across the dead-line the soldier passed, and soon a bullet passed through his brain, and his crushed spirit was free with God. What a sad picture.

We remember when we stood there and gazed upon that hallowed acre of God's and liberty's. We thought of those wicked men who whelmed this land into those dark nights of war; who told us then that the Union soldier died in vain; that the names of those uncoffined sleepers there would be forgotten and unsung, and as my comrades and myself stood there revolving these thoughts in our minds, we vowed over those graves, before heaven, to be the enemies of traitors. "Died in vain! sacrificed their lives for naught! their names to be forgotten and unsung!" Who uttered those words in application to the noble sleepers there? Who spoke thus to the weeping mother and stricken sister? Traitors in the North! Traitors on the legislative floors uttered these words! We speak the sentiment of the Seventh when we say that we would not take millions for what we hate these men, contemptible in nature, pusillanimous in soul, with hearts as black as the "steeds of night."[200] Like Brownlow, were we not afraid of springing a theological question, we would say that better men have been going down with the wailing hosts for the last eighteen hundred years.

A few days after going into camp at Fort Brown, Major Johnson is ordered with Companies A, H and K, to proceed down the river to Bonniventure, about five miles from Savannah. Arriving, we take up our quarters in the old Bonniventure mansion, a fashionable resort for the chivalry in the days that have flown. During our stay here we live chiefly on oysters, which are obtained in great abundance by the boys. Major Johnson and his detachment will not soon forget how they gamboled and loitered beneath the shades of those live oaks down by the great Atlantic's shore.[201]

The Seventh remains in camp at Fort Brown and Bonniventure until the latter part of January, 1865. In the mean time Captain Norton, with the mounted portion of the regiment, was ordered across the Savannah river into South Carolina, Joining Howard's command at Pocataligo.[202]

About the twenty-fifth of January, Major Johnson, with his detachment, leaves Bonniventure, and joins the regiment at Fort Brown. Receiving marching orders, General Corse, with his division, who were now isolated and alone from the corps, leaves Savannah, marching up the Savannah river as far as Sister's Ferry, where we find Gen. Slocum struggling with the floods.[203] We remain here until the fourth of February. In the evening we cross over into the Palmetto State and go into camp three miles from the river; we doubt if ever an army encountered more difficulties than did Slocum's command and General Corse's Division encounter in crossing the Savannah. The river was up, and for three long miles the army was compelled to build a solid road.

February 5th.—In the evening we move about four miles across an almost impassable swamp and go into camp. The seventy thousand are now making a terrible stride in South Carolina, moving through the swamps, the favorite haunts of the slave hunter and his blood hounds. But the tables are turning; other hounds will soon yelp down here—Sherman's fierce hounds of war,—they will go sweeping on their path for freedom and law, making John C. Calhoun restless in his tomb.

February 6th.—We move early this morning; our Division is moving by itself upon a lone road, General Corse having orders to move across the country and form a junction with the corps now moving from Pocataligo. The roads are desperate; we only succeed in getting about eight miles to-day.

February 7th. We cross Black Water swamps and go into camp at Hickory Hill, making a distance of ten miles.

February 8th.—We cross Whippie Swamp about noon to-day and go into camp for the night.

February 9th.—The roads still continue desperate, and in consequence we move slowly. In the evening we cross the little Saltkatchie swamp.

February 10th.—We move early this morning, but very slow; these swamps prove to be terrible obstacles to Sherman's seventy thousand. We soon come to the great Saltkatchie swamp at Beaufort's Bridge; we find the swamp all flooded, about one mile wide, and the bridge in the middle. Weak commanders would have faltered; things indeed look frightful, but General Corse gave the command forward. The Seventh led, and into the great Swamp the Fourth Division passed, and through it they waded, the water, winter cold, ranging from waist to neck deep. It did seem that some of the men would perish; that they would be left in that great swamp; but all passed safely through, and gaining a footing on the opposite side, drove the enemy far away, who were all the while disputing our passage. The ammunition train is now ordered to move across (the ammunition being raised out of water's reach); about midway they swamp, and the soldiers of Corse's Division are compelled to go back into the swamp and carry the ammunition boxes out to land.

Remaining here until the trains are crossed, we move forward and join the corps at Midway, on the South Carolina Railroad. Then began the movement on Orangeburg.[204] We notice that Black Jack is at the head of the Fifteenth Corps, having arrived from his campaign on the northern line and assumed command at Pocataligo. We also find that the mounted portion of the Seventh are now (as the boys say) members of his staff. We cross the South Fork of the Edisto River at Halmond's bridge and move to Poplar Springs to support the Seventeenth Army Corps, moving straight to Orangeburg, which is taken by a dash of the Seventeenth.

From Poplar Springs we cross the North Edisto River at Skilling's bridge, and on the fifteenth we find the enemy in strong position at Little Congaree bridge, but the gallant Logan with his thundering Fifteenth, soon ousts them, when we move across and go into camp in front of Columbia. During the night our camp is shelled from a battery on the east side of the Congaree, above Grundy, causing considerable stir in the Fifteenth Corps' camp.

February 16th—This morning we move our camp and shift around more to the left. Brisk skirmishing is now going on along the river, with some cannonading. In the evening we again move our position more to the left. The capitol of South Carolina is now in full view. The Saluda river being pontooned, we cross this evening, which throws us between two rivers, the Saluda and the Broad, which two form a junction at Columbia and make the Congaree.

During the night, under cover of Stone's Brigade, of the Fifteenth Corps, which was crossed in the afternoon, a pontoon bridge was laid across the Broad River, three miles above Columbia. On the morning of the seventeenth, Colonel Stone, of the Twenty-fifth Iowa, commanding Third Brigade, First Division, Fifteenth Corps, moves towards the city.[205] At eleven o'clock the Mayor comes out and makes a formal surrender of the city to Col. Stone. In anticipation of General Howard, with the army of the Tennessee, entering the city, General Sherman's orders are to spare all dwellings, colleges, asylums, and harmless private property.

General Logan, who stood at the end of the pontoon bridge when the last pontoon was laid, says to Howard, with his black eyes flashing: "I will now move into this hell of treason. But say the word and I will sweep this city from the earth." It is now past noon. Generals Sherman and Howard have rode into the city. The Fifteenth Corps is now moving across Broad river. The Seventh is ordered to stay back and guard the train.

It is now night; the wind is raging furiously; the heavens are all aglow; Columbia is enveloped in flames; her beautiful architecture is crumbling; her gorgeous mansions are falling; the work and labor of a century is being destroyed.[206] At four o'clock A.M. February 18th, the Seventh cross Broad River and go into camp near the doomed city. We can now see the great conflagration. Oh! how terrible those sweeping elements, causing innocent ones to cry as they behold their childhood's place of play crumbling into ashes. But such is war! Terrible in its legitimate vengeance, powerful in its tread, it harkens not to the cries for mercy. The question is now asked, "Who will be held responsible for the burning of the capitol of South Carolina." The impartial historian will tell the world that Wade Hampton burned his own city of Columbia by filling the streets with lint, cotton and tinders, and setting fire to it, which was spread by the raging wind. But it matters not with the seventy thousand who will be charged with the burning of South Carolina's capitol, for this great army who had swept a continent thus far, smiled and felt glad in their hearts when they beheld this city laid low in ashes, where rebellion was born, and where pampered and devilish treason first lifted its mad head and made its threats against the Union and freedom.[207]

From the 23d to the 26th heavy rains fall, swelling the rivers and making the roads almost impassable. Passing through Camden, we arrive at Cheraw on the 2d of March. Colonel Perrin is now in command of the mounted portion of the regiment, and Major Johnson the non-mounted portion.[208] We remain in camp here one day and two nights. From this point an expedition of cavalry and mounted infantry was sent down to Florence, which was joined by Colonel Perrin and the mounted portion of the Seventh, but it encountered both cavalry and infantry, and returned having only broken up in part the branch road from Florence to Cheraw.[209]

Leaving Cheraw, and after crossing the Pedee river we are again put in motion, moving towards Fayetteville, North Carolina. On the 11th of March we arrive at Fayetteville, and while approaching, the advance was for awhile engaged in skirmishing with Wade Hampton's cavalry, that covered the rear of Hardee's retreating army.

March 12th.—The army tug Davenson reaches Fayetteville from Wilmington to-day. We remain here until the 14th, when we again move. We proceed to the Cape Fear river one mile below town where we remain until noon waiting for the 17th Army Corps to cross, after which General Corse leads his division upon the long pontoon bridge. After crossing we move on and go into camp two miles from the river.

March 15th.—The 4th Division take the advance this morning. The advance encounter Hampton's cavalry, but by a little skirmishing they are soon scattered. We move only ten miles to-day, going into camp for the night one mile from South river, where the rebels are said to be in force.

March 16th.—By advancing this morning we discover that the rebels have all made their exit from South river. General Corse again takes the advance. The South river bottoms are overflowed. The bridge across the main channel having been damaged is now repaired, but the troops are compelled to wade the bottoms which are about knee deep. Our advance encounters rebels all day—Butler's and Wade Hampton's cavalry.[210] We go into camp at 3 o'clock P.M. It is now raining. Everything looks frightful in these swamps where the men of war are tramping. Mud and water everywhere.

March 17th.—The 4th Division still moves in the adv ance. We take the main Goldsboro road this morning. The roads are desperate, the troops are compelled to corduroy the roads almost entirely with rails. We march about seven miles and go into camp at Clinton cross roads. Being now in close proximity to Johnson's rebel army we are ordered to throw up fortifications and remain here the remainder of the day and night to wait for the left wing to move up.[211]

March 18th.—9 o'clock A.M. we move. The roads still desperate—corduroying almost every step. A great many refugees are now following the army, seeking to be freed from the Davis tyranny; they are enduring much suffering. We go into camp to-night about sun down. We are now about twenty-six miles from Goldsboro, North Carolina.

March 19th.—To-day we reach Falling Creek, where the mounted portion of the Seventh is thrown forward to the river bridge, where they encounter the enemy in a brisk skirmish, which for dash and vim elicits the compliments of "Black Jack." Advancing, General Slocum discovered that Johnson with his army was strongly posted in the vicinity of Bentonville.

March 20th.—We advance early this morning. The Seventh are soon deployed on the skirmish line, and are soon skirmishing, for on such occasions the Seventh with their sixteen-shooters are always called upon. The Fifteenth Corps gaining position, we commence throwing up breastworks within cannon range of the enemy's works. By 4 o'clock P.M. Johnson finds himself confronted with a complete and strong line of battle.

March 21st.—This morning the armies are menacing each other face to face, each remaining behind their works. The design of Sherman is to hold him there until Schofield and Terry can advance from Kingston, North Carolina.[212] Skirmishing has been going on all day. In the evening the Seventh is ordered forward on the skirmish line, and moving forward under the command of Major Johnson, into a creek bottom, we provoked a fierce fire from the enemy stationed on the opposite side. In this encounter Privates Jacob Groch and Gotleib Burkhardt, of Company H, were wounded. Other noble men were also wounded, but we have been unable to obtain their names.[213]

It is now raining and night has let her curtains fall. We are ordered to dig rifle-pits and remain on the line all night. It is a dark night, a cold March rain is falling upon the tired soldiers. The chilling winds make mournful music through the branches of the tall pines. The rebels are entrenched close to our lines and until three o'clock in the morning there is a continual firing. The Seventh pumped the death dealing elements from their sixteen-shooters with such a vim that it made the enemy think that the whole army was on the line of battle. Three o'clock in the morning the firing ceased, and at the first gray dawn of morning light the enemy is discovered to be gone and on the retreat. Thus ends our battle near Bentonville, North Carolina, which proves to be our last encounter with the rebel army in the war for the Union.[214]

After the battles around and in the vicinity of Bentonville, we move towards Goldsboro, where we arrive March 20th. As we move into Goldsboro we are reviewed by General Sherman, thus ending our campaign in the Carolinas,—a campaign that will furnish history with many startling events—events that will tell of privations endured, and of a fortitude developed in Sherman's seventy thousand that had never been developed before by the world in all its martial history.[215]

This evening some of the soldiers who were wounded at Allatoona, join the regiment, having been at Goldsboro waiting our arrival for some days. We are glad to see our genial friend and boon companion, the gallant Captain Hackney, lately commissioned for his bravery at Allatoona. We notice that he has a beautiful mark on his beautiful face, the compliment of a rebel's whizzing minie. But as Grace Greenwood says, this will be his patent of nobility. While here three companies lately recruited for the Seventh join the regiment from Illinois, which are lettered and officered as follows: Company B,

Captain Hugh J. Cosgrove, First Lieutenant George H. Martin, Second Lieutenant M. D. F. Wilder; Company D, Captain William A. Hubbard, First Lieutenant John H. Gay, Second Lieutenant William M. Athey; Company G, Captain S. W. Hoyt, First Lieutenant Andrew J. Moore, Second Lieutenant W. J. Hamlin.

To make room for these new companies orders are issued to consolidate old Company B with Company A, Captain Sweeny commanding; old Company D with Company C, Captain Roberts commanding; old Company G, with Company I, Captain Norton commanding.[216]

Chapter XVIII.

[April 10, 1865–July 18, 1865]

Leaving Goldsboro—News of Lee's surrender—Arrival at Raleigh, North Carolina—March to Morrisville—Entire regiment to be mounted—The assassination of Abraham Lincoln—The effect of the news upon Sherman's army—The march back towards Raleigh—Camp on Crab Creek—The march to Petersburg—The march to Richmond—The arrival at Alexandria—The grand review—Our camp near Washington—Leaving Washington—Arrival at Louisville, Kentucky—Camp near Louisville—Camp in the City—Mustered out—Returning to peaceful life.

After building houses and making our camp pleasant and comfortable, we move from Goldsboro on the tenth of April and march towards Raleigh, North Carolina. On the twelfth we arrive at Lowell, and while here we receive the first news of Lee's surrender to General Grant. Sherman's grand army seems wild to-night. The pineries ring for Grant and the Union. Victory has come at last, and the bronzed and stalwart men who have tramped across a continent, make the air vocal with their happy cheers. The morning of peace cometh; we already see its welcome light peering from behind the curtains of war's long dark night.

April 14th.—We enter Raleigh, the capitol of North Carolina, pass through the city and go into camp one mile from the outer works.[217] To-day Companies A and K leave for headquarters to be mounted. The dismounted portion of the regiment is now very small. Company H and the three new companies, B, D and G, are the only ones now remaining to plod their way on "terra firma;" but we all hope soon to be mounted; especially old company H, who, from past experience, know what virtue there is in mules.

April 15th.—This morning we are ordered from our camp at three o'clock; it soon commences to rain very hard; the old North Carolina clay roads soon become terrible. During the morning we hear heavy cannonading, said to be along the front to Jeff. C.

Davis' Fourteenth Corps. We march hard all day, wading a good portion of the time in mud and water, from knee to waist deep. Night coming on, we go into camp at Morrisville on the North Carolina Railroad, having traveled twenty miles since morning.[218]

April 16th.—This morning the dismounted portion of the regiment receives orders to report to regimental headquarters to be mounted. Oh! how welcome the news, notwithstanding we do find the stock and the riding material somewhat on the decline; but anything to ride is the word that goes forth now from Company H and the new companies. To-night, for the first time since we crossed the Ocmulgee river, November 19th, 1864, the Seventh Regiment is all together in camp.

April 17th.—This morning Sherman's great army bow their heads in mournful silence over the startling news of the assassination. While we write we remember how we were made glad when the news was read to us "Richmond has fallen!" "Lee has surrendered!" Yes, we were made glad, for we knew then that the rebellion was dead, that the war would soon end, and wild, loud and long were the shouts that rang through the forests of North Carolina, in honor of those glorious events. But now we find the army possessed of a different feeling: all seem downcast and sad; a veil of gloom hangs like a midnight curtain. And why this gloom? Why do the tall dark pines seem to wail so mournfully as, tossed by the wind, they sway hither and fro? Why this sorrow when the harbinger of peace seems so nigh? Ah, our chief, our ruler, our friend, the Union's friend, the world's friend, humanity's truest friend on earth, has been stricken down in the hour of his greatest triumph by the cowardly hand of the assassin. We loved the good, the noble, the merciful LINCOLN, who had led the millions of the western world through so terrible a war with the end so nigh. But the great mission designed for him by the Creator he has accomplished—the freedom of a chained race. May we ever remember that Abraham Lincoln died a martyr to freedom, a martyr to law, a martyr to right; and above all let us remember that the minions of slavery slew him; slew him because he was the world's champion for the rights of man; because he loved his country, and had a heart that went out to the lonely cottage homes where the disconsolate widow and fatherless child sat weeping for the loved and lost who had been swept away by war's dark wave; slew him because he defied the world;

> "While the thunders of War did rattle,
> And the Soldiers fought the battle;"

slew him because his democracy would not embrace the slaveholder's aristocracy; because his democracy was too broad; because it breathed a spirit of love and compassion towards earth's chained millions, and a spirit of hatred towards pampered royalty and cruel tyranny. Although he is dead; although his name, spotless and pure, has gone to the christian calendar, yet that liberty for which he died still moves on, and will move on until every throne beneath the circle of the sun shall have been shaken to its fall. Moving on where the Danube and the Volga move; moving on where the south wind makes music along the Tiber's winding way; it will move on until equal rights, the darling theme of Lincoln's life, shall be established, and the clanking of chains forever silenced, for the consummation of such an end is certain. God, not man, created men equal, and deep laid in the solid foundation of God's eternal throne and great principles of man's equality are established indestructible and immortal. When that time comes, when liberty shall unfurl her beautiful banner of stars over the crumbling tombs of empires, heaven and earth will rejoice and the generations that follow will look back upon the past, (perhaps it will be a century or more,) and say of Abraham Lincoln, he was the world's leading spirit for freedom, truth and the rights of man, and the world's bitterest foe against treason and imperialism.

The memory of Lincoln, his model manhood, his exalted virtues, his heroic endeavors amid darkness and disparagements; his sublime devotion to the cause he had espoused; his love towards the Union army; his great sympathy for the widow and the orphan boy whose father fell with Wadsworth and Sedgwick in the wilderness,[219] whose life blood made crimson Rappahannock's rippling waters, whose lamp of life flickered out in Andersonville and Libby prisons as victims to a ferocious tyranny; these all will be forever linked with the memory of the patriot pilgrims, who, in years to come, will bow their heads in silent reverence before the marble cenotaph that marks the place where the martyred champion sleeps. May Americans ever love to applaud his virtues, for virtues he had as pure as the driven snow. *"Vivit post funera virtus"*: may the Illinois soldiers tread lightly around his tomb; may the prairie winds ever chant requiems to his memory, and may the great American people remember the day when their leading light went out—when their brightest star went home to God.

The Seventh remained in camp at Morrisville, until after the surrender of Johnson, when we retraced our steps and went into camp on Crab Creek, five miles from Raleigh. On the 20th, prior to leaving Morrisville, Colonel Rowett, who was wounded at Allatoona, returns to the regiment. Never was a colonel's return to his regiment more welcome than was Colonel Rowett, and as we approach him and take him by the hand we remember Allatoona—remember how he fought there—remember how he fell! how he bled! how he cheered his men on to victory. He now assumes command of his old 3d Brigade, 4th Division, 15th A. C. We remain quietly in camp on Crab Creek until the 29th, when Sherman's army break up their camp around Raleigh and take up the line of march for Washington City. The Seventh being now mounted with the exception of three new companies, we lead the advance of the 15th Corps. We arrive at Petersburg on the 6th of May. Things around here tell very plainly that war's mad machine has been at work here, leaving marks that will be seen a century hence. We remain at Petersburg until the 9th, when we move towards Richmond. We go into camp for the night near Fort Darling on the James river.

On the morning of the 10th we move towards Richmond. For some cause unknown we do not enter the city, but are ordered into camp three miles from the bridge that spans the James river. We remain in camp here until the 14th, when Sherman's victorious army enters Richmond. We pass Libby Prison, which seemed to send an appeal from her dark recesses to Sherman's army to sweep the city from the earth. But Sherman held the rein, and Richmond fell not a victim to their wrath. We pass on through the city, moving on the road leading to Fredericksburg, where we arrive and cross the Rappahannock on the 16th. Night coming on, we go into camp on the banks of the

Potomac. In the evening we look away in the distance and behold its winding way. What a tale of blood could this river tell. But the story will never be known until a book unscanned by mortal eyes shall be unfolded before the assembled universe.

On the 17th we arrive at Alexandria and go into camp two miles from the city, and from our camp we can behold the Union's capital this evening. The flag looks beautiful as we see it waving in the wind from the old Capitol dome. It looks beautiful because beneath it treason has fallen, and it tells us that the old Union still lives,—showing to the world the possibilities and capabilities of institutions based on the voice of men echoing the voice of God.

On the 20th we turn over our stock, saddles and bridles to the A. Q. M., 4th Division. We part from our mules this time without any regrets, inasmuch as we need them no more, having finished our work in the south-land. But the Seventh will ever feel grateful to Major General Logan for permitting them to retain their stock until their arrival at Washington, thereby saving them from a long weary march.

On the 24th of May we cross the long bridge spanning the Potomac and enter Washington City and pass up Pennsylvania Avenue, and by the White House, with Sherman's army in the grand review. This was a proud day for Sherman and his army. Flowers and wreaths, plucked and formed by the hands of the nation's fair ones, fell thick and fast at the feet of the tramping army as it surged like an ocean wave in the great avenue. Passing by the stand where stood the nation's great men, General Sherman turns to his wife and says, "There are the Seventh Illinois and the sixteen-shooters that helped to save my army in the great battle on the Allatoona hills."

On that day there were men in the national capital who were loud in denouncing Sherman as a traitor, for his actions in his conference with General Joe Johnson. Generals Howard, Logan, Blair and Slocum are familiar with the circumstances that controlled Sherman in that conference. The seventy thousand who with him tramped the continent, have learned the history of those negotiations, and their expression is unanimous for Sherman, and to-day they are wild in denouncing all who oppose him.[220] Catching the spirit of these stalwart men, Lieutenant Flint, of Company G, writes thus:

Back to your kennels! 'tis no time
To snarl upon him now,
Ye cannot tear the blood-earned bays
From off his regal brow.

Along old Mississippi's stream,
We saw his banner fly;
We followed where from Georgia's peaks
It flapped against the sky.

And forward! vain her trackless swamps,
Her wilderness of pines,
He saw the sun rise from the sea
Flash on his serried lines!

Back to your kennels! 'tis too late
To sully Sherman's name;
To us it is the synonym
Of valor, worth and fame.

A hundred fights, a thousand miles
Of glory, blood and pain,
From our dear valley of the west,
To Carolina's plain,

Are his and ours; and peace or war,
Let his old pennon reel,
And ten times ten thousand men
Will thunder at his heel."

After the grand review, we go into camp a few miles from
the capital near the Soldier's Home. Treason and rebellion being prostrate, and the Union saved, the western troops are ordered to rendezvous at Louisville, Kentucky, preparatory to
their muster-out of the United States service.

About the first of June we leave Washington by rail, taking the
Baltimore & Ohio Railroad, and while passing by Harper's Ferry
the men make the welkin ring by singing "John Brown's soul is
marching on." Upon arriving at Parkensburg, Va., we embark on
a Government steamer and are soon floating down the Ohio.

Sitting upon the deck of the proud steamer, Lieutenant
Flint, ever full of his poetical genius, writes:

Beautiful river; well named they of old
Thee, the blue flood that pours o'er thy channel of gold,
Speed down from the mountains, thou fairest of daughters,
That meet on the breast of the father of waters.

Rush down from thy mountains and bear us along,
With bugle and drum note, and wild burst of song,
Our eyes will grow dim as they follow thy shore,
And thy waves bear us downward and homeward once more.

Bring out the old flags; their rents and their scars,
Are as dear to our hearts as their stripes and their stars,
Wave your old flags, men, point them towards home,
Proudly in victory and honor we come.

O! mothers and sisters, and sweethearts and wives,
Glean our prairies of flowers for this crown of our lives;
Strew a path for the war-horse that moves at our head,
For his rider is dear to the legions he led.

Know ye our leader? Aye, millions shall tell
How the strongholds of Treason like Jerichos fell,
From the streams of the west to the furthermost shore,
His story is writ on the banners he bore.

Shake out your old flags and point to their scars,
Sherman is leading his host from the wars;
Wave your old flags, men, point them towards home,
Shout! for in victory and honor we come.

The weather is pleasant and the boys seem happy as they
remember that blood has ceased to flow, and that a conquered
peace is drawing nigh. As we stand upon the steamer moving
so queenly, we cast our eyes towards the Kentucky shore; the
hills are green and our feelings tell us they never were so

beautiful before. Years ago, one could not help thinking of the many sad hearts that throbbed over there. But now the song of freedom is sung on that side of the river as well as on this side. Yet there are memories associated with those hills that will make us sad years to come, for many brave hearts are stilled in death over there. Over and around their graves the green grass is growing, and the freedman will weave chaplets of flowers and spread over the graves of the lone soldiers; and may be he will sing a song in grateful remembrance of his fallen benefactor. Arriving at Louisville we pass through the city and go into camp about five miles up the river.

We now notice that Colonel Rowett wears the well merited stars, which are honors fitly bestowed, and which should have fallen upon his shoulder long ere this. But as it happened he was no sycophant, and never crawled at the feet of power. After remaining in camp here a short time the Seventh is ordered to proceed to Louisville and report to the post commander for provost guard duty. We go into camp upon one of the vacant lots in the city where we remain performing the aforesaid duty, until we receive orders to prepare to be mustered out and discharged from the United States service. After weeks of anxious waiting for the orders and the completing of the rolls, on the ninth day of July, 1865, the Seventh Illinois Veteran Volunteer Infantry is mustered out of the United States service. The same evening we cross the Ohio river and take the cars at Jeffersonville, Indiana, for Springfield, Illinois, where we arrive on the 11th of July and go into camp near Camp Butler, and remain there until the 18th, when we receive our pay and final discharge, and to our homes return to enjoy again the peace and quiet of civil life.

Kind reader, our task is done; through more than four years of war and carnage unknown to but few nations, we have gone step by step to tell the story of the Seventh in those turbulent years—"years that saw this nation brought up from darkness and bondage, to light and liberty." Our mind now reverts, and we remember when they fell—remember where their life blood ebbed away, while it was yet the spring-time of life with them.

"But it was duty."
"Some things are worthless, and some others so good,
That nations who buy them pay only in blood;
For Freedom and Union each man owes his part,
And these warriors have paid their share all warm from the heart.
"For it was duty."

As the years of peace roll in, may America's triumphant and happy people cherish their names, and passing the scenes of their glory and their last struggle in their country's cause, may they drop tears to their memory, remembering that they helped to save this union in those days of war's wrathful power. In uncoffined graves, among strangers they are now resting, and no chiseled stones stand there to tell the wandering pilgrims of freedom where they sleep. Hence no epitaphs are theirs, but they need none, for these are written in the hearts of their countrymen. Farewell, ye brave-hearted men! Farewell, bright hopes of the past; farewell! farewell, noble comrades who sleep in the sunny south! Peace to the ashes of the Seventh's noble fallen; peace, eternal peace to the ashes of every fallen soldier who went down in America's great crusade for freedom, truth, and the rights of men!

"How sleep the brave who sink to rest,
With all their country's wishes blest!
When spring with dewy fingers cold,
Returns to deck the hallowed mound,
She then shall dress a sweeter sod,
Than fancy's feet have ever trod.
By fairy hands their knell is rung,
By forms unseen their dirge is sung,
Their honor comes a pilgrim gray,
To bless the turf that wraps their clay,
And freedom shall awhile repair,
To dwell a weeping hermit there.

"On fame's eternal camping ground,
Their silent tents are spread,
And glory guards with solemn rounds,
The bivouac of the dead."

NOTES TO AMBROSE'S WORK

1. This famous phrase comes from Abraham Lincoln's Second Inaugural Address, not his first.

2. Located on the fairgrounds at Springfield, and named for Illinois governor Richard Yates, Camp Yates was one of several early rendezvous points and training camps for the state's volunteers.

3. The regiment was first accepted as three-month volunteers, mustered in by Capt. (later Gen.) John Pope. A summary of its history during this time, Apr. 25–July 25, 1861, may be found in *OR Supplement,* pt. 2, 8:512–22.

4. Because Harvey and Dunsmore died while serving as three-month volunteers, their names do not appear on the final regimental roster.

5. Col. John McArthur, who would soon be a general, commanded the 12th Illinois Infantry.

6. Gen. Benjamin M. Prentiss, formerly colonel of the 10th Illinois Infantry, commanded the troops at Cairo. Col. Richard J. Oglesby, who would be elected governor of Illinois in 1864, commanded the 8th Illinois Infantry. Col. Eleazer A. Paine, who would later be promoted to general, commanded the 9th Illinois Infantry.

7. Jesse P. Davis served as the original chaplain for the regiment. He resigned in September 1862.

8. Bird's Point is in Missouri, across the Mississippi River from Cairo.

9. Gen. Meriwether "Jeff" Thompson led a largely irregular rebel force in southeast Missouri and northeast Arkansas for most of the war.

10. Colonel Cook suddenly found himself in command of the brigade (although it is unclear which regiments composed it) because General Prentiss was embroiled in a dispute over seniority with Gen. Ulysses S. Grant, who now commanded the district around Cairo. Prentiss tendered his resignation on September 1, and on September 2 he placed himself under arrest. Grant directed Cook to lead the expedition. See U.S. War Department, *War of the Rebellion: Official Records of the Union and Confederate Armies,* 128 vols. (Washington, D.C.: Government Printing Office, 1880–1901), ser. 1, 3:145–46 (hereafter cited as *OR*).

11. The "buck and gag" was a form of physical punishment for Civil War soldiers found guilty of minor crimes, such as theft. Ambrose's implication that Union soldiers often ignored strictures against pilfering civilian property is accurate.

12. Lt. Col. David Bayles, not Boyle, commanded the 11th Missouri Infantry, although orders replacing him had been issued on September 24 (*OR*, ser. 1, 3:505).

13. Capt. Joseph B. Plummer, a West Point graduate, was given command of the 11th Missouri on September 24. He commanded the post at Cape Girardeau until promoted to general in March 1862.

14. With its arrival at Fort Holt, Ky., the 7th Illinois was assigned to its first formal brigade on Oct. 14, 1861. The regiment now formed part of the Fourth Brigade, District of Southeast Missouri, along with the 28th Illinois Infantry, McAllister's Light Artillery Company, Delano's Cavalry, and one company of the 2nd Illinois Cavalry, all commanded by Cook (*OR*, ser. 1, 3:523, 534).

15. Grant was defeated by Gen. Leonidas Polk on Nov. 7, 1861, at Belmont, Mo. For the orders that directed the march of the 7th Illinois, see *OR*, ser. 1, 3:271–72.

16. For Colonel Cook's report on this episode, which involved three Confederate gunboats on Dec. 1, 1861, see *OR*, ser. 1, 7:6–7.

17. Gen. John A. McClernand, an Illinois congressman before the war, commanded a brigade at this time. The 7th Illinois and the rest of Colonel Cook's brigade would ultimately be assigned to a different division.

18. Gen. Charles F. Smith, an 1825 graduate of West Point, had been ordered by Grant on Jan. 3, 1862, to organize the Second Division, District of Cairo, from troops then scattered at Paducah, Fort Holt, and Smithland, Ky.; but Ambrose errs when he implies that the 7th Illinois joined Smith on January 15. Colonel Cook's entire brigade advanced toward Blandville, Ky., under separate orders from Grant, who commanded the District of Cairo, on Jan. 15, 1862. The regiment would not join Smith's division officially until February 3, and it would not come under Smith's personal command until February 5. See Frank J. Welcher, *The Union Army, 1861–1865: Organization and Operations*, 2 vols. (Bloomington: Indiana University Press, 1989–1993), 2:89; *OR*, ser. 1, 7:127–29, 219, 552.

19. For these movements on January 15, see *OR*, ser. 1, 7:69.

20. For the order directing this movement, see *OR*, ser. 1, 7:559–60.

21. Colonel Cook was given command of the Third Brigade of Smith's Second Division, District of West Tennessee, on February 3. In addition to the 7th Illinois, the brigade included the 7th Iowa Infantry, 12th Iowa Infantry, 13th Missouri Infantry, 50th Illinois Infantry, and 1st Missouri Light Artillery. The 13th Missouri, however, was reassigned on February 8, the 7th Iowa on February 11. In re-

turn, Cook received on February 11 the 52nd Indiana Infantry (*OR*, ser. 1, 7:219–20).

22. Gen. Henry W. Halleck had been appointed commander of the mammoth Department of the Missouri, which included Kentucky west of the Cumberland River, in November 1861. McClernand, who led the First Division in Grant's advance against Fort Henry, claimed to have given Camp Halleck its name (*OR*, ser. 1, 7:127–28).

23. The small Confederate garrison at Fort Henry, which guarded the Tennessee River south of the Kentucky state line, surrendered on Feb. 6, 1862, after offering light resistence. As Ambrose implies, the 7th Illinois took no active role in the fighting. See Colonel Cook's report, *OR*, ser. 1, 7:219–20.

24. Gen. Lloyd Tilghman had commanded Fort Henry. He would be exchanged in August 1862.

25. Fort Donelson, which defended the Cumberland River on the Tennessee-Kentucky border, was Grant's next target in the campaign. Operations against the fort continued from February 12 until the garrison surrendered on Feb. 16, 1862.

26. Col. Jacob J. Lauman and Colonel MacArthur commanded the Fourth and First Brigades of Smith's division. Col. Richard J. Oglesby commanded a brigade in McClernand's division.

27. For Colonel Cook's report on his brigade's role at Fort Donelson—although without reference to the dramatic remarks Ambrose attributes to General Smith—see *OR*, ser. 1, 7:220–22.

28. Gen. Simon B. Buckner surrendered Fort Donelson to his former West Point classmate Grant. Grant received the nickname Unconditional Surrender Grant—which happened to coincide with his first two initials, U. S.—as a result of his rigid terms of capitulation, although Ambrose quotes the first sentence inaccurately: "No terms except unconditional and immediate surrender can be accepted" (*OR*, ser. 1, 7:161). For the Henry and Donelson campaign generally, see Benjamin Franklin Cooling, *Forts Henry and Donelson: The Key to the Confederate Heartland* (Knoxville: University of Tennessee Press, 1987).

29. British poet Thomas Campbell wrote "Battle of the Baltic" to celebrate Horatio Nelson's victory over Denmark in 1801.

30. Official figures show that the 7th Illinois had 22, not 20, casualties (*OR*, ser. 1, 7:168). Further details are known about three of the wounded men. Cpl. William Boring of Springfield had a portion of his right leg amputated; Pvts. Dilivan (or Dilavan) B. Daniels and Charles Huffman, both from Carlinville, were discharged from service on May 1, 1862, after having portions of their right legs amputated. Huffman was seventeen years old. See U.S. War Department, *Medical*

and Surgical History of the Civil War, 12 vols. (1870–1883; rpt., Wilmington, N.C.: Broadfoot, 1991), 11:246, 12:484, 496 (cited hereafter as *Medical and Surgical History*).

31. The regiment's medical staff at this time consisted of Dr. Richard L. Metcalf, surgeon, and James Hamilton, assistant surgeon (*OR,* ser. 1, 7:222).

32. Lt. James M. Munn resigned from the army May 30, 1862.

33. On this day, too, the composition of the Third Brigade was changed to include the 7th Illinois, 50th Illinois Infantry, 57th Illinois Infantry, 58th Illinois Infantry, and two companies of the 2nd Illinois Cavalry (*OR,* ser. 1, 7:649).

34. There may be more to this episode with the Clarksville tobacco factories than Ambrose allows. By early March 1862, Colonel Cook was suspected in Washington, D.C., of participating in a fraudulent scheme with army sutlers. He supposedly used the 7th Illinois to confiscate commodities like tobacco—rice, sugar, and coffee are mentioned specifically in the complaint—then delivered these goods to the sutlers who, in turn, sold them for large profits. "[T]hey tell me," an anonymous informer explained, "that Cook has no part of the profits, but he is very clever and accommodating to his friends, one of whom is a personal friend of Cook's, and lives in Springfield, Ill." Indeed, Cook had no end of political and business connections, being the son of a congressman, grandson of a governor, and himself a former mayor of Springfield. The rumors appear to have ended his promising military career. Praised as a hero and soon promoted to general for his actions at Fort Donelson, Cook never held another important field command. See *OR,* ser. 1, 10(pt. 2):13–15; Ezra J. Warner, *Generals in Blue: Lives of the Union Commanders* (Baton Rouge: Louisiana State University Press, 1964), 89.

35. When the Confederates fled Nashville following the surrender of Fort Donelson, Grant ordered Gen. William Nelson, who commanded a division under Gen. Don Carlos Buell, to occupy the city.

36. Ambrose consistently misspells the last name of Gen. Albert Sidney Johnston, who, as commander of the Western Department, would lead Confederate forces against Grant in the upcoming Shiloh campaign. Gen. Pierre G. T. Beauregard served as Johnston's second in command.

37. The Army of the Tennessee was not officially created until October 1862, even though at the battle of Shiloh, fought Apr. 6–8, 1862, Grant's Army in the Field, District of West Tennessee, was often referred to by that name (Welcher, *Union Army,* 2:220, 229).

38. It is hard to imagine the taciturn Grant shouting these words.

39. Johnston died needlessly on the battlefield when his staff failed to stop the flow of blood from a relatively minor wound.

40. A controversy arose after the battle and continued long after the war as to whether Grant or General Buell deserved credit for the victory. For Buell's case, see Stephen D. Engle, *Don Carlos Buell: Most Promising of Them All* (Chapel Hill: University of North Carolina Press, 1999), 235–37.

41. For the regiment's role at Shiloh, see Major Rowett's report in *OR*, ser. 1, 10(pt. 1):162–63. Ambrose does not mention that the Third Brigade was commanded in the battle by Col. (later Gen.) Thomas W. Sweeny of the 52nd Illinois Infantry. The brigade consisted of the 7th Illinois, 8th Iowa Infantry, 50th Illinois Infantry, 52nd Illinois Infantry, 57th Illinois Infantry, and 58th Illinois Infantry. John Cook, who had been promoted to general in March, returned to the army on April 5, but he did not command any troops in the battle (*OR*, ser. 1, 10[pt. 1]:184). For the Shiloh campaign generally, see Wiley Sword, *Shiloh: Bloody April* (New York: Morrow, 1974); and Larry J. Daniel, *Shiloh: The Battle That Changed the Civil War* (New York: Simon & Schuster, 1997).

42. Alden Bates of Wayne, Ill., is listed as a corporal on the regiment's roster.

43. In fact, the 7th Illinois suffered 99 casualties at Shiloh: 17 killed, 81 wounded, and 1 captured. This was not, however, the heaviest sacrifice by an Illinois regiment in a battle—one of the bloodiest of the war—that totaled 23,740 casualties. The 9th Illinois Infantry, fighting in the Second Brigade of the Second Division, lost 366 men. Illinois contributed 28 of the 65 Union regiments at Shiloh. See *OR*, ser. 1, 10(pt. 1):101; Hicken, *Illinois in the Civil War*, 70.

44. Dr. James R. Zearing, surgeon of the 57th Illinois Infantry, described these conditions in a letter to his wife dated Apr. 8, 1862: "The wounded of the whole army were brought to the landing at the river, where we erected tents and used steamboats for putting them in. You may imagine the scene of from two to three thousand wounded men at one point calling to have their wounds dressed. . . . [T]he crowded state of everything and the absence of extensive preparations for such an event caused a great deal of suffering. . ." ("Letters Written by Dr. James R. Zearing to His Wife Lucinda Helmer Zearing during the Civil War, 1861–1865," *Publications of the Illinois State Historical Library*, no. 28 [Springfield, Ill.: Phillips Brothers, 1922], 156).

45. Casualties and resignations required these changes in the regiment's leadership. Former sergeant John E. Sullivan, mentioned earlier by Ambrose, was promoted to second lieutenant of Company I in February 1862 and to first lieutenant in March; but Lt. John A. Smith of Company E did not become a captain until November 1862. Men not already mentioned in the text are former sergeant Benjamin F. Sweeny

of Company A, whose commission was not dated until June 1862, and former sergeant Henry Ahern of Company F, although the regiment's roster mistakenly lists his commission as coming in 1864. Ira A. Church was made captain of Company D when Captain Munn resigned his commission; Church, too, would resign in September 1862.

46. *OR,* ser. 1, 10(pt. 2):152, 185, show the 52nd Illinois Infantry but not the 22nd Ohio Infantry as part of the Third Brigade, Second Division. Col. Silas D. Baldwin of the 57th Illinois Infantry replaced Sweeny, who had been wounded at Shiloh, as brigade commander. Gen. Thomas A. Davies led the division.

47. Gen. William T. Sherman commanded the Fifth Division.

48. Gen. John Pope, who had mustered the 7th Illinois into service as a captain, was a rising military star with victories at New Madrid, Mo., and Island No. 10 in April. Now directing a wing of the advancing army, his men won the first of several skirmishes around Farmington, Miss., in May 1862 (*OR,* ser. 1, 10[pt. 1]:801–2).

49. For the controversy surrounding Grant after Shiloh, see Brooks D. Simpson, *Ulysses S. Grant: Triumph over Adversity, 1822–1865* (New York: Houghton Mifflin, 2000), 135–38, 140–42. As a result of these charges, General Halleck had taken personal command of the Union force that advanced toward Corinth.

50. Gen. George B. McClellan was in the midst of his Peninsula campaign in Virginia.

51. Governor Yates was one of several Northern governors and other dignitaries who visited the army in the weeks after the battle of Shiloh.

52. Pvt. Ethan Drake of Company G must have been one of the men fired at while on picket duty, for even though Ambrose fails to mention the episode Drake lost his left eye to a gunshot wound on May 5. He was discharged from the army on Nov. 3, 1862 (*Medical and Surgical History,* 8:334).

53. Gen. Stephen A. Hurlbut commanded the Fourth Division of Halleck's force, which had been divided into two wings and a reserve. Gen. George Thomas directed the Right Wing, which included the divisions of Davies, Hurlbut, William Sherman, Thomas J. McKean, and Thomas W. Sherman (*OR,* ser. 1, 10[pt. 2]:185–86).

54. The Confederates under Beauregard abandoned Corinth on the night of May 29–30 and retreated to Tupelo, thus ending a Union siege of Corinth that had begun in late April.

55. Gen. Earl Van Dorn had commanded the Confederate troops around Farmington.

56. Sterling Price was another Confederate general operating at this time under Beauregard in northern Mississippi. By the end of July, he would command the District of Tennessee, based at Tupelo, Miss.

57. Ambrose is premature in referring to Pvt. William P. Hackney as a captain, a rating he would not achieve until October 1864. He also served for a time as a sergeant in Company H (see chap. XI).

58. Gen. Edward O. C. Ord commanded the post and garrison at Corinth. One member of the 7th Illinois expressed regret that the previous commander, Gen. George Cadwalader, had been relieved, but concluded, "I suppose we will get along just as well for there is not much difference who commands, for they are all 'birds of one feather'" (David B. Givler to Frank, Sept. 21, 1862, in Givler, "Intimate Glimpses of Army Life").

59. The First and Second Confiscation Acts, passed by the U.S. Congress on Aug. 6, 1861, and July 17, 1862, authorized armies in the field to confiscate "property" used to support the Confederacy. This definition included slaves, who were soon referred to euphemistically as "contraband" of war, and gave them protection within Union lines.

60. Ambrose is premature in promoting Lt. Thomas McGuire, who was not made captain of Company A until January 1863 (see end of this chapter). George T. Sayles did not receive his commission until December 1862.

61. Gen. William S. Rosecrans defeated Price in the battle of Iuka on Sept. 19, 1862.

62. Having felt political pressure through the preceding summer to take some dramatic step against slavery, Abraham Lincoln issued his preliminary emancipation proclamation on Sept. 22, 1862, following George McClellan's "victory" at the battle of Antietam. As Ambrose suggests later in the narrative, however, many Illinois soldiers opposed emancipation. See Hicken, *Illinois in the Civil War,* 128–32.

63. Some of these promotions are reflected in the reorganization of the Third Brigade, Second Division, which on Sept. 30, 1862, operated as part of the Army of West Tennessee. The brigade now included the 7th Illinois, 9th Illinois Infantry, 50th Illinois Infantry, 2nd Iowa Infantry, 7th Iowa Infantry, and 14th Missouri (later known as the 66th Illinois) Infantry, although its composition would change within the week (*OR,* ser. 1, 17[pt. 2]:249).

64. Col. John McDermott commanded the 15th Michigan Infantry; Col. John M. Oliver (not Olive), who was also from the 15th Michigan, commanded the entire brigade (Second) as part of the Sixth Division. Ambrose describes the opening of the battle of Corinth, fought Oct. 3–4, 1862.

65. Gen. Pleasant A. Hackleman commanded the First Brigade. The Third Brigade had only three regiments at the battle of Corinth: 7th Illinois, 50th Illinois Infantry, and 57th Illinois Infantry.

66. Rosecrans commanded the Army of the Mississippi, the second of the two Union armies engaged at the battle of Corinth. Gen. David S. Stanley and Gen. Charles S. Hamilton commanded divisions in the army. For Rosecrans's report on the battle, see *OR*, ser. 1, 17(pt. 1):166–70.

67. Maj. Albert M. Powell commanded the artillery of the Third Division, Army of the Mississippi, in the fighting at Corinth, and his old Battery M, known as Powell's Battery, also fought with that army. Artillery support for the Army of West Tennessee, which could have supported Davies's brigade, was supplied by the four other batteries of the 1st Missouri Artillery, commanded by Maj. George H. Stone.

68. Col. John V. DuBois took command of the brigade when Baldwin was wounded.

69. Col. John S. Birge's (not Berge's) Sharpshooters had been transferred to Grant's command from Missouri in February, assigned to the Fourth Brigade of the Second Division. They were led at Corinth by Col. Patrick E. Burke and known both as the Western Sharpshooters and the 14th Missouri Infantry. They were designated the 66th Illinois Infantry in November 1862.

70. Men in new positions include the following: A. D. Knowlton of Company F had been a lieutenant. Seth Raymond of Litchfield, Ill., had been a sergeant in Company D; he would later become captain of the company. Thomas B. Atchinson had been a sergeant in Company F. William C. Gillison had been promoted from sergeant of Company K, although the regiment's roster lists his commission as January 1863; he would later become captain of his company. John A. Smith did not receive his commission as captain of Company E until November 1862.

71. Gen. William L. Cabell commanded a Confederate brigade in the battle of Corinth.

72. Sgt. Laban Wheeler of Lincoln, Ill.

73. Captain J. Lovell was an assistant adjutant general in the Second Division.

74. Col. William P. Rogers of the 2nd Texas Infantry led a brigade at the battle of Corinth.

75. Capt. William Hanna of the 50th Illinois Infantry was an aide-de-camp to General DuBois.

76. Sgt. Isaac D. Newell appears on the regiment's roster as Corporal Dewell; Cpl. Joseph Bordwell was from Atlanta, Ill. Colonel Babcock praised both men in his report (see n. 77).

77. See Colonel Babcock's report for the regiment's role in the fighting of Oct. 3–4, 1862, at Corinth, *OR*, ser. 1, 17(pt. 1):292–94. For the battle of Corinth generally, see Peter Cozzens, *The Darkest Days*

of the War: The Battles of Iuka and Corinth (Urbana: University of Illinois Press, 1997). For the entire operation that began at Fort Henry and concluded at Corinth, see Stephen D. Engle, *Struggle for the Heartland: The Campaigns from Fort Henry to Corinth* (Lincoln: University of Nebraska Press, 2001).

78. Ambrose slightly understates the regiment's losses àt Corinth, which official reports put at 77 (*OR*, ser. 1, 17[pt. 1]:175). More can be said about two of the wounded men. Pvt. Jasper Eveland of Atlanta, Ill., had a bone broken in his right leg from a gunshot wound. Partial amputation was required, and the remaining loose skin was cut off on Jan. 10, 1863. He was discharged from the army. Pvt. Roswell C. Staples of Bunker Hill, Ill., had already been wounded at Fort Donelson. At Corinth, he was wounded in the right thigh. Dr. Metcalf, the regiment's surgeon, personally amputated his leg, and Staples was discharged from service on Nov. 26, 1862 (*Medical and Surgical History*, 11:217, 255).

79. Large numbers of troops and the difficulty of protecting long supply lines required that Illinois soldiers, along with the rest of the army, forage and confiscate food from Southern civilians by the autumn of 1862. Like Ambrose, most men saw this means of subsisting themselves as just retribution for the South. Another member of the 7th Illinois told a friend that foraging put "new zeal into the soldiers for they think they have protected rebel property about long enough now, they intend to help themselves to anything that will add to their comfort!" (quoted in Hicken, *Illinois in the Civil War*, 80–81).

80. Sgt. Eugene Frank Morse of Mattoon, Ill., would be promoted to lieutenant and adjutant in February 1865.

81. This unidentified Confederate appears to have belonged to the 42nd Alabama Infantry, which was brigaded with the 2nd Texas Infantry of Colonel Rogers. For a report of his regiment's action against Battery or Redoubt (not Fort) Robinett, see *OR*, ser. 1, 17(pt. 1):167–70.

82. If brigaded with these regiments at this time, it could have been only a temporary assignment. See n. 85.

83. W.D.B. was William Denison Bickham, a reporter for Murat Halstead's *Cincinnati Commercial*. Ambrose was especially unhappy with Bickham's article because the *Commercial*, known as the "soldier's paper," was so widely read in the western armies. See J. Cutler Andrews, *The North Reports the Civil War* (Pittsburgh: University of Pittsburgh Press, 1955), 28.

84. Rosecrans's congratulatory order to the army, which included the remark about Davies's division, is in *OR*, ser. 1, 17(pt. 1):172–73.

85. By December 1862, the 7th Illinois formed part of the Third Brigade, District of Corinth, along with the 50th Illinois Infantry, 57th Illinois Infantry, and 18th Missouri Infantry. Colonel Rowett commanded the regiment, Col. Moses M. Bane of the 50th Illinois led the brigade, and Gen. Grenville M. Dodge headed the district (*OR,* ser. 1, 17[pt. 2]:517). Colonel Babcock, as Ambrose reveals at the end of the next chapter, had been assigned to a Military Commission that was hearing cases at Corinth.

86. Gen. Nathan Bedford Forrest commanded a brigade of Confederate cavalry in West Tennessee that was engaged in a particularly destructive expedition against Union supply and communication lines—mostly railroads—between Dec. 11, 1862, and Jan. 3, 1863 (*OR,* ser. 1, 17[pt. 1]:593–97). General Dodge, a noted civil engineer before the war, was ordered to repair the railroads in West Tennessee and northern Mississippi and then protect them against raiders like Forrest.

87. Ambrose conveys the hardening mood in Union armies everywhere toward Confederate civilians and their property. As he suggests, much of the changed attitude was inspired by growing frustration over the inability of Union soldiers to catch or control elusive foes like Forrest, the mounting fatigue of campaigning, the seemingly endless nature of the war, and the apparent material abundance of rebel communities in comparison to the slim rations available to the army. An officer in another Illinois regiment decided, "I begin to think the better way would be to *utterly desolate wherever we went. . ."* (quoted in Hicken, *Illinois in the Civil War,* 79–81). See generally Mark Grimsley, *The Hard Hand of War: Union Military Policy toward Southern Civilians, 1861–1865* (Cambridge: Cambridge University Press, 1995). General Dodge emphasized the good behavior of his men in the official report of this seven-day reconnaissance, as though to suggest that restraint was not the norm: "Great credit is due the officers and men of the command for the . . . orderly manner in which they conducted themselves on the march, being entirely free from pillaging or unauthorized depredations of any kind" (*OR,* ser. 1, 17[pt. 1]:550).

88. By "present mode of warfare," Ambrose refers to legitimate cavalry raids, to be distinguished from the bushwhacking and guerrilla tactics against which he and his comrades would later contend.

89. Gen. Ambrose Burnside had been beaten back across the Rappahannock River by Gen. Robert E. Lee following the battle of Fredericksburg in December 1862. In early January 1863, Burnside still contemplated an aggressive move against Lee and the Confederate capital.

90. These are references to the battles of Stones River (or Murfreesboro), Tenn., fought Dec. 31, 1862–Jan. 2, 1863, and Fredericksburg, Va., fought Dec. 11–15, 1862.

91. These are references to the variety of reading habits of Civil War soldiers. The "Waverlys" allude to the novels of Sir Walter Scott; "Harper's cuts" were the illustrations (woodcuts) in *Harper's Weekly* newspaper.

92. The P.M. is probably the postmaster (linked to the P.O.— post office—mentioned in the preceding paragraph), but it might also refer to the provost marshal, an officer commanding the military police of Civil War armies.

93. Henry Hampton was a private in Company K.

94. The M.D.s were the mule drivers.

95. Ambrose refers to the debate—still carried on among historians—about the relative merits of the Union's eastern and western armies. See Michael C. C. Adams, *Our Masters the Rebels: A Speculation on Union Military Failure in the East, 1861–1865* (Cambridge, Mass.: Harvard University Press, 1978). For a similar—and related— debate on the Confederate side, see Richard M. McMurry, *Two Great Rebel Armies: An Essay in Confederate Military History* (Chapel Hill: University of North Carolina Press, 1989).

96. The officers who have not yet been identified are Col. Augustus L. Chetlain, Lt. Col. John S. Wilcox, Col. August Mersey (not Merser), and Lt. Col. John Morrill. Colonel Burke's 14th Missouri Infantry had been redesignated the 66th (not 65th) Illinois Infantry. James Zearing of the 57th Illinois Infantry told his wife that the resolutions were published in the Chicago newspapers, and he insisted in mid-February, "The army is as determined as ever to fight until the rebellion is crushed. There is scarcely a symptom of disaffection" ("Letters Written by Dr. James R. Zearing," 169).

97. Lt. Col. J. J. Phillips of the committee. Such testimonials were common in 1863, after the Copperhead movement had gained momentum with significant Democratic electoral gains against Republicans in the autumn of 1862.

98. Praise for Rev. W. Perkins, who ministered to the 7th Illinois from December 1862 to April 1864, came from outside the regiment, too. An officer in the 59th Illinois Infantry wrote of Perkins a year later, "He gave us a good sermon and the meeting was a good one. He gave officers a scoring as to morality. Between 50 and 60 men spoke of their religious experience and five or six men stood up and asked to be prayed for" (Arnold Gates, ed., *The Rough Side of War: The Civil War Journal of Chesley A. Mosman, 1st Lieutenant, Company D, 59th Illinois Volunteer Infantry Regiment* [Garden City, N.Y.: Basin

Publishing, 1987], 159). Not all chaplains were so inspirational. Zearing told his wife on Feb. 14, 1863, "I find there are a great many things practiced in the army that would not be considered strictly correct at home. I suppose it is because we are seldom instructed by our chaplains. They grow as lazy in their habits as the rest of us. . ." ("Letters Written by Dr. James R. Zearing," 169).

99. Other parts of Dodge's command were not so inactive in February and March 1863, as they kept busy operating against Confederate cavalry. For example, see *OR,* ser. 1, 23(pt. 1):63–64.

100. One of the cases likely being heard by the commission involved Colonel Baldwin, Babcock's former brigade commander, who was subsequently dismissed from military service. See "Letters Written by Dr. James R. Zearing," 165–66, 168, 171.

101. Col. (later Gen.) Philip Dale Roddey was not a guerrilla but a very effective Confederate raider who served under both Forrest and Gen. Joseph Wheeler, most often in northern Alabama, his home state. Dodge, who proved to be very effective in protecting railroads against rebel raiders and guerrillas, was beginning his Courtland, Ala., expedition, Apr. 15–May 5, 1863 (*OR,* ser. 1, 23[pt. 1]:241–61).

102. Ambrose consistently misspells the name of Col. Abel D. Streight, who conducted an unsuccessful raid from Tuscumbia, Ala., toward Rome, Ga., Apr. 26–May 3, 1863.

103. Ambrose refers to the reputation earned by units of Kansans and Southern unionists for treating Confederate civilians even more harshly than did Federal troops from the North. The two units mentioned by Ambrose were the 1st Alabama Cavalry and 7th Kansas Cavalry. The latter unit was also known as Jennison's Jayhawkers, after its erstwhile commander, Charles R. Jennison.

104. Ambrose supplies much more information about the role of the regiment in this campaign, especially the fighting on Apr. 28, 1863, than does the report of brigade commander Colonel Bane (*OR,* ser. 1, 23[pt. 1]:259–60).

105. Again, Ambrose gives a more detailed account of this four-day march from Town Creek to Corinth than does Colonel Bane (*OR,* ser. 1, 23[pt. 1]:260).

106. General Burnside's General Orders No. 38 led to the arrest, eventual trial, and exile of former Democratic Ohio congressman Clement L. Vallandigham, the North's most notorious Copperhead. See William Marvel, *Burnside* (Chapel Hill: University of North Carolina Press, 1991), 231–38.

107. Ambrose M. Miller was one of two representatives in the Illinois legislature from the counties of Sangamon and Logan.

108. Grace Greenwood was the pen name of Sarah Jane Clarke

Lippincott (1823–1904), a popular writer and newspaper correspondent. She gave patriotic lectures in Union army camps and hospitals during the war.

109. These various references to Union heroism include Gen. Lewis "Lew" Wallace, who led a division at Shiloh; Gen. Joseph Hooker in the battle of Lookout Mountain (although it did not occur until November 1863); the principal Confederate prison in Richmond, Va.; and the ironclad warship USS *Monitor*.

110. Vallandigham was, indeed, banished by President Lincoln, but Ambrose knew full well, as he acknowledges in the next chapter, that Gen. Robert E. Lee defeated Joseph Hooker at the battle of Chancellorsville, May 1–6, 1863. Part of Hooker's strategic plan called for Gen. George Stoneman to lead a cavalry raid in Lee's rear. A portion of Stoneman's command reached the outskirts of Richmond, but he never seriously threatened the city. Ambrose here tries to show how camp rumors were constantly causing hopes to rise and fall within the army.

111. A member of the 7th Iowa Infantry had a different view of Ambrose and his comrades. In a letter dated May 27, 1863, from Bethel, Tenn., he wrote, "[T]he 7th Ill is . . . familiarly known as 'Cooks Crampers' the term is significant implying that any thing alying loose has an extreme liability to stick to their fingers." The Iowan did agree with Ambrose, however, when he added that "the two 7's will make a strong team." See John K. Mahon, ed., "The Civil War Letters of Samuel Mahon, Seventh Iowa Infantry," *Iowa Journal of History* 51 (1953): 244. That the soldiers still associated the regiment with General Cook nearly a year after he had left it is also interesting, given the old suspicions about Cook's mercantile dealings.

112. Gen. Lorenzo Thomas was appointed adjutant general of the U.S. Army in August 1861 and held the post until 1869.

113. Col. Jacob D. Biffle commanded the 9th (also known as the 19th) Tennessee Cavalry under Forrest.

114. D.D. refers to a doctor of divinity, but the identity of R.A.Y. is uncertain.

115. For Col. Florence M. Cornyn's report on his destructive raid from Corinth, Miss., to Florence, Ala., May 26–31, 1863, see *OR*, ser. 1, 23(pt. 1):349–51.

116. Converting infantry to mounted infantry, either on mules or horses, was not uncommon, as Union field commanders found it extremely difficult to contain Confederate guerrillas with foot soldiers. At least one company in the regiment—Company C—appears to have been mounted on horses (David B. Givler to Frank, Dec. 9, 1863, in Givler, "Intimate Glimpses of Army Life").

117. Neither Captain Aldridge nor Colonel Horton can be identified, although a Lt. Col. George H. Morton operated at this time with the 2nd Tennessee Cavalry on the Tennessee-Mississippi border.

118. The garrison at Vicksburg, Miss., surrendered to Grant after a 47-day siege on July 4, 1863.

119. Thomas Moore (1779–1852) was an Irish poet.

120. Colonel Phillips of the 9th Illinois Infantry, also serving now as mounted infantry, and Col. (later Gen.) Edward Hatch, who commanded a cavalry brigade, were on Biffle's trail in the summer of 1863.

121. Commanders in both armies frequently ordered their men to witness the execution of comrades in hopes that the experience would serve as a deterrent to desertion and other serious crimes.

122. Sgt. Solomon C. Leatherman can be identified but not the other two men.

123. Col. John F. Newsom had been authorized to recruit a cavalry regiment within Union lines earlier that year. By late July 1863, he had raised eight companies, known collectively as Newsom's Tennessee Cavalry Regiment. See Thomas A. Wigginton et al., *Tennesseans in the Civil War: A Military History of Confederate and Union Units with Available Rosters of Personnel*, 2 vols. (Nashville: Civil War Centennial Commission, 1964), 1:110–11.

124. S. L. Ross was the only member of the Tennessee legislature with that surname between 1857 and 1861, but there were a Joseph L. Rosson and a James G. Rose, the latter serving as lieutenant colonel of the 61st Tennessee Mounted Infantry. See Philip M. Hamer, ed., *Tennessee: A History, 1673–1932*, 4 vols. (New York: American Historical Society, 1933), 2:1019, 1021.

125. For Major Estabrook's report on the expedition from La Grange to Toone's Station, Tenn., Sept. 11–16, 1863, see *OR*, ser. 1, 30(pt. 2):652–53.

126. Gen. Quincy A. Gillmore had begun a bombardment of Charleston, S.C., in late August 1863 that would continue for nearly 600 days. One of the earliest benefits of his campaign came with the surrender of Fort Wagner on Sept. 8, 1863.

127. The name of Sergeant Pickott does not appear on the regiment's roster.

128. For Colonel Rowett's report on the expedition from Corinth into West Tennessee, Sept. 27–Oct. 1, 1863, see *OR*, ser. 1, 30(pt. 2):662. Interestingly, Ambrose provides the same dates as Rowett for this expedition, whereas the regiment's published Record of Events says the scout took place on September 21–25. See *OR Supplement*, pt. 2, 8:487.

129. See *OR*, ser. 1, 30(pt. 4):55.

130. This episode refers to the defeat of Clement Vallandigham, who campaigned in Ohio's gubernatorial election from exile in Canada.

131. The identity of the guerrilla Smith is uncertain.

132. The commands of Col. George E. Spencer and Gen. Samuel W. Ferguson skirmished at Vincent's Crossroads, Miss., on Oct. 26, 1863 (*OR*, ser. 1, 31[pt. 1]:37–38).

133. Sherman now commanded the Department and Army of the Tennessee, with the 7th Illinois serving in General Hurlbut's XVI Corps. On Oct. 31, 1863, the corps formed part of the army's Left Wing, led by General Dodge, with the regiment part of the Third Brigade, led by Colonel Bane. The other regiments of the brigade were the 50th Illinois Infantry, 57th Illinois Infantry, 113th Illinois Infantry, 120th Illinois Infantry, 39th Iowa Infantry, and 18th Missouri Infantry (*OR*, ser. 1, 31[pt. 1]:281).

134. Orders for the march directed the First Brigade and "Seventh Illinois Mounted Infantry" to bring up the rear, but official reports make no further mention of the regiment's role on the expedition (*OR*, ser. 1, 31[pt. 3]:82).

135. A report of the movements of the Second Division of XVI Corps for Oct. 31–Nov. 11, 1863, states, as mentioned by Ambrose, that the 7th Illinois and 9th Illinois "were kept in advance and on the flanks of the column during the entire march" to Pulaski (*OR*, ser. 1, 31[pt. 3]:289).

136. Col. James B. Weaver commanded the 2nd Iowa Infantry.

137. Col. (later Gen.) Adam Rankin Johnson had escaped capture with a few hundred men during John Hunt Morgan's disastrous Indiana-Ohio raid in the summer of 1863. At this time, he operated under Forrest in East Tennessee.

138. Ferdinand Yeager had been promoted to captain in December 1862. As Ambrose states, parts of the regiment were again operating separately. Rowett's headquarters was at Pulaski, Tenn., on Nov. 25, 1863, several dozen miles northeast of Waterloo, Ala. Assigned to repair the damage done by raiders to the railroad between Columbia, Tenn., and Decatur, Ala., Rowett reported that Newsom was again operating in the area (*OR*, ser. 1, 31[pt. 3]:251).

139. By November 28, Rowett had returned to Eastport, where he was to help assemble "mounted men enough" to pursue Roddy, who was thought to command two regiments near Florence, Ala. (*OR*, ser. 1, 31[pt. 3]:264).

140. George Moore commanded a company of Alabama cavalry, but he apparently operated only loosely under the control of Nathan B. Forrest. An Iowa soldier described him as "Chief of a band of *robbers*." He was a slippery character, too. Captured at least twice in early 1864, he always managed to escape. See James I. Robertson, Jr.,

ed., "'Such Is War': The Letters of an Orderly in the 7th Iowa Infantry," *Iowa Journal of History* 58 (1960): 325–28 and notes 16 and 22.

141. The scout Lowery cannot be further identified.

142. Rowett had orders to take eight squadrons "for the purpose of making a reconnaissance in the vicinity of Lexington, and protecting Union families who desire to obtain refuge inside our lines" (*OR*, ser. 1, 31[pt. 3]:373).

143. Ambrose refers to Lt. Col. M. D. Moreland, who commanded a battalion of Alabama cavalry under Roddey.

144. Mounted infantry units were kept busy with numerous duties that winter. Grenville Dodge summarized their activities in a report dated Dec. 15, 1863: "The mounted infantry have been employed watching the Tennessee River and the country toward Eastport, and have captured in several skirmishes some 300 prisoners, including 21 officers. The work upon the railroad has been immense, and the running of mills, guarding trains, etc., have kept the command very busy and very healthy" (*OR*, ser. 1, 31[pt. 3]:413; see also 451).

145. The regiment's roster indicates that Henry Ahern did not receive his commission as captain of Company F until November 1864, as Ambrose himself states in the following chapter.

146. The Veteran Volunteer Act granted men who reenlisted for the war a $400 bounty, a month's furlough, and transportation home. Several Illinois regiments became caught up in the enthusiastic atmosphere, although a measure of peer pressure was necessary to get some men to reenlist. Even then, not a few veterans were motivated less by patriotism than by *"green back* fever," as a member of Company C observed (Hicken, *Illinois in the Civil War,* 240–45).

147. At the start of 1864, the 7th Illinois still formed part of Dodge's Left Wing of XVI Corps, but the Third Brigade had been assigned to the Second Division, which was commanded by General Sweeny. Additionally, the 113th and 120th Illinois Infantry had been dropped from the brigade (*OR*, ser. 1, 31[pt. 3]:567).

148. General Cook headed the District of Illinois with his headquarters at Springfield.

149. The regiment did, in fact, receive a tumultuous welcome, although Ambrose neglects to mention that, on the trip to Springfield, some men became so rowdy that provost marshal guards had to be summoned aboard the train. An altercation followed (Hicken, *Illinois in the Civil War,* 244).

150. Even before leaving Camp Butler, located in Springfield, to rejoin the army in Alabama, the 7th Illinois had been reassigned to its earlier place in the Third Brigade of Sweeny's division, although

the brigade was now commanded by Col. Madison Miller (*OR,* ser. 1, 32[pt. 3]:103).

151. *OR,* ser. 1, 32(pt. 3):103.

152. Major Estabrook reported the regiment's progress on Mar. 23, 1864, to division headquarters and delivered eight prisoners of war, six of them Confederate deserters. In return, he received orders to guard the roads leading to Pulaski from the west and southwest (*OR,* ser. 1, 32[pt. 3]:126–27).

153. The regiment received orders to advance on this day (*OR,* ser. 1, 32[pt. 3]:141).

154. Samuel E. Fergus received his commission as a second lieutenant in Company H in November 1862. Forrest was busy conducting a raid though parts of western Tennessee and Kentucky in March–April 1864, but he did not enter Memphis. Gen. James Longstreet led an independent command in operations against Union-occupied Knoxville, Tenn., in November–December 1863, but he was on the defensive in East Tennessee by March 1864, and he and his men would rejoin the Army of Northern Virginia in April.

155. Captain R is Captain Ring, and Sergeant A is probably John F. Adams of Company H, although Sgt. Eldridge Atchison served in Company F. Neither Sergeant N nor the South's literary star can be identified.

156. Ambrose's description fails to convey the larger picture. Confederate guerrilla bands and cavalry units swarmed through the area at this time, and several communications from army and corps headquarters show that the 7th Illinois was almost constantly deployed on picket duty and reconnaissance patrols. See *OR,* ser. 1, 32(pt. 3):309, 349, 389, 442, 525–26, 535. The Confederates were also well aware of the regiment's strength and position, as shown by a report to Roddey dated Apr. 25, 1864 (*OR,* ser. 1, 32[pt. 3]:830).

157. There were two lieutenants in the detachment who might be so identified, Henry Ahern and Thomas B. Atchison of Company F. Ambrose would not be commissioned until July 1864.

158. With Colonel Bane back in command, the brigade no longer contained the 18th Missouri Infantry (*OR,* ser. 1, 32[pt. 3]:564).

159. Josiah Lee is listed as a corporal on the roster of Company F.

160. Rowett's situation is communicated in *OR,* ser. 1, 38(pt. 4):86, 110.

161. Thomas McGuire received his commission as captain in January 1863; Edward R. Roberts received his commission barely two weeks before being captured. The story of Captain Roberts's capture and subsequent escape, based on his own recollections of the events, is told in Josephine Craven Chandler, "An Episode of the Civil War: A

Romance of Coincidence," *Publications of the Illinois State Historical Library,* no. 31 (Springfield, Ill.: Phillips Brothers, 1924), 112–22, although Chandler misleadingly refers to Edwards as Colonel Edwards.

162. Further details of the attack that drove Rowett's command out of Florence are in *OR,* ser. 1, 38(pt. 4):110, 142–43. The Confederate force, which clearly took the regiment by surprise, was led by Adam Johnson (*OR,* ser. 1, 38[pt. 4]:247).

163. Both the 7th Illinois and the 9th Ohio Cavalry were ordered back to Florence on May 13, 1864, but brigade headquarters still underestimated the size of Confederate cavalry forces in the area. Gen. James B. McPherson, who assumed command of the Army of the Tennessee in March 1864, called the 9th Ohio Cavalry "a green regiment but well officered" (*OR,* ser. 1, 38[pt. 4]:172).

164. General Sherman announced to the three armies he commanded that Secretary of War Edwin M. Stanton had informed him of a Union victory at Spotsylvania, Va. (ibid.).

165. The Confederate major Williams cannot be identified.

166. Adam Johnson, leading a brigade under Roddey, commanded the Confederates who opposed Rowett, and they withdrew not so much because of the 7th Illinois and 9th Ohio Cavalry as because Gen. Walter Q. Gresham was approaching with his infantry (*OR,* ser. 1, 38[pt. 4]:230).

167. These three men cannot be identified, although Buckee and Foster were evidently outspoken secessionists.

168. *OR,* ser. 1, 38(pt. 4):231.

169. General Gresham reported the arrival of Rowett on May 18: "He met the enemy and drove him across the Tennessee River, killing and wounding a number of men. He has 24 prisoners with him" (*OR,* ser. 1, 38[pt. 4]:245). The initial report on the skirmish at Centre Star, Ala., May 15, 1864, said that Rowett's command had taken 35 prisoners (*OR,* ser. 1, 39[pt. 1]:16). For Rowett's report on his brigade's actions between Apr. 30 and May 22, 1864, see *OR,* ser. 1, 38(pt. 3):464–65.

170. Lt. Joseph Rowett of Company K received his commission in August 1861.

171. The A.Q.M. was the assistant quartermaster. Orders for the 7th Illinois to surrender its mounts and return to the brigade were issued on May 19, 1864, by General McPherson. The mounts— McPherson refers to horses—were to be turned over to the 9th Ohio Cavalry and 1st Alabama Cavalry (U.S.), although the regiment apparently did not finally surrender its animals until June 16 (*OR,* ser. 1, 38[pt. 4]:258, 38[pt. 3]:465).

172. Rowett reported that the regiment did not leave Athens, Ala., until June 16, 1864, although this may have been his way of saying that the movement was not *completed* until the early morning hours of that day (*OR,* ser. 1, 38[pt. 3]:465).

173. Ambrose refers in the foregoing paragraphs to events in the battles of Chickamauga (Sept. 19–20, 1863), Lookout Mountain (Nov. 24, 1863), and Missionary Ridge (Nov. 25, 1863).

174. Ambrose refers to the hit-and-run tactics of Confederate cavalry leader Joseph Wheeler.

175. Colonel Rowett verifies the arrival of the regiment at Rome, Ga., on July 9, 1864, by which time Sherman's armies were well into the Atlanta campaign, having departed Chattanooga in early May (*OR,* ser. 1, 38[pt. 3]:465).

176. Ambrose so compresses events between June 25 and July 10, 1864, as to neglect an exciting episode in which about fifty men from the 7th Illinois, assigned to picket duty along the railroad, drove off a Confederate force, possibly guerrillas, that had derailed a locomotive and partially burned a dozen cars six miles north of Tilton, Ga., on July 5 (*OR,* ser. 1, 38[pt. 3]:269, 274, 466–67).

177. Men mentioned here but not yet identified are Oscar Poole, Michael McEvoy, and Washington Judy, all of whom enlisted in 1862.

178. The regiment's place in the Army of the Tennessee was still XVI Corps (now commanded by General Dodge), Second Division, Third Brigade, the composition of which remained unchanged. Several men had commanded the brigade at various times since mid-June, when Moses Bane had apparently resigned "for the purposes of embarking in the political affairs of the day." He was replaced by Gen. William Vandever from June 20 to August 2; Col. Henry J. B. Cummings then led the brigade until Colonel Rowett took over on August 15. Lt. Col. Hector Perrin took command of the regiment (*OR,* ser. 1, 38[pt. 1]:107). Ambrose appears to have liked Rowett, but a soldier in Company C called the colonel "a man in form but not in principle." He portrayed Rowett as a martinet who surrounded himself with "congenial spirits akin to his—such as horse stealing and horse racing in which he is proficient but beyond which I could not now or never could recommend him" (David B. Givler to Frank, Aug. 8, 1864, in Givler, "Intimate Glimpses of Army Life")

179. Thomas W. Billington was the first sergeant of Company C; William Ross, from Litchfield, Ill., had reenlisted as a veteran of the regiment, but Private Frits does not appear on the regiment's roster. Dr. Felty was not one of the regiment's regular medical officers. Another member of Company C attributed the attack to "a squad of

Rebel cavalry," rather than guerrillas, and he reported that Billington was killed "by a ball from the rear through his vetals, the ball lodging in the center of his breast outside" (David B. Givler to Frank, Aug. 31, 1864, in Givler, "Intimate Glimpses of Army Life")

180. Ambrose refers to the prelude of the battle of Allatoona, Oct. 5, 1864, which he describes fully in the following chapter. Gen. John Bell Hood had evacuated Atlanta on September 7. Rather than continuing to oppose Sherman's larger force in Georgia, Hood moved north around the Union armies in late September in hopes of severing their supply lines and possibly regaining a foothold in Tennessee. After missing the Atlanta campaign, in which most of the rest of its division had participated, the 7th Illinois would form part of the first Union command to block Hood's northward march.

181. Gen. John M. Corse had led the Second Division of XVI Corps from July 26 to Sept. 6, 1864, when the Army of the Tennessee was consolidated into two corps, XV and XVII. At that time, Corse received command of the Fourth Division, XV Corps. On September 29, he also assumed command of the post at Rome, Ga., where most of his troops had assembled, from Colonel Rowett. On October 4, as Ambrose states, Sherman ordered Corse by means of signal flags to block Hood's advance at Allatoona Pass (*OR,* ser. 1, 39[pt. 1]:761–62). For the broader context of the story Ambrose now tells, see Anne J. Bailey, *The Chessboard of War: Sherman and Hood in the Autumn Campaigns of 1864* (Lincoln: University of Nebraska Press, 2000), 26–33.

182. Gen. Samuel G. French led the attacking Confederate force.

183. John Etterline was a new recruit who had only enlisted in the regiment in February 1864.

184. Capt. Charles Rattray of the 57th Illinois Infantry was the acting assistant inspector-general of the Third Brigade.

185. Lt. Col. John E. Tourtellotte of the 4th Minnesota Infantry commanded the post at Allatoona. Before the arrival of Corse, his garrison numbered just 890 men from his own regiment, the 93rd Illinois Infantry, 18th Wisconsin Infantry, and 12th Wisconsin Battery. Col. William Hanna led the 50th Illinois Infantry.

186. In fact, the 7th Illinois suffered 141 casualties at Allatoona Pass, with 16 percent of the regiment being killed. The fight was, as Ambrose states, the regiment's bloodiest combat of the war (Hicken, *Illinois in the Civil War,* 300–302). Sherman described it as "a very hard fight, but complete success" (*OR,* ser. 1, 39[pt. 3]:125). For the reports of General Corse and Colonel Perrin, see *OR,* ser. 1, 39(pt. 1):761–66, 777–78.

More details are available for some of the casualties. Thirty-five-year-old Colonel Rowett was treated at the corps hospital before

being evacuated to the Officer's Hospital in Nashville, Tenn. Lt. John
S. Robinson, who had served as the regiment's adjutant since November 1862, had a rib broken by a bullet that entered his left lung. Hem-
orrhaging kept him in the division's field hospital for four weeks before he could be evacuated to Chattanooga, where he died on Jan. 4,
1865. Sgt. James O'Donnell of Company A lost his right eye to a gunshot wound, but he returned to duty on Feb. 9, 1865. John Hunter of
Company B (listed as a corporal in medical records but as a private
on the regiment's roster) hailed from Mattoon. His amputated left leg
demonstrated "exhaustive suppuration," and he died on Oct. 21, 1864.
Pvt. John McAlpine of Vandalia did not enlist in Company C until October 1863; he died on Oct. 8, 1864, from a gunshot wound that frac-
tured one of his hips. Pvt. Edwin R. Jones, a twenty-three-year-old
from Springfield, enlisted in Company E in August 1862. He had been
wounded previously at Corinth; at Allatoona he lost his right eye to a
gunshot wound. Jones returned to duty on Feb. 28, 1865. Pvts.
Nathan D. Atchison and Bernard Keely both died from their wounds,
Keely following the amputation of a leg on the day of battle, Atchison
on Oct. 10, 1864, from a bullet wound to the head. Pvt. Richard P.
Graham, age twenty-three from Lincoln, Ill., had his right leg amputated at the thigh on November 9 after receiving a wound to a knee
joint. He remained in the hospital until discharged from the army on
May 22, 1865. Pvt. William T. Massey of Richland did not enlist in
Company I until January 1864. A gunshot wound in his upper left leg
required amputation, which led to his discharge from the army on
Mar. 12, 1865 (*Medical and Surgical History,* 7:136, 257, 8:337, 339,
527, 9:320, 10:84, 12:476, 510, 789).

187. The A.A.A.G. was the acting assistant adjutant general.

188. Actually, the 39th Iowa Infantry lost more men—170—than
the 7th Illinois (*OR,* ser. 1, 39[pt. 1]:766).

189. For the return to Rome and the regiment's activities between October 6 and November 10, when Ambrose resumes his narrative, see *OR,* ser. 1, 39(pt. 1):767–71, 778–79, 782–84, 39(pt. 3):188.
The men spent most of their time strengthening the fortifications
around Rome, although they also engaged in some skirmishing, most
notably in an engagement on Oct. 13, 1864.

190. Pvts. John White and William J. White of Lincoln had both
been mustered into the regiment in February 1864.

191. Gen. George Thomas commanded the Army of the Cumberland.

192. A major reorganization of the Department of the Tennessee
on October 31, 1864, retained the 7th Illinois and the rest of the Third
Brigade as part of the Fourth Division, XV Corps, where it had been
assigned for the battle of Allatoona. However, Gen. Oliver O. Howard

now commanded the Army of the Tennessee, Gen. Peter J. Osterhaus led the corps, and Lt. Col. Frederick J. Hurlbut had charge of the brigade (*OR*, ser. 1, 39[pt. 3]:565).

193. Ambrose refers to the battle of Kenesaw (or Kennesaw) Mountain, fought June 27, 1864, during the Union advance toward Atlanta. Gen. John A. Logan, an Illinois native and former congressman, commanded a corps in the battle.

194. Ambrose refers to General Howard, who would lead two corps from the Army of the Tennessee—XV and XVII—as the Right Wing of Sherman's march across Georgia. Gen. Henry R. Slocum led XIV and XX Corps of the newly created Army of Georgia as the Left Wing. Ambrose says as much a few pages later.

195. An A.C. was an army corps. For Sherman's March to the Sea, conducted Nov. 15–Dec. 21, 1864, see Bailey, *Chessboard of War;* Joseph T. Glatthaar, *The March to the Sea and Beyond: Sherman's Troops in the Savannah and Carolinas Campaigns* (New York: New York University Press, 1985); and Lee Kennett, *Marching through Georgia: The Story of Soldiers and Civilians during Sherman's Campaign* (New York: HarperCollins, 1995).

196. Gen. Judson Kilpatrick led the cavalry division of Slocum's Left Wing.

197. Colonel Perrin reported that he was ordered on Nov. 19, 1864, to mount the entire regiment, but he could find sufficient animals and equipment for only 5 officers and 120 men. Thus, the regiment was again divided as it advanced through the Carolinas, this time with half of the men mounted and half on foot (*OR*, ser. 1, 44:146–47).

198. Gen. William B. Hazen's Second Division, XV Corps, captured Fort McAllister, located fifteen miles south of Savannah, on Dec. 13, 1864. The fort had been crucial to the defense of the city.

199. To put in context the role of the 7th Illinois during the campaign that began on November 15 see the reports of Generals Corse and Hurlbut in *OR*, ser. 1, 44:125–28, 144–46.

200. William G. Brownlow of Knoxville, Tenn., known as Parson Brownlow, was a Methodist minister, newspaper editor, and staunch unionist who spoke forcefully against the Confederacy throughout the war.

201. Major Johnson was ordered to occupy Fort Bonaventure with the four dismounted companies of the regiment on Dec. 26, 1864 (*OR*, ser. 1, 44:147, 814).

202. The 7th Illinois and the rest of the Third Brigade remained in the Fourth Division, but General Logan commanded XV Corps on the march from Savannah through the Carolinas (*OR*, ser. 1, 47[pt. 1]:46–48).

203. Meantime, the still mounted half of the regiment, which General Logan referred to as the 7th Illinois Mounted Infantry, had been sent ahead and across the Savannah River for purposes of reconnaissance on Jan. 16, 1865 (*OR,* ser. 1, 47[pt. 1]:220).

204. Logan was known as "Black Jack" because of his dark eyes and hair and swarthy complexion.

205. This was Col. George A. Stone.

206. Contrary to the impression of Logan given in the preceding paragraph—willing to "sweep" Columbia from the map—the general's report on the campaign expressed regret over the burning of the city (*OR,* ser. 1, 47[pt. 1]:227–28).

207. Controversy continues over whether Sherman's advancing army or Gen. Wade Hampton's retreating Confederates burned Columbia, S.C., on Feb. 17–19, 1865. See Marion B. Lucas, *Sherman and the Burning of Columbia* (College Station: Texas A&M University Press, 1976); and Walter B. Edgar and Deborah K. Woolley, *Columbia: Portrait of a City* (Norfolk, Va.: Donning, 1986). Regardless, the state of South Carolina probably suffered more destruction than North Carolina or Georgia at the hands of Sherman's soldiers.

208. General Corse ordered Perrin to assume command of the mounted troops and Johnson the foot soldiers on Feb. 23, 1865 (*OR,* ser. 1, 47[pt. 1]:367).

209. See *OR,* ser. 1, 47(pt. 1):230, 254–55, 363–64, 368, for the expeditions of Mar. 3–7, 1865.

210. Gen. Matthew G. Butler commanded a division under General Hampton.

211. Gen. Joseph E. Johnston (not Johnson) was responsible for coordinating the Confederate defense of the Carolinas, Georgia, and Florida from February to April 1865.

212. Sherman added a Center column to complement his Right and Left Wings on Mar. 21, 1865. Gen. John M. Schofield commanded the Center, and Gen. Alfred Terry commanded X Corps under him.

213. Groch (or Grosch) and Burkhardt, both from Lincoln, Illinois, had served through the war with the 7th Illinois and reenlisted as Veterans. Burkhardt, age twenty-six, had his left arm amputated after being shot in the shoulder. He died of typhoid fever while in the hospital on May 5, 1865. One of the unnamed wounded was Pvt. II. (or possibly William) Egbert, who suffered a head contusion when thrown from his horse near Fayetteville, N.C., on Mar. 14, 1865 (*Medical and Surgical History,* 7:39, 10:536).

214. For the regiment's role in the fighting on Mar. 19–22, 1865, near Bentonville, N.C., see *OR,* ser. 1, 47(pt. 1):69, 368–69. The 7th Illinois had seven men wounded.

215. For reports on the entire campaign by Generals Logan, Corse, and Hurlbut, see *OR,* ser. 1, 47(pt. 1):220–37, 336–42, 359–67.

216. These "old" companies had been reduced by casualties, discharges, and resignations to below effective strength.

217. The 7th Illinois was specifically assigned to guard the supply, ordnance, and ambulance trains when the division entered Raleigh (*OR,* ser. 1, 47[pt. 3]:194).

218. The move to Morrisville came at the request of Colonel Perrin (ibid., 223).

219. Both Gen. James S. Wadsworth and Gen. John Sedgwick were killed during the fighting in the Wilderness, May 1864.

220. General Sherman was criticized by some politicians for the generous terms he offered to Joseph Johnston in the surrender on Apr. 26, 1865, near Durham, N.C.

INDEX